Marketing: A Managerial Perspective

Marketing: A Managerial Perspective

Stella Stephenson

Larsen & Keller
www.larsen-keller.com

Marketing: A Managerial Perspective
Stella Stephenson
ISBN: 978-1-64172-627-6 (Hardback)

Larsen & Keller
Published by Larsen and Keller Education,
5 Penn Plaza,
19th Floor,
New York, NY 10001, USA

Cataloging-in-Publication Data

Marketing : a managerial perspective / Stella Stephenson.
p. cm.
Includes bibliographical references and index.
ISBN 978-1-64172-627-6
1. Marketing. 2. Marketing--Management. 3. Industrial management.
I. Stephenson, Stella.
HF5415 .M37 2021
658.8--dc23

For more information regarding Larsen and Keller Education and its products, please visit the publisher's website www.larsen-keller.com

TABLE OF CONTENTS

PREFACE

It is with great pleasure that I present this book. It has been carefully written after numerous discussions with my peers and other practitioners of the field. I would like to take this opportunity to thank my family and friends who have been extremely supporting at every step in my life.

The study and management of exchange relationships is known as marketing. It is a business process that focuses on creating relationships with customers and fulfilling their expectations. Marketing is one of the fundamental and essential components of business management. Some of the major aspects of marketing are market orientations, marketing mix and deciding the methods which will be used to market the product. The most common market orientations are product, sales, production, etc. Marketing mix refers to the set of actions which a company uses to promote its brand. This book is compiled in such a manner, that it will provide in-depth knowledge about the theory and practice of marketing. While understanding the long-term perspectives of the topics, the book makes an effort in highlighting their impact as a modern tool for the growth of the discipline. It will provide comprehensive knowledge to the readers.

The chapters below are organized to facilitate a comprehensive understanding of the subject:

Chapter - What is Marketing?

The study and management of exchange relationships is known as marketing. It is particularly used to create relationships with customers and satisfying them. This is an introductory chapter which will introduce briefly all the significant aspects of marketing such as the importance of marketing and marketing management.

Chapter - Types of Marketing

Some of the common types of marketing are direct marketing, guerrilla marketing, online advertising, evangelism marketing, multi-level marketing and global marketing. The topics elaborated in this chapter will help in gaining a better perspective about these diverse types of marketing.

Chapter - Fundamental Concepts of Marketing

There are numerous concepts which are studied and applied in the field of marketing. Some of them are pricing strategies, marketing mix, distribution, retail, brand licensing, marketing activation and social marketing. The topics elaborated in this chapter will help in gaining a better perspective about these fundamental concepts of marketing.

Chapter - Market Structure

The main types of market structure are perfect competition, imperfect competition, oligopoly, monopoly and monopsony. All the diverse principles and concepts related to these types of market structure such as monopsonistic competition and monopolistic competition have been carefully analyzed in this chapter.

Chapter - Services Marketing

The specialized branch of marketing that is involved in identifying, creating, communicating and delivering value to customers is known as services marketing. Some of its major focus areas are relationship marketing, customer satisfaction and customer experience. This chapter discusses in detail these aspects of service marketing.

Stella Stephenson

What is Marketing? 1

• Marketing Management

The study and management of exchange relationships is known as marketing. It is particularly used to create relationships with customers and satisfying them. This is an introductory chapter which will introduce briefly all the significant aspects of marketing such as the importance of marketing and marketing management.

Marketing is the sum of activities involved in directing the flow of goods and services from producers to consumers.

Marketing's principal function is to promote and facilitate exchange. Through marketing, individuals and groups obtain what they need and want by exchanging products and services with other parties. Such a process can occur only when there are at least two parties, each of whom has something to offer. In addition, exchange cannot occur unless the parties are able to communicate about and to deliver what they offer. Marketing is not a coercive process: all parties must be free to accept or reject what others are offering. So defined, marketing is distinguished from other modes of obtaining desired goods, such as through self-production, begging, theft, or force.

Marketing is not confined to any particular type of economy, because goods must be exchanged and therefore marketed in all economies and societies except perhaps in the most primitive. Furthermore, marketing is not a function that is limited to profit-oriented business; even such institutions as hospitals, schools, and museums engage in some forms of marketing. Within the broad scope of marketing, merchandising is concerned more specifically with promoting the sale of goods and services to consumers (i.e., retailing) and hence is more characteristic of free-market economies.

Based on these criteria, marketing can take a variety of forms: it can be a set of functions, a department within an organization, a managerial process, a managerial philosophy, and a social process.

Roles of Marketing

As marketing developed, it took a variety of forms. It was noted above that marketing can be viewed as a set of functions in the sense that certain activities are traditionally associated with the exchange process. A common but incorrect view is that selling and advertising are the only marketing activities. Yet, in addition to promotion, marketing includes a much broader set of functions, including product development, packaging, pricing, distribution, and customer service.

Many organizations and businesses assign responsibility for these marketing functions to a specific group of individuals within the organization. In this respect, marketing is a unique and separate entity. Those who make up the marketing department may include brand and product managers, marketing researchers, sales representatives, advertising and promotion managers, pricing specialists, and customer service personnel.

As a managerial process, marketing is the way in which an organization determines its best opportunities in the marketplace, given its objectives and resources. The marketing process is divided into a strategic and a tactical phase. The strategic phase has three components—segmentation, targeting, and positioning (STP). The organization must distinguish among different groups of customers in the market (segmentation), choose which group(s) it can serve effectively (targeting), and communicate the central benefit it offers to that group (positioning). The marketing process includes designing and implementing various tactics, commonly referred to as the "marketing mix," or the "4 Ps": product, price, place (or distribution), and promotion. The marketing mix is followed by evaluating, controlling, and revising the marketing process to achieve the organization's objectives.

The managerial philosophy of marketing puts central emphasis on customer satisfaction as the means for gaining and keeping loyal customers. Marketers urge their organizations to carefully and continually gauge target customers' expectations and to consistently meet or exceed these expectations. In order to accomplish this, everyone in all areas of the organization must focus on understanding and serving customers; it will not succeed if all marketing occurs only in the marketing department. Marketing, consequently, is far too important to be done solely by the marketing department. Marketers also want their organizations to move from practicing transaction-oriented marketing, which focuses on individual exchanges, to relationship-driven marketing, which emphasizes serving the customer over the long term. Simply getting new customers and losing old ones will not help the organization achieve its objectives.

Finally, marketing is a social process that occurs in all economies, regardless of their political structure and orientation. It is the process by which a society organizes and distributes its resources to meet the material needs of its citizens. However, marketing activity is more pronounced under conditions of goods surpluses than goods shortages. When goods are in short supply, consumers are usually so desirous of goods that the exchange process does not require significant promotion or facilitation. In contrast, when there are more goods and services than consumers need or want, companies must work harder to convince customers to exchange with them.

The Marketing Process

The marketing process consists of four elements: strategic marketing analysis, marketing-mix planning, marketing implementation, and marketing control.

Strategic Marketing Analysis

Market Segments

The aim of marketing in profit-oriented organizations is to meet needs profitably. Companies must therefore first define which needs—and whose needs—they can satisfy. For example, the personal transportation market consists of people who put different values on an automobile's cost, speed, safety, status, and styling. No single automobile can satisfy all these needs in a superior fashion; compromises have to be made. Furthermore, some individuals may wish to meet their personal transportation needs with something other than an automobile, such as a motorcycle, a bicycle, or a bus or other form of public transportation. Because of such variables, an automobile company must identify the different preference groups, or segments, of customers and decide which group(s) they can target profitably.

Market Niches

Segments can be divided into even smaller groups, called subsegments or niches. A niche is defined as a small target group that has special requirements. For example, a bank may specialize in serving the investment needs of not only senior citizens but also senior citizens with high incomes and perhaps even those with particular investment preferences. It is more likely that larger organizations will serve the larger market segments (mass marketing) and ignore niches. As a result, smaller companies typically emerge that are intimately familiar with a particular niche and specialize in serving its needs.

Marketing to Individuals

A growing number of companies are now trying to serve "segments of one." They attempt to adapt their offer and communication to each individual customer. This is understandable, for instance, with large industrial companies that have only a few major customers. For example, The Boeing Company (United States) designs its 747 planes differently for each major customer, such as United Airlines, Inc., or American Airlines, Inc. Serving individual customers is increasingly possible with the advent of database marketing, through which individual customer characteristics and purchase histories are retained in company information systems. Even mass-marketing companies, particularly large retailers and catalog houses, compile comprehensive data on individual customers and are able to customize their offerings and communications.

Positioning

A key step in marketing strategy, known as positioning, involves creating and communicating a message that clearly establishes the company or brand in relation to competitors. Thus, Volvo Aktiebolaget (Sweden) has positioned its automobile as the "safest," and Daimler-Benz AG (Germany), manufacturer of Mercedes-Benz vehicles, has positioned its car as the best "engineered." Some products may be positioned as "outstanding" in two or more ways. However, claiming superiority along several dimensions may hurt a company's credibility because consumers will not believe that any single offering can excel in all dimensions. Furthermore, although the company may communicate a particular position, customers may perceive a different image of the company as a result of their actual experiences with the company's product or through word of mouth.

Marketing-mix Planning

Having developed a strategy, a company must then decide which tactics will be most effective in achieving strategy goals. Tactical marketing involves creating a marketing mix of four components—product, price, place, promotion—that fulfills the strategy for the targeted set of customer needs.

Product

Product Development

The first marketing-mix element is the product, which refers to the offering or group of offerings that will be made available to customers. In the case of a physical product, such as a car, a company will gather information about the features and benefits desired by a target market. Before assembling a product, the marketer's role is to communicate customer desires to the engineers who design the product or service. This is in contrast to past practice, when engineers designed a product based on their own preferences, interests, or expertise and then expected marketers to find as many customers as possible to buy this product. Contemporary thinking calls for products to be designed based on customer input and not solely on engineers' ideas.

In traditional economies, the goods produced and consumed often remain the same from one generation to the next—including food, clothing, and housing. As economies develop, the range of products available tends to expand, and the products themselves change. In contemporary industrialized societies, products, like people, go through life cycles: birth, growth, maturity, and decline. This constant replacement of existing products with new or altered products has significant consequences for professional marketers. The development of new products involves all aspects of a business—production, finance, research and development, and even personnel administration and public relations.

Packaging and Branding

Packaging and branding are also substantial components in the marketing of a product. Packaging in some instances may be as simple as customers in France carrying long loaves of unwrapped bread or small produce dealers in Italy wrapping vegetables in newspapers or placing them in customers' string bags. In most industrialized countries, however, the packaging of merchandise has become a major part of the selling effort, as marketers now specify exactly the types of packaging that will be most appealing to prospective customers. The importance of packaging in the distribution of the product has increased with the spread of self-service purchases—in wholesaling as well as in retailing. Packaging is sometimes designed to facilitate the use of the product, as with aerosol containers for room deodorants. In Europe such condiments as mustard, mayonnaise, and ketchup are often packaged in tubes. Some packages are reusable, making them attractive to customers in poorer countries where metal containers, for instance, are often highly prized.

Marketing a Service Product

The same general marketing approach about the product applies to the development of service offerings as well. For example, a health maintenance organization (HMO) must design a contract for its members that describes which medical procedures will be covered, how much physician choice will be available, how out-of-town medical costs will be handled, and so forth. In creating a successful service mix, the HMO must choose features that are preferred and expected by target customers, or the service will not be valued in the marketplace.

Price

The second marketing-mix element is price. Ordinarily companies determine a price by gauging the quality or performance level of the offer and then selecting a price that reflects how the market values its level of quality. However, marketers also are aware that price can send a message to a customer about the product's presumed quality level. A Mercedes-Benz vehicle is generally considered to be a high-quality automobile, and it therefore can command a high price in the marketplace. But, even if the manufacturer could price its cars competitively with economy cars, it might not do so, knowing that the lower price might communicate lower quality. On the other hand, in order to gain market share, some companies have moved to "more for the same" or "the same for less" pricing, which means offering prices that are consistently lower than those of their competitors. This kind of discount pricing has caused firms in such industries as airlines and pharmaceuticals (which used to charge a price premium based on their past brand strength and reputation) to significantly reevaluate their marketing strategies.

Place

Place, or where the product is made available, is the third element of the marketing mix and is most commonly referred to as distribution. When a product moves along its path from producer to consumer, it is said to be following a channel of distribution. For example, the channel of distribution for many food products includes food-processing plants, warehouses, wholesalers, and supermarkets. By using this channel, a food manufacturer makes its products easily accessible by ensuring that they are in stores that are frequented by those in the target market. In another example, a mutual funds organization makes its investment products available by enlisting the assistance of brokerage houses and banks, which in turn establish relationships with particular customers. However, each channel participant can handle only a certain number of products: space at supermarkets is limited, and investment brokers can keep abreast of only a limited number of mutual funds. Because of this, some marketers may decide to skip steps in the channel and instead market directly to buyers through factory outlets, direct mail, and shopping via the Internet (a significant trend from the late 20th century).

Promotion

Promotion, the fourth marketing-mix element, consists of several methods of communicating with and influencing customers. The major tools are sales force, advertising, sales promotion, and public relations.

Sales Force

Sales representatives are the most expensive means of promotion, because they require income, expenses, and supplementary benefits. Their ability to personalize the promotion process makes salespeople most effective at selling complex goods, big-ticket items, and highly personal goods—for example, those related to religion or insurance. Salespeople are trained to make presentations, answer objections, gain commitments to purchase, and manage account growth. Some companies have successfully reduced their sales-force costs by replacing certain functions (for example, finding new customers) with less expensive methods.

Advertising

Advertising includes all forms of paid nonpersonal communication and promotion of products, services, or ideas by a specified sponsor. Advertising appears in such media as print (newspapers, magazines, billboards, flyers), broadcast (radio, television), and the Internet, including e-mail and the World Wide Web. Print advertisements typically consist of a picture, a headline, information about the product, and occasionally a response coupon. Broadcast advertisements consist of an audio or video narrative that can range from short 15-second spots to longer segments known as infomercials, which generally last 30 or 60 minutes. E-mail advertisements are similar in content to print advertisements and contain hyperlinks to the retailer of the product or service. Advertisements on Web sites consist of static or moving pictures and words, sometimes presented in so-called pop-up windows, and brief videos, with or without an audio narrative, along with hyperlinks. A notorious form of advertising over the Internet is spam, consisting of unsolicited commercial messages sent to e-mail accounts, blogs, social-networking sites, and cellular telephones.

Sales Promotion

While advertising presents a reason to buy a product, sales promotion offers a short-term incentive to purchase. Sales promotions often attract brand switchers (those who are not loyal to a specific brand) who are looking primarily for low price and good value. Thus, especially in markets where brands are highly similar, sales promotions can cause a short-term increase in sales but little permanent gain in market share. Alternatively, in markets where brands are quite dissimilar, sales promotions can alter market shares more permanently. The use of promotions rose considerably during the late 20th century. This was due to a number of factors within companies, including an increased sophistication in sales promotion techniques and greater pressure to increase sales. Several market factors also fostered this increase, including a rise in the number of brands (especially similar ones) and a decrease in the efficiency of traditional advertising due to increasingly fractionated consumer markets.

Public Relations

Public relations, in contrast to advertising and sales promotion, generally involves less commercialized modes of communication. Its primary purpose is to disseminate information and opinion to groups and individuals who have an actual or potential impact on a company's ability to achieve its objectives. In addition, public relations specialists are responsible for monitoring these individuals and groups and for maintaining good relationships with them. One of their key activities is to work with news and information media to ensure appropriate coverage of the company's activities and products. Public relations specialists create publicity by arranging press conferences, contests, meetings, and other events that will draw attention to a company's products or services. Another public relations responsibility is crisis management—that is, handling situations in which public awareness of a particular issue may dramatically and negatively impact the company's ability to achieve its goals. For example, when it was discovered that some bottles of Perrier sparkling water might have been tainted by a harmful chemical, Source Perrier, SA's public relations team, had to ensure that the general consuming public did not thereafter automatically associate Perrier with tainted water. Other public relations activities include lobbying, advising management about public issues, and planning community events.

Because public relations does not always seek to impact sales or profitability directly, it is sometimes seen as serving a function that is separate from marketing. However, some companies recognize that public relations can work in conjunction with other marketing activities to facilitate the exchange process directly and indirectly. These organizations have established marketing public relations departments to directly support corporate and product promotion and image management.

Marketing Implementation

Companies have typically hired different agencies to help in the development of advertising, sales promotion, and publicity ideas. However, this often results in a lack of coordination between elements of the promotion mix. When components of the mix are not all in harmony, a confusing message may be sent to consumers. For example, a television advertisement for an automobile may emphasize the car's exclusivity and luxury, while a Web-site advertisement may stress rebates and sales, clashing with this image of exclusivity. Alternatively, by integrating the marketing elements, a company can more efficiently utilize its resources. Instead of individually managing four or five different promotion processes, the company manages only one. In addition, promotion expenditures are likely to be better allocated, because differences among promotion tools become more explicit. This reasoning has led to integrated marketing communications, in which all promotional tools are considered to be part of the same effort, and each tool receives full consideration in terms of its cost and effectiveness.

Marketing Evaluation and Control

No marketing process, even the most carefully developed, is guaranteed to result in maximum benefit for a company. In addition, because every market is changing constantly, a strategy that is effective today may not be effective in the future. It is important to evaluate a marketing program periodically to be sure that it is achieving its objectives.

Marketing Control

There are four types of marketing control, each of which has a different purpose: annual-plan control, profitability control, efficiency control, and strategic control.

Annual-plan Control

The basis of annual-plan control is managerial objectives—that is to say, specific goals, such as sales and profitability, that are established on a monthly or quarterly basis. Organizations use five tools to monitor plan performance. The first is sales analysis, in which sales goals are compared with actual sales and discrepancies are explained or accounted for. A second tool is market-share analysis, which compares a company's sales with those of its competitors. Companies can express their market share in a number of ways, by comparing their own sales to total market sales, sales within the market segment, or sales of the segment's top competitors. Third, marketing expense-to-sales analysis gauges how much a company spends to achieve its sales goals. The ratio of marketing expenses to sales is expected to fluctuate, and companies usually establish an acceptable range for this ratio. In contrast, financial analysis estimates such expenses (along with others) from a corporate perspective. This includes a comparison of profits to sales (profit margin), sales to assets (asset turnover), profits to assets (return on assets), assets to worth (financial leverage), and, finally, profits to worth (return on net worth). Finally, companies measure customer satisfaction as a means of tracking goal achievement. Analyses of this kind are generally less quantitative than those described above and may include complaint and suggestion systems, customer satisfaction surveys, and careful analysis of reasons why customers switch to a competitor's product.

Profitability Control

Profitability control and efficiency control allow a company to closely monitor its sales, profits, and expenditures. Profitability control demonstrates the relative profit-earning capacity of a company's different products and consumer groups. Companies are frequently surprised to find that a small percentage of their products and customers contribute to a large percentage of their profits. This knowledge helps a company allocate its resources and effort.

Efficiency Control

Efficiency control involves micro-level analysis of the various elements of the marketing mix, including sales force, advertising, sales promotion, and distribution. For example, to understand its sales-force efficiency, a company may keep track of how many sales calls a representative makes each day, how long each call lasts, and how much each call costs and generates in revenue. This type of analysis highlights areas in which companies can manage their marketing efforts in a more productive and cost-effective manner.

Strategic Control

Strategic control processes allow managers to evaluate a company's marketing program from a critical long-term perspective. This involves a detailed and objective analysis of a company's organization and its ability to maximize its strengths and market opportunities. Companies can use two types of strategic control tools. The first, which a company uses to evaluate itself, is called a marketing-effectiveness rating review. In order to rate its own marketing effectiveness, a company examines its customer philosophy, the adequacy of its marketing information, and the efficiency of its marketing operations. It will also closely evaluate the strength of its marketing strategy and the integration of its marketing tactics.

Marketing Audit

The second evaluation tool is known as a marketing audit. This is a comprehensive, systematic, independent, and periodic analysis that a company uses to examine its strengths in relation to its current and potential market(s). Such an analysis is comprehensive because it covers all aspects of the marketing climate (unlike a functional audit, which analyzes one marketing activity), looking at both macro-environment factors (demographic, economic, ecological, technological, political, and cultural) and micro- or task-environment factors (markets, customers, competitors, distributors, dealers, suppliers, facilitators, and publics). The audit includes analyses of the company's marketing strategy, marketing organization, marketing systems, and marketing productivity. It must be systematic in order to provide concrete conclusions based on these analyses. To ensure objectivity, a marketing audit is best done by a person, department, or organization that is independent of the company or marketing program. Marketing audits should be done not only when the value of a company's current marketing plan is in question; they must be done periodically in order to isolate and solve problems before they arise.

The Marketing Actors

The elements that play a role in the marketing process can be divided into three groups: customers, distributors, and facilitators. In addition to interacting with one another, these groups must interact within a business environment that is affected by a variety of forces, including governmental, economic, and social influences.

Customers

In order to understand target customers, certain questions must be answered: Who constitutes the market segment? What do they buy and why? And how, when, and where do they buy? Knowing who constitutes the market segment is not simply a matter of knowing who uses a product. Often, individuals other than the user may participate in or influence a purchasing decision. Several individuals may play various roles in the decision-making process. For instance, in the decision to purchase an automobile for a small family business, the son may be the initiator, the daughter may be an influencer, the wife may be the decider, the purchasing manager may be the buyer, and the husband may be the user. In other words, the son may read on a Web site that businesses can save money and decrease tax liability by owning or leasing company transportation. He may therefore initiate the product search process by raising this issue at a weekly business meeting. However, the son may not be the best-qualified person to gather and process information about automobiles, because the daughter worked for several years in the auto industry before joining the family business. Although the daughter's expertise and research efforts may influence the process, she may not be the key decision maker. The mother, by virtue of her position in the business and in the family, may make the final decision about which car to purchase. However, the family uncle may have good negotiation skills, and he may be the purchasing agent. Thus, he will go to different car dealerships in order to buy the chosen car at the best possible price. Finally, despite the involvement of all these individuals in the purchase process, none of them may actually drive the car. It may be purchased so that the father may use it for his frequent sales calls. In other instances, an individual may handle more than one of these purchasing functions and may even be responsible for all of them. The key is that a marketer must recognize that different people have different influences on the purchase decision, and these factors must be taken into account in crafting a marketing strategy.

In addition to knowing to whom the marketing efforts are targeted, it is important to know which products target customers tend to purchase and why they do so. Customers do not purchase "things" as much as they purchase services or benefits to satisfy needs. For instance, a conventional oven allows users to cook and heat food. Microwave oven manufacturers recognized that this need could be fulfilled—and done so more quickly—with a technology other than conventional heating. By focusing on needs rather than on products, these companies were able to gain a significant share in the food cooking and heating market.

Knowledge of when, where, and how purchases are made is also useful. A furniture store whose target customers tend to make major purchases in the spring may send its mailings at the beginning of this season. A food vendor may set up a stand near the door of a busy office complex so that employees must pass the stand on their way to lunch. And a jeweler who knows that customers prefer to pay with credit cards may ensure that all major credit cards are accepted at the store. In other cases, marketers who understand specifics about buying habits and preferences also may try to alter them. Thus, a remotely situated wholesale store may use deeply discounted prices to lure customers away from local shopping malls or online stores.

Customers can be divided into two categories: consumer customers, who purchase goods and services for use by themselves and by those with whom they live; and business customers, who purchase goods and services for use by the organization for which they work. Although there are a number of similarities between the purchasing approaches of each type of customer, there are important differences as well.

Consumer Customers

Factors Influencing Consumers

Four major types of factors influence consumer buying behaviour: cultural, social, personal, and psychological.

Cultural Factors

Cultural factors have the broadest influence, because they constitute a stable set of values, perceptions, preferences, and behaviours that have been learned by the consumer throughout life. For example, in Western cultures consumption is often driven by a consumer's need to express individuality, while in Eastern cultures consumers are more interested in conforming to group norms. In addition to the influence of a dominant culture, consumers may also be influenced by several subcultures. In Quebec the dominant culture is French-speaking, but one influential subculture is English-speaking. Social class is also a subcultural factor: members of any given social class tend to share similar values, interests, and behaviours.

Social Factors

A consumer may interact with several individuals on a daily basis, and the influence of these people constitutes the social factors that affect the buying process. Social factors include reference groups—that is, the formal or informal social groups against which consumers compare themselves. Consumers may be influenced not only by their own membership groups but also by reference groups of which they wish to be a part. Thus, a consumer who wishes to be considered a successful white-collar professional may buy a particular kind of clothing because the people in this reference group tend to wear that style. Typically, the most influential reference group is the family. In this case, family includes the people who raised the consumer (the "family of orientation") as well as the consumer's spouse and children (the "family of procreation"). Within each group, a consumer will be expected to play a specific role or set of roles dictated by the norms of the group. Roles in each group generally are tied closely to status.

Personal Factors

Personal factors include individual characteristics that, when taken in aggregate, distinguish the individual from others of the same social group and culture. These include age, life-cycle stage, occupation, economic circumstances, and lifestyle. A consumer's personality and self-conception will also influence his or her buying behaviour.

Psychological Factors

Finally, psychological factors are the ways in which human thinking and thought patterns influence buying decisions. Consumers are influenced, for example, by their motivation to fulfill a need. In addition, the ways in which an individual acquires and retains information will affect the buying process significantly. Consumers also make their decisions based on past experiences—both positive and negative.

Consumer Buying Tasks

A consumer's buying task is affected significantly by the level of purchase involvement. The level of involvement describes how important the decision is to the consumer; high involvement is usually associated with purchases that are expensive, infrequent, or risky. Buying also is affected by the degree of difference between brands in the product category. The buying task can be grouped into four categories based on whether involvement is high or low and whether brand differences are great or small.

High-involvement Purchases

Complex buying behaviour occurs when the consumer is highly involved with the purchase and when there are significant differences between brands. This behaviour can be associated with the purchase of a new home or a personal computer. Such tasks are complex because the risk is high (significant financial commitment), and the large differences between brands or products require gathering a substantial amount of information prior to purchase. Marketers who wish to influence this buying task must help the consumer process the information as readily as possible. This may include informing the consumer about the product category and its important attributes, providing detailed information about product benefits, and motivating sales personnel to influence final brand choice. For instance, realtors' Web sites typically offer extensive photographs and videos and full descriptions of each available home. And a computer sales representative is likely to spend time providing information to customers who have questions.

Dissonance-reducing buying behaviour occurs when the consumer is highly involved but sees little difference between brands. This is likely to be the case with the purchase of a lawn mower or a diamond ring. After making a purchase under such circumstances, a consumer is likely to experience the dissonance that comes from noticing that other brands would have been just as good, if not slightly better, in some dimensions. A consumer in such a buying situation will seek information or ideas that justify the original purchase.

Low-involvement Purchases

There are two types of low-involvement purchases. Habitual buying behaviour occurs when involvement is low and differences between brands are small. Consumers in this case usually do not form a strong attitude toward a brand but select it because it is familiar. In these markets, promotions tend to be simple and repetitive so that the consumer can, without much effort, learn the association between a brand and a product class. Marketers may also try to make their product more involving. For instance, toothpaste was at one time purchased primarily out of habit, but Proctor and Gamble Co. introduced a brand, Crest toothpaste, that increased consumer involvement by raising awareness about the importance of good dental hygiene.

Brand Differences

Variety-seeking buying behaviour occurs when the consumer is not involved with the purchase, yet there are significant brand differences. In this case, the cost of switching products is low, and so the consumer may, perhaps simply out of boredom, move from one brand to another. Such is often the case with frozen desserts, breakfast cereals, and soft drinks. Dominant firms in such a market situation will attempt to encourage habitual buying and will try to keep other brands from being considered by the consumer. These strategies reduce customer switching behaviour. Challenger firms, on the other hand, want consumers to switch from the market leader, so they will offer promotions, free samples, and advertising that encourage consumers to try something new.

Consumer Buying Process

The purchase process is initiated when a consumer becomes aware of a need. This awareness may come from an internal source such as hunger or an external source such as marketing communications. Awareness of such a need motivates the consumer to search for information about options with which to fulfill the need. This information can come from personal sources, commercial sources, public or government sources, or the consumer's own experience. Once alternatives have been identified through these sources, consumers evaluate the options, paying particular attention to those attributes the consumer considers most important. Evaluation culminates with a purchase decision, but the buying process does not end here. In fact, marketers point out that a purchase represents the beginning, not the end, of a consumer's relationship with a company. After a purchase has been made, a satisfied consumer is more likely to purchase another company product and to say positive things about the company or its product to other potential purchasers. The opposite is true for dissatisfied consumers. Because of this fact, many companies continue to communicate with their customers after a purchase in an effort to influence post-purchase satisfaction and behaviour.

For example, a plumber may be motivated to consider buying a new set of tools because his old set of tools is getting rusty. To gather information about what kind of new tool set to buy, this plumber may examine the tools of a colleague who just bought a new set, read advertisements in plumbing trade magazines, and visit different stores to examine the sets available. The plumber then processes all the information collected, focusing perhaps on durability as one of the most important attributes. In making a particular purchase, the plumber initiates a relationship with a particular tool company. This company may try to enhance post-purchase loyalty and satisfaction by sending the plumber promotions about new tools.

Business Customers

Business customers, also known as industrial customers, purchase products or services to use in the production of other products. Such industries include agriculture, manufacturing, construction, transportation, and communication, among others. They differ from consumer markets in several respects. Because the customers are organizations, the market tends to have fewer and larger buyers than consumer markets. This often results in closer buyer-seller relationships, because those who operate in a market must depend more significantly on one another for supply and revenue. Business customers also are more concentrated; for instance, in the United States more than half of the country's business buyers are concentrated in only seven states. Demand for business goods is derived demand, which means it is driven by a demand for consumer goods. Therefore, demand for business goods is more volatile, because variations in consumer demand can have a significant impact on business-goods demand. Business markets are also distinctive in that buyers are professional purchasers who are highly skilled in negotiating contracts and maximizing efficiency. In addition, several individuals within the business usually have direct or indirect influence on the purchasing process.

Factors Influencing Business Customers

Although business customers are affected by the same cultural, social, personal, and psychological factors that influence consumer customers, the business arena imposes other factors that can be even more influential. First, there is the economic environment, which is characterized by such factors as primary demand, economic forecast, political and regulatory developments, and the type of competition in the market. In a highly competitive market such as airline travel, firms may be concerned about price and therefore make purchases with a focus on saving money. In markets where there is more differentiation among competitors—e.g., in the hotel industry—many firms may make purchases with a focus on quality rather than on price.

Second, there are organizational factors, which include the objectives, policies, procedures, structures, and systems that characterize any particular company. Some companies are structured in such a way that purchases must pass through a complex system of checks and balances, while other companies allow purchasing managers to make more individual decisions. Interpersonal factors are more salient among business customers, because the participants in the buying process—perhaps representing several departments within a company—often have different interests, authority, and persuasiveness. Furthermore, the factors that affect an individual in the business buying process are related to the participant's role in the organization. These factors include job position, risk attitudes, and income.

Business Buying Process

The business buying process mirrors the consumer buying process, with a few notable exceptions. Business buying is not generally need-driven and is instead problem-driven. A business buying process is usually initiated when someone in the company sees a problem that needs to be solved or recognizes a way in which the company can increase profitability or efficiency. The ensuing process follows the same pattern as that of consumers, including information search, evaluation of alternatives, purchase decision, and post-purchase evaluation. However, in part because business purchase decisions require accountability and are often closely analyzed according to cost and efficiency, the process is more systematic than consumer buying and often involves significant documentation. Typically, a purchasing agent for a business buyer will generate documentation regarding product specifications, preferred supplier lists, requests for bids from suppliers, and performance reviews.

Marketing Intermediaries: The Distribution Channel

Many producers do not sell products or services directly to consumers and instead use marketing intermediaries to execute an assortment of necessary functions to get the product to the final user. These intermediaries, such as middlemen (wholesalers, retailers, agents, and brokers), distributors, or financial intermediaries, typically enter into longer-term commitments with the producer and make up what is known as the marketing channel, or the channel of distribution. Manufacturers use raw materials to produce finished products, which in turn may be sent directly to the retailer, or, less often, to the consumer. However, as a general rule, finished goods flow from the manufacturer to one or more wholesalers before they reach the retailer and, finally, the consumer. Each party in the distribution channel usually acquires legal possession of goods during their physical transfer, but this is not always the case. For instance, in consignment selling, the producer retains full legal ownership even though the goods may be in the hands of the wholesaler or retailer—that is, until the merchandise reaches the final user or consumer.

Channels of distribution tend to be more direct—that is, shorter and simpler—in the less industrialized nations. There are notable exceptions, however. For instance, the Ghana Cocoa Marketing Board collects cacao beans in Ghana and licenses trading firms to process the commodity. Similar marketing processes are used in other West African nations. Because of the vast number of small-scale producers, these agents operate through middlemen who, in turn, enlist sub-buyers to find runners to transport the products from remote areas. Japan's marketing organization was, until the late 20th century, characterized by long and complex channels of distribution and a variety of wholesalers. It was possible for a product to pass through a minimum of five separate wholesalers before it reached a retailer.

Companies have a wide range of distribution channels available to them, and structuring the right channel may be one of the company's most critical marketing decisions. Businesses may sell products directly to the final customer, as is the case with most industrial capital goods. Or they may use one or more intermediaries to move their goods to the final user. The design and structure of consumer marketing channels and industrial marketing channels can be quite similar or vary widely.

The channel design is based on the level of service desired by the target consumer. There are five primary service components that facilitate the marketer's understanding of what, where, why, when, and how target customers buy certain products. The service variables are quantity or lot size (the number of units a customer purchases on any given purchase occasion), waiting time (the amount of time customers are willing to wait for receipt of goods), proximity or spatial convenience (accessibility of the product), product variety (the breadth of assortment of the product offering), and service backup (add-on services such as delivery or installation provided by the channel). It is essential for the designer of the marketing channel—typically the manufacturer—to recognize the level of each service point that the target customer desires. A single manufacturer may service several target customer groups through separate channels, and therefore each set of service outputs for these groups could vary. One group of target customers may want elevated levels of service (that is, fast delivery, high product availability, large product assortment, and installation). Their demand for such increased service translates into higher costs for the channel and higher prices for customers.

Channel Functions and Flows

In order to deliver the optimal level of service outputs to their target consumers, manufacturers are willing to allocate some of their tasks, or marketing flows, to intermediaries. As any marketing channel moves goods from producers to consumers, the marketing intermediaries perform, or participate in, a number of marketing flows, or activities. The typical marketing flows, listed in the usual sequence in which they arise, are collection and distribution of marketing research information (information), development and dissemination of persuasive communications (promotion), agreement on terms for transfer of ownership or possession (negotiation), intentions to buy (ordering), acquisition and allocation of funds (financing), assumption of risks (risk taking), storage and movement of product (physical possession), buyers paying sellers (payment), and transfer of ownership (title).

Each of these flows must be performed by a marketing intermediary for any channel to deliver the goods to the final consumer. Thus, each producer must decide who will perform which of these functions in order to deliver the service output levels that the target consumers desire. Producers delegate these flows for a variety of reasons. First, they may lack the financial resources to carry out the intermediary activities themselves. Second, many producers can earn a superior return on their capital by investing profits back into their core business rather than into the distribution of their products. Finally, intermediaries, or middlemen, offer superior efficiency in making goods and services widely available and accessible to final users. For instance, in overseas markets it may be difficult for an exporter to establish contact with end users, and various kinds of agents must therefore be employed. Because an intermediary typically focuses on only a small handful of specialized tasks within the marketing channel, each intermediary, through specialization, experience, or scale of operation, can offer a producer greater distribution benefits.

Management of Channel Systems

Although middlemen can offer greater distribution economy to producers, gaining cooperation from these middlemen can be problematic. Middlemen must continuously be motivated and stimulated to perform at the highest level. In order to gain such a high level of performance, manufacturers need some sort of leverage. Researchers have distinguished five bases of power: coercive (threats if the middlemen do not comply), reward (extra benefits for compliance), legitimate (power by position—rank or contract), expert (special knowledge), and referent (manufacturer is highly respected by the middlemen).

As new institutions emerge or products enter different life-cycle phases, distribution channels change and evolve. With these types of changes, no matter how well the channel is designed and managed, conflict is inevitable. Often this conflict develops because the interests of the independent businesses do not coincide. For example, franchisers, because they receive a percentage of sales, typically want their franchisees to maximize sales, while the franchisees want to maximize their profits, not sales. The conflict that arises may be vertical, horizontal, or multichannel in nature. When the Ford Motor Company comes into conflict with its dealers, this is a vertical channel conflict. Horizontal channel conflict arises when a franchisee in a neighbouring town feels a fellow franchisee has infringed on its territory. Finally, multichannel conflict occurs when a manufacturer has established two or more channels that compete against each other in selling to the same market. For example, a major tire manufacturer may begin selling its tires through mass merchandisers, much to the dismay of its independent tire dealers.

Wholesalers

Wholesaling includes all activities required to sell goods or services to other firms, either for resale or for business use, usually in bulk quantities and at lower-than-retail prices. Wholesalers, also called distributors, are independent merchants operating any number of wholesale establishments. Wholesalers are typically classified into one of three groups: merchant wholesalers, brokers and agents, and manufacturers' and retailers' branches and offices.

Merchant Wholesalers

Merchant wholesalers, also known as jobbers, distributors, or supply houses, are independently owned and operated organizations that acquire title ownership of the goods that they handle. There are two types of merchant wholesalers: full-service and limited-service.

Full-service Wholesalers

Full-service wholesalers usually handle larger sales volumes; they may perform a broad range of services for their customers, such as stocking inventories, operating warehouses, supplying credit, employing salespeople to assist customers, and delivering goods to customers. General-line wholesalers carry a wide variety of merchandise, such as groceries; specialty wholesalers, on the other hand, deal with a narrow line of goods, such as coffee and tea or seafood.

Limited-service Wholesalers

Limited-service wholesalers, who offer fewer services to their customers and suppliers, emerged in order to reduce the costs of service. There are several types of limited-service wholesalers. Cash-and-carry wholesalers usually handle a limited line of fast-moving merchandise, selling to smaller retailers on a cash-only basis and not delivering goods. Truck wholesalers or jobbers sell and deliver directly from their vehicles, often for cash. They carry a limited line of semiperishables such as milk, bread, and snack foods. Drop shippers do not carry inventory or handle the merchandise. Operating primarily in bulk industries such as lumber, coal, and heavy equipment, they take orders but have manufacturers ship merchandise directly to final consumers. Rack jobbers, who handle nonfood lines such as housewares or personal goods, primarily serve drug and grocery retailers. Rack jobbers typically perform such functions as delivery, shelving, inventory stacking, and financing. Producers' cooperatives—owned by their members, who are farmers—assemble farm produce to be sold in local markets and share profits at the end of the year.

In less-developed countries, wholesalers are often the sole or primary means of trade; they are the main elements in the distribution systems of many countries in Latin America, East Asia, and Africa. In such countries the business activities of wholesalers may expand to include manufacturing and retailing, or they may branch out into nondistributive ventures such as real estate, finance, or transportation. Until the late 1950s, Japan was dominated by wholesaling. Even relatively large manufacturers and retailers relied principally on wholesalers as their intermediaries. However, in the late 20th century, Japanese wholesalers declined in importance. Even in the most highly industrialized countries, however, wholesalers remain essential to the operations of significant numbers of small retailers.

Brokers and Agents

Manufacturers may use brokers and agents, who do not take title possession of the goods, in marketing their products. Brokers and agents typically perform only a few of the marketing flows, and their main function is to ease buying and selling—that is, to bring buyers and sellers together and negotiate between them. Brokers, most commonly found in the food, real estate, and insurance industries, may represent either a buyer or a seller and are paid by the party who hires them. Brokers often can represent several manufacturers of noncompeting products on a commission basis. They do not carry inventory or assume risk.

Unlike merchant wholesalers, agent middlemen do not take legal ownership of the goods they sell; nor do they generally take physical possession of them. The three principal types of agent middlemen are manufacturers' agents, selling agents, and purchasing agents. Manufacturers' agents, who represent two or more manufacturers' complementary lines on a continuous basis, are usually compensated by commission. As a rule, they carry only part of a manufacturer's output, perhaps in areas where the manufacturer cannot maintain full-time salespeople. Many manufacturers' agents are businesses of only a few employees and are most commonly found in the furniture, electric, and apparel industries. Sales agents are given contractual authority to sell all of a manufacturer's output and generally have considerable autonomy to set prices, terms, and conditions of sale. Sometimes they perform the duties of a manufacturer's marketing department, although they work on a commission basis. Sales agents often provide market feedback and product information to the manufacturers and play an important role in product development. They are found in such product areas as chemicals, metals, and industrial machinery and equipment. Purchasing agents, who routinely have long-term relationships with buyers, typically receive, inspect, store, and ship goods to their buyers.

Manufacturers' and Retailers' Branches and Offices

Wholesaling operations conducted by the sellers or buyers themselves rather than by independent wholesalers comprise the third major type of wholesaling. Manufacturers may engage in wholesaling through their sales branches and offices. This allows manufacturers to improve the inventory control, selling, and promotion flows. Numerous retailers also establish purchasing offices in major market centres such as Chicago and New York City that play a role similar to that of brokers and agents. The major difference is that they are part of the buyer's own organization.

Retailers

Retailing, the merchandising aspect of marketing, includes all activities required to sell directly to consumers for their personal, nonbusiness use. The firm that performs this consumer selling—whether it is a manufacturer, wholesaler, or retailer—is engaged in retailing. Retailing can take many forms: goods or services may be sold in person, by mail, telephone, television, or the Internet, or even through vending machines. These products can be sold on the street, in a physical or online store, or in the consumer's home. However, businesses that are classified as retailers secure the vast majority of their sales volume from store-based retailing.

Retailing

For centuries most merchandise was sold in marketplaces or by peddlers. In many countries, hawkers still sell their wares while traveling from one village to the next. Marketplaces are still the primary form of retail selling in these villages. This was also true in Europe until the Renaissance, when market stalls in certain localities became permanent and eventually grew into stores and business districts.

Retail chains are known to have existed in China several centuries before the Common Era and in some European cities in the 16th and 17th centuries. However, the birth of the modern chain store can be traced to 1859, with the inauguration of what is now the Great Atlantic & Pacific Tea Company, Inc. (A&P), in New York City. During the 15th and 16th centuries the Fugger family of Germany was the first to carry out mercantile operations of a chain-store variety. In 1670 the Hudson's Bay Company chartered its chain of outposts in Canada.

Department stores also were seen in Europe and Asia as early as the 17th century. The famous Bon Marché in Paris grew from a large specialty store into a full-fledged department store in the mid-1800s. By the middle of the 20th century, department stores existed in major U.S. cities, although small independent merchants still constitute the majority of retailers.

Shopping malls, a late 20th-century development in retail practices, were created to provide for a consumer's every need in a single, self-contained shopping area. Although they were first created for the convenience of suburban populations, they can now also be found on main city thoroughfares. A large branch of a well-known retail chain usually serves as a mall's retail flagship, which is the primary attraction for customers. In fact, few malls can be financed and built without a flagship establishment already in place.

Underground mall at the main railway station in Leipzig, Germany.

Other mall proprietors have used recreation and entertainment to attract customers. Movie theatres, holiday displays, and live musical performances are often found in shopping malls. In Asian countries, malls also have been known to house swimming pools, arcades, and amusement parks. Hong Kong's City Plaza shopping mall includes one of the territory's two ice rinks. Some malls, such as the Mall of America in Bloomington, Minn., U.S., may offer exhibitions, sideshows, and other diversions.

Amusement park rides at the Mall of America, Bloomington, Minn.

Although there is a great variety of retail enterprises, with new types constantly emerging, they can be classified into three main types: store retailers, nonstore retailers, and retail organizations.

Store Retailers

Several different types of stores participate in retail merchandising. The following is a brief description of the most important store retailers.

Specialty Stores

A specialty store carries a deep assortment within a narrow line of goods. Furniture stores, florists, sporting-goods stores, and bookstores are all specialty stores. Stores such as Athlete's Foot (sports shoes only) and Tall Men (clothing for tall men) are considered superspecialty stores because they carry a very narrow product line.

Department Stores

Department stores carry a wider variety of merchandise than most stores but offer these items in separate departments within the store. These departments usually include home furnishings and household goods, as well as clothing, which may be divided into departments according to gender and age. Department stores in western Europe and Asia also have large food departments, such as the renowned food court at Harrods in the United Kingdom. Departments within each store are usually operated as separate entities, each with its own buyers, promotions, and service personnel. Some departments, such as restaurants and beauty parlours, are leased to external providers.

Department stores generally account for less than 10 percent of a country's total retail sales, but they draw large numbers of customers in urban areas. The most influential of the department stores may even be trendsetters in various fields, such as fashion. Department stores such as Sears,

Roebuck and Company have also spawned chain organizations. Others may do this through mergers or by opening branch units within a region or by expanding to other countries.

Supermarkets

Supermarkets are characterized by large facilities (15,000 to 25,000 square feet [1,394 to 2,323 square metres] with more than 12,000 items), low profit margins (earning about 1 percent operating profit on sales), high volume, and operations that serve the consumer's total needs for items such as food (groceries, meats, produce, dairy products, baked goods) and household sundries. They are organized according to product departments and operate primarily on a self-service basis. Supermarkets also may sell wines and other alcoholic beverages (depending on local licensing laws) and clothing.

The first true supermarket was opened in the United States by Michael Cullin in 1930. His King Kullen chain of large-volume food stores was so successful that it encouraged the major food-store chains to convert their specialty stores into supermarkets. When compared with the conventional independent grocer, supermarkets generally offered greater variety and convenience and often better prices as well. Consequently, in the two decades after World War II, the supermarket drove many small food retailers out of business, not only in the United States but throughout the world. In France, for example, the number of larger food stores grew from about 50 in 1960 to 4,700 in 1982, while the number of small food retailers fell from 130,000 to 60,000.

Convenience Stores

Located primarily near residential areas, convenience stores are relatively small outlets that are open long hours and carry a limited line of high-turnover convenience products at high prices. Although many have added food services, consumers use them mainly for "fill-in" purchases, such as bread, milk, or miscellaneous goods.

Superstores

Superstores, hypermarkets, and combination stores are unique retail merchandisers. With facilities averaging 35,000 square feet, superstores meet many of the consumer's needs for food and nonfood items by housing a full-service grocery store as well as such services as dry cleaning, laundry, shoe repair, and cafeterias. Combination stores typically combine a grocery store and a drug store in one facility, utilizing approximately 55,000 square feet of selling space. Hypermarkets combine supermarket, discount, and warehousing retailing principles by going beyond routinely purchased goods to include furniture, clothing, appliances, and other items. Ranging in size from 80,000 to 220,000 square feet, hypermarkets display products in bulk quantities that require minimum handling by store personnel.

Discount Stores

Selling merchandise below the manufacturer's list price is known as discounting. The discount store has become an increasingly popular means of retailing. Following World War II, a number of retail establishments in the United States began to pursue a high-volume, low-profit strategy designed to attract price-conscious consumers. A key strategy for keeping operating costs (and therefore prices) low was to locate in low-rent shopping districts and to offer minimal service assistance. This no-frills approach was used at first only with hard goods, or consumer durables, such as electrical household appliances, but it has since been shown to be successful with soft goods, such as clothing. This practice has been adopted for a wide variety of products, so that discount stores have essentially become department stores with reduced prices and fewer services. In the late 20th century, discount stores began to operate outlet malls. These groups of discount stores are usually located some distance away from major metropolitan areas and have facilities that make them indistinguishable from standard shopping malls. As they gained popularity, many discount stores improved their facilities and appearances, added new lines and services, and opened suburban branches. Coupled with attempts by traditional department stores to reduce prices in order to compete with discounters, the distinction between many department and discount stores has become blurred. Specialty discount operations have grown significantly in electronics, sporting goods, and books.

Off-price Retailers

Off-price retailers offer a different approach to discount retailing. As discount houses tried to increase services and offerings in order to upgrade, off-price retailers invaded this low-price, high-volume sector. Off-price retailers purchase at below-wholesale prices and charge less than retail prices. This practice is quite different from that of ordinary discounters, who buy at the market wholesale price and simply accept lower margins by pricing their products below retail costs. Off-price retailers carry a constantly changing collection of overruns, irregulars, and leftover goods and have made their biggest forays in the clothing, footwear, and accessories industries. The three primary examples of off-price retailers are factory outlets, independent carriers, and warehouse clubs. Stocking manufacturers' surplus, discontinued, or irregular products, factory outlets are owned and operated by the manufacturer. Independent off-price retailers carry a rapidly changing collection of higher-quality merchandise and are typically owned and operated by entrepreneurs or divisions of larger retail companies. Warehouse (or wholesale) clubs operate out of enormous, low-cost facilities and charge patrons an annual membership fee. They sell a limited selection of brand-name grocery items, appliances, clothing, and miscellaneous items at a deep discount. These warehouse stores, such as Wal-Mart-owned Sam's, Price Club, and Costco (in the United States), maintain low costs because they buy products at huge quantity discounts, use less labour in stocking, and typically do not make home deliveries or accept credit cards.

Nonstore Retailers

Some retailers do not operate stores, and these nonstore businesses have grown much faster than store retailers. The major types of nonstore retailing are direct selling, direct marketing, and automatic vending.

Direct Selling

This form of retailing originated several centuries ago and has mushroomed into a multibillion-dollar industry consisting of companies selling door-to-door, office-to-office, or at private-home sales meetings. The forerunners in the direct-selling industry include The Fuller Brush Company (brushes, brooms, etc.), Electrolux (vacuum cleaners), and Avon (cosmetics). In addition, Tupperware pioneered the home-sales approach, in which friends and neighbours gather in a home where Tupperware products are demonstrated and sold. Network marketing, a direct-selling approach similar to home sales, is also gaining prevalence in markets worldwide. In the model used by companies such as Amway and Shaklee, distributors are rewarded not only for their direct sales but also for the sales of those they have recruited to become distributors. In 2007 Amway's parent company tested an Internet recruitment model by launching Fanista, a Web site that sells entertainment media such as books, movies, and music while rewarding users for bringing other customers to the site.

Direct Marketing

Direct marketing is direct contact between a seller (manufacturer or retailer) and a consumer. Generally speaking, a seller can measure response to an offer because of its direct addressability. Although direct marketing gained wide popularity as a marketing strategy only in the late 20th century, it has been successfully utilized for more than one hundred years. Sears, Roebuck and Company and the now-defunct Montgomery Ward & Co. began as direct marketers in the late 1880s, selling their products solely by mail order. A century later, however, both companies were conducting most of their business in retail stores; Montgomery Ward ceased operations in the early 21st century. Many contemporary department stores and specialty stores supplement their store operations with direct-marketing transactions by mail, telephone, or the Internet. Mail-order firms grew rapidly in the 1950s and '60s in continental Europe, Great Britain, and certain other highly industrialized nations. Modern direct marketing is generally supported by advanced database technologies that track each customer's purchase behaviour. These technologies are used by established retail firms, such as Quelle and Neckermann in Germany, and are the foundation of mail-order businesses such as J. Crew, The Sharper Image, and L.L. Bean (all in the United States). Direct marketing is not a worldwide business phenomenon, however, because mail-order operations require infrastructure elements that are still lacking in many countries, such as efficient transportation networks and secure methods for transmitting payments.

Direct marketing has expanded from its early forms, among them direct mail and catalog mailings, to include such vehicles as telemarketing, direct-response radio and television, and Internet shopping. Unlike many other forms of promotion, a direct-marketing campaign is quantitatively measurable.

Automatic Vending

Automatic vending is a unique area in nonstore merchandising because the variety of merchandise offered through automatic vending machines continues to grow. Initially, impulse goods with high convenience value such as cigarettes, soft drinks, candy, newspapers, and hot beverages were offered. However, a wide array of products such as hosiery, cosmetics, food snacks, postage stamps, paperback books, record albums, camera film, and even fishing worms are becoming available through machines.

Vending-machine operations are usually offered in sites owned by other businesses, institutions, and transportation agencies. They can be found in offices, gasoline stations, large retail stores, hotels, restaurants, and many other locales. In Japan vending machines now dispense frozen beef, fresh flowers, whiskey, jewelry, and even names of prospective dating partners. In Sweden vending machines have developed as a supplementary channel to retail stores, where hours of business are restricted by law. High costs of manufacturing, installation, and operation have somewhat limited the expansion of vending-machine retailing. In addition, consumers typically pay a high premium for vended merchandise.

Retail Organizations

While merchants can sell their wares through a store or nonstore retailing format, retail organizations can also structure themselves in several different ways. The major types of retail organizations are corporate chains, voluntary chains and retailer cooperatives, consumer cooperatives, franchise organizations, and merchandising conglomerates.

Corporate Chains

Two or more outlets that have common ownership and control, centralized buying and merchandising operations, and similar lines of merchandise are considered corporate chain stores. Corporate chain stores appear to be strongest in the food, drug, shoe, variety, and women's clothing industries. Managed chain stores have a number of advantages over independently managed stores. Because managed chains buy large volumes of products, suppliers are willing to offer cost advantages that are not usually available to other stores. These savings can be passed on to consumers in the form of lower prices and better sales. In addition, because managed chains operate on such a large scale, they can hire more specialized and experienced personnel, who may be better able to take full advantage of purchasing and promotion opportunities. Chain stores also have the opportunity to take advantage of economies of scale in the areas of advertising, store design, and inventory control. However, a corporate chain may have disadvantages as well. Its size and bureaucracy often weaken staff members' personal interest, drive, creativity, and customer-service motivation.

Voluntary Chains and Retailer Cooperatives

These are associations of independent retailers, unlike corporate chains. Wholesaler-sponsored voluntary chains of retailers who engage in bulk buying and collective merchandising are prevalent in many countries. True Value hardware stores represent this type of arrangement in the United States. In western Europe there are several large wholesaler-sponsored chains of retailers located across multiple countries, each store using the same name and, as a rule, offering the same brands of products but remaining an independent enterprise. Wholesaler-sponsored chains offer the same types of services for their clients as do the financially integrated retail chains. Retailer cooperatives, such as ACE hardware stores, are grouped as independent retailers who establish a central buying organization and conduct joint promotion efforts.

Consumer Cooperatives

Consumer cooperatives, or co-ops, are retail outlets that are owned and operated by consumers for their mutual benefit. The first consumer cooperative store was established in Rochdale, Eng., in 1844, and most co-ops are modeled after the same, original principles. They are based on open consumer membership, equal voting among members, limited customer services, and shared profits among members in the form of rebates generally related to the amounts of their purchases. Consumer cooperatives have gained widespread popularity throughout western and northern

Europe, particularly in Denmark, Finland, Iceland, Norway, Sweden, and Great Britain. Co-ops typically emerge because community residents believe that local retailers' prices are too high or service is substandard.

Franchise Organizations

Franchise arrangements are characterized by a contractual relationship between a franchiser (a manufacturer, wholesaler, or service organization) and franchisees (independent entrepreneurs who purchase the right to own and operate any number of units in the franchise systems). Typified by a unique product, service, business method, trade name, or patent, franchises have been prominent in many industries, including fast foods, video stores, health and fitness centres, hair salons, auto rentals, motels, and travel agencies. McDonald's Corporation is a prominent example of a franchise retail organization, with franchises all over the world.

Merchandising Conglomerates

Merchandising conglomerates combine several diversified retailing lines and forms under central ownership, as well as integrate distribution and management of functions. Merchandising conglomerates are relatively free-form corporations.

Marketing Facilitators

Because marketing functions require significant expertise, it is often both efficient and effective for an organization to use the assistance of independent marketing facilitators. These are organizations and consultants whose sole or primary responsibility is to handle marketing functions. In many larger companies, all or some of these functions are performed internally. However, this is not necessary or justifiable in most companies, which usually require only part-time or periodic assistance from marketing facilitators. Also, most companies cannot afford to support the salaries and operating expenses required to maintain marketing facilitators as a permanent part of their staff. Furthermore, independent marketing contractors can be more effective than an internal department because nonemployee facilitators can have broader expertise and more objective perspectives. In addition, independent contractors often are more motivated to perform at high standards, because competition in the facilitator market is usually aggressive, and poor performance could mean lost business.

There are four major types of marketing facilitators: advertising agencies, market research firms, transportation firms, and warehousing firms.

Advertising Agencies

Advertising agencies are responsible for initiating, managing, and implementing paid marketing communications. In addition, some agencies have diversified into other types of marketing communications, including public relations, sales promotion, interactive media, and direct marketing. Agencies typically consist of four departments: account management, a creative division, a research group, and a media planning department. Those in account management act as liaisons between the client and the agency, ensuring that client needs are communicated to the agency and that agency recommendations are clearly understood by the client. Account managers also manage the flow of work within the agency, making sure that projects proceed according to schedule. The creative department is where advertisements are conceived, developed, and produced. Artists, writers, and producers work together to craft a message that meets agency and client objectives. In this department, slogans, jingles, and logos are developed. The research department gathers and processes data about the target market and consumers. This information provides a foundation for the work of the creative department and account management. Media planning personnel specialize in selecting and placing advertisements in print and broadcast media.

Market Research Firms

Market research firms gather and analyze data about customers, competitors, distributors, and other actors and forces in the marketplace. A large portion of the work performed by most market research firms is commissioned by specific companies for particular purposes. However, some firms also routinely collect a wide spectrum of data and then attempt to sell some or all of it to companies that may benefit from such information. For example, the A.C. Nielsen Co. in the United States specializes in supplying marketing data about consumer television viewing habits, and Information Resources, Inc. (IRI), has an extensive database regarding consumer supermarket purchases.

Marketing research may be quantitative, qualitative, or a combination of both. Quantitative research is numerically oriented, requires significant attention to the measurement of market phenomena, and often involves statistical analysis. For example, when a restaurant asks its customers to rate different aspects of its service on a scale from 1 (good) to 10 (poor), this provides quantitative information that may be analyzed statistically. Qualitative research focuses on descriptive words and symbols and usually involves observing consumers in a marketing setting or questioning them about their product or service consumption experiences. For example, a marketing researcher may stop a consumer who has purchased a particular type of detergent and ask him why that detergent was chosen. Qualitative and quantitative research each provides different insights into consumer behaviour, and research results are ordinarily more useful when the two methods are combined.

Market research can be thought of as the application of scientific method to the solution of marketing problems. It involves studying people as buyers, sellers, and consumers, examining their attitudes, preferences, habits, and purchasing power. Market research is also concerned with the channels of distribution, with promotion and pricing, and with the design of the products and services to be marketed.

Transportation Firms

As a product moves from producer to consumer, it must often travel long distances. Many products consumed in the United States have been manufactured in another area of the world, such as Asia or Mexico. In addition, if the channel of distribution includes several firms, the product must be moved a number of times before it becomes accessible to consumers. A basic home appliance begins as a raw material (iron ore at a steel mill, for example) that is transported from a processing plant to a manufacturing facility.

Transportation firms assist marketers in moving products from one point in a channel to the next. An important matter of negotiation between companies working together in a channel is whether the sender or receiver of goods is responsible for transportation. Movement of products usually involves significant cost, risk, and time management. Thus, when firms consider a transportation option, they carefully weigh its dependability and price, frequency of operation, and accessibility. A firm that has its own transportation capabilities is known as a private carrier. There are also contract carriers, which are independent transportation firms that can be hired by companies on a long- or short-term basis. A common carrier provides services to any and all companies between predetermined points on a scheduled basis. The U.S. Postal Service is a common carrier, as are Federal Express and the Amtrak railway system.

Warehousing Firms

Because products are not usually sold or shipped as soon as they are produced or delivered, firms require storage facilities. Two types of warehouses meet this need: storage warehouses hold goods for longer periods of time, and distribution warehouses serve as way stations for goods as they pass from one location to the next. Like the other marketing functions, warehouses can be wholly owned by firms, or space can be rented as needed. Although companies have more control over wholly owned facilities, warehouses of this sort can tie up capital and firm resources. Operations within warehouses usually require inspecting goods, tracking inventories, repackaging goods, shipping, and invoicing.

Consumer-goods Marketing

Consumer goods can be classified according to consumer shopping habits.

Convenience Goods

Convenience goods are those that the customer purchases frequently, immediately, and with minimum effort. Soaps and newspapers are considered convenience goods, as are common staples like ketchup or pasta. Convenience-goods purchasing is usually based on habitual behaviour, where the consumer will routinely purchase a particular product. Some convenience goods, however, may be purchased impulsively, involving no habit, planning, or search effort. These goods, usually displayed near the cash register in a store in order to encourage quick choice and purchase, include candy, razors, and batteries. A slightly different type of convenience product is the emergency good, which is purchased when there is an urgent need. Such goods include umbrellas and snow shovels, and these are usually distributed at a wide variety of outlets so that they will be readily available when necessary.

Shopping Goods

A second type of product is the shopping good, which usually requires a more involved selection process than convenience goods. A consumer usually compares a variety of attributes, including suitability, quality, price, and style. Homogeneous shopping goods are those that are similar in quality but different enough in other attributes (such as price, brand image, or style) to justify a search process. These products might include automobile tires or a stereo or television system. Homogeneous shopping goods are often sold strongly on price.

With heterogeneous shopping goods, product features become more important to the consumer than price. Such is often the case with the purchase of major appliances, clothing, furniture, and high-tech equipment. In this situation, the item purchased must be a certain size or colour and must perform very specific functions that cannot be fulfilled by all items offered by every supplier. With goods of this sort, the seller has to carry a wide assortment to satisfy individual tastes and must have well-trained salespeople to provide both information and advice to consumers.

Specialty Goods

Specialty goods have particularly unique characteristics and brand identifications for which a significant group of buyers is willing to make a special purchasing effort. Examples include specific brands of fancy products, luxury cars, professional photographic equipment, and high-fashion clothing. For instance, consumers who favour merchandise produced by a certain shoe manufacturer or furniture maker will, if necessary, travel considerable distances in order to purchase that particular brand. In specialty-goods markets, sellers do not encourage comparisons between options; buyers invest time to reach dealers carrying the product desired, and these dealers therefore do not necessarily need to be conveniently located.

Unsought Goods

Finally, an unsought good is one that a consumer does not know about—or knows about but does not normally think of buying. New products, such as new frozen-food concepts or new smartphones, are unsought until consumers learn about them through word-of-mouth influence or advertising. In addition, the need for unsought goods may not seem urgent to the consumer, and purchase is often deferred. This is frequently the case with life insurance, preventive car maintenance, and cemetery plots. Because of this, unsought goods require significant marketing efforts, and some of the more sophisticated selling techniques have been developed from the challenge to sell unsought goods.

Services Marketing

A service is an act of labour or a performance that does not produce a tangible commodity and does not result in the customer's ownership of anything. Its production may or may not be tied to a physical product. Thus, there are pure services that involve no tangible product (as with psychotherapy), tangible goods with accompanying services (such as a computer software package with free software support), and hybrid product-services that consist of parts of each (for instance, restaurants are usually patronized for both their food and their service).

Services can be distinguished from products because they are intangible, inseparable from the production process, variable, and perishable. Services are intangible because they can often not be seen, tasted, felt, heard, or smelled before they are purchased. A person purchasing plastic surgery cannot see the results before the purchase, and a lawyer's client cannot anticipate the outcome of a case before the lawyer's work is presented in court. To reduce the uncertainty that results from this intangibility, marketers may strive to make their service tangible by emphasizing the place, people, equipment, communications, symbols, or price of the service. For example, consider the insurance slogan "You're in good hands with Allstate."

Services are inseparable from their production because they are typically produced and consumed simultaneously. This is not true of physical products, which are often consumed long after the product has been manufactured, inventoried, distributed, and placed in a retail store. Inseparability is especially evident in entertainment services or professional services. In many cases, inseparability limits the production of services because they are so directly tied to the individuals who perform them. This problem can be alleviated if a service provider learns to work faster or if the service expertise can be standardized and performed by a number of individuals or in some cases by software that the consumer purchases or uses online for a fee.

The variability of services comes from their significant human component. Not only do humans differ from one another, but their performance at any given time may differ from their performance at another time. The mechanics at a particular auto service garage, for example, may differ in terms of their knowledge and expertise, and each mechanic will have "good" days and "bad" days. Variability can be reduced by quality-control measures. These measures can include good selection and training of personnel and allowing customers to communicate dissatisfaction (e.g., through customer suggestion and complaint systems) so that poor service can be detected and corrected.

Finally, services are perishable because they cannot be stored. Because of this, it is difficult for service providers to manage anything other than steady demand. When demand increases dramatically, service organizations face the problem of producing enough output to meet customer needs. When a large tour bus unexpectedly arrives at a restaurant, its staff must rush to meet the demand, because the food services (taking orders, making food, taking money, etc.) cannot be "warehoused" for such an occasion. To manage such instances, companies may hire part-time employees, develop efficiency routines for peak demand occasions, or ask consumers to participate in the service-delivery process. On the other hand, when demand drops off precipitously, service organizations are often burdened with a staff of service providers who are not performing. Organizations can maintain steady demand by offering differential pricing during off-peak times, anticipating off-peak hours by requiring reservations, and giving employees more flexible work shifts.

Business Marketing

Business marketing, sometimes called business-to-business marketing or industrial marketing, involves those marketing activities and functions that are targeted toward organizational customers. This type of marketing involves selling goods (and services) to organizations (public and private) to be used directly or indirectly in their own production or service-delivery operations. Some of the major industries that comprise the business market are construction, manufacturing, mining, transportation, public utilities, communications, and distribution. One of the key points that differentiates business from consumer marketing is the magnitude of the transactions. For example, in the early 21st century, a Boeing 747 airliner, selling for more than $300 million, could take up to four years to manufacture and deliver once the order was placed. Often a major airline company will order several aircraft at one time, making the purchase price as high as several billion dollars.

Customers for industrial goods can be divided into three groups: user customers, original-equipment manufacturers, and resellers. User customers make use of the goods they purchase in their own businesses. An automobile manufacturer, for example, might purchase a metal-stamping press to produce parts for its vehicles. Original-equipment manufacturers incorporate the purchased goods into their final products, which are then sold to final consumers. Industrial resellers are middlemen—essentially wholesalers but in some cases retailers—who distribute goods to user customers, to original-equipment manufacturers, and to other middlemen. Industrial-goods wholesalers include mill-supply houses, steel warehouses, machine-tool dealers, paper jobbers, and chemical distributors.

Nonprofit Marketing

Marketing scholars began exploring the application of marketing to nonprofit organizations in 1969. Since then, nonprofit organizations have increasingly turned to marketing for growth, funding, and prosperity.

Although it is difficult to define "nonprofit" organizations because of the existence of a number of quasi-governmental organizations, a study in the early 21st century found more than 1.5 million private, nonprofit organizations in the United States. Some experts believe that the way to distinguish between organizations is according to their sources of funding. The three major sources are profits, government revenues (such as grants or taxes), and voluntary donations. In addition, a legally defined nonprofit organization is one that has been granted tax-exempt status by the Internal Revenue Service. However, while nonprofit groups can be defined legally, it is more helpful to focus on the specific marketing activities that need to be performed within the organization's environment. Museums, hospitals, universities, and churches are all examples of nonprofit organizations. Although many individuals may believe that nonprofit organizations have only a small impact on the economy, the operating expenditures of private nonprofit organizations now represent a significant percentage of the U.S. gross national product. In addition, many of these are substantial enterprises.

Social Marketing

Social marketing employs marketing principles and techniques to advance a social cause, idea, or behaviour. It entails the design, implementation, and control of programs aimed at increasing the acceptability of a social idea or practice that would benefit the adoptors or society. Social ideas can take the form of beliefs, attitudes, and values, such as human rights. Whether social marketers are promoting ideas or social practices, their ultimate goal is to alter behaviour. In order to accomplish this behaviour change, social marketers set measurable objectives, research their target group's needs, target their "products" to these particular "consumers," and effectively communicate their benefits. In addition, social-marketing organizations have to be constantly aware of changes in their environments and must be able to adapt to these changes. One very significant change of environment took place in the early 2000s with the advent of social networking via the Internet, which encompassed blogs, Web sites such as Facebook and LinkedIn, and instant-messaging services such as Twitter. A large proportion of social marketing has since been conducted through these media.

Place Marketing

Place marketing employs marketing principles and techniques to advance the appeal and viability of a place (town, city, state, region, or nation) to tourists, businesses, investors, and residents.

Among the "place sellers" are economic development agencies, tourist promotion agencies, and mayors' offices. Place sellers must gain a deep understanding of how place buyers make their purchasing decisions. Place-marketing activities can be found in both the private and public sectors at the local, regional, national, and international levels. They can range from activities involving downtrodden cities trying to attract businesses to vacation spots seeking to attract tourists. In implementing these marketing activities, each locale must adapt to external shocks and forces beyond its control (intergovernmental power shifts, increasing global competition, and rapid technological change) as well as to internal forces and decline cycles.

Economic and Social Aspects of Marketing

Sometimes criticized for its impact on personal economic and social well-being, marketing has been said to affect not only individual consumers but also society as a whole.

Marketing and Individual Welfare

Criticisms have been leveled against marketers, claiming that some of their practices may damage individual welfare. While this may be true in certain circumstances, it is important to recognize that, if a business damages individual welfare, it cannot hope to continue in the marketplace for long. As a consequence, most unfavourable views of marketing are criticisms of poor marketing, not of strategically sound marketing practices.

Others have raised concerns about marketing by saying that it increases prices by encouraging excessive markups. Marketers recognize that consumers may be willing to pay more for a product—such as a necklace from Tiffany & Co.—simply because of the associated prestige. This not only results in greater costs for promotion and distribution, but it allows marketers to earn profit margins that may be significantly higher than industry norms. Marketers counter these concerns by pointing out that products provide not only functional benefits but symbolic ones as well. By creating a symbol of prestige and luxury, Tiffany offers a symbolic benefit that, according to some consumers, justifies the price. In addition, brands may symbolize not only prestige but also quality and functionality, which gives consumers greater confidence when they purchase a branded product. Finally, advertising and promotions are often very cost-effective methods of informing the general public about items and services that are available in the marketplace.

A few marketers have been accused of using deceptive practices, such as misleading promotional activities or high-pressure selling. These deceptive practices have given rise to legislative and administrative remedies, including guidelines offered by the Federal Trade Commission (FTC) regarding advertising practices, automatic 30-day guarantee policies by some manufacturers, and "cooling off" periods during which a consumer may cancel any contract signed. In addition, professional marketing associations, such as the Direct Marketing Association, have promulgated a set of professional standards for their industry, including a requirement that marketers provide consumers with the opportunity to modify or decline future mail or e-mail solicitations.

Marketing and Societal Welfare

Concern also has been raised that some marketing practices may encourage excessive interest in material possessions, create "false wants," or promote the purchase of nonessential goods. For example, in the United States, children's Saturday morning television programming came under fire for promoting materialistic values. The Federal Communications Commission (FCC) responded in the early 1990s by regulating the amount of commercial time per hour. In many of these cases, however, the criticisms overstate the power of marketing communications to influence individuals and portray members of the public as individuals unable to distinguish between a good decision and a bad one. In addition, such charges cast marketing as a cause of social problems when often the problems have much deeper societal roots.

Marketing activity also has been sometimes criticized because of its control by strong private interests and its neglect of social and public concern. For example, while companies in the oil and alcohol industries may have significant influence on legislation, media, and individual behaviour, organizations that focus on environmental, health, or education concerns are not able to wield such influence and often fail to receive appropriate recognition for their efforts. While there is clearly an imbalance of power between private interests and public ones, since the late 20th century private companies have received more praise for their marketing efforts for social causes.

Marketing's Contribution to Individuals and Society

Although some have questioned the appropriateness of the marketing philosophy in an age of environmental deterioration, resource shortages, world hunger and poverty, and neglected social services, numerous firms are commendably satisfying individual consumer demands as well as acting in the long-term interests of the consumer and society. These dual objectives of many of today's companies have led to a broadening of the "marketing concept" to become the "societal marketing concept." Generating customer satisfaction while at the same time attending to consumer and societal well-being in the long run are the core concepts of societal marketing.

In practicing socictal marketing, marketers try to balance company profits, consumer satisfaction, and public interest in their marketing policies. Many companies have achieved success in adopting societal marketing. Two companies that were among the pioneers of societal marketing are The Body Shop International PLC, based in England, and Ben & Jerry's Homemade Inc., which produces ice cream and is based in the U.S. state of Vermont. Body Shop's cosmetics and personal hygiene products, based on natural ingredients, are sold in recycled packaging. The products are formulated without animal testing, and a percentage of profits each year is donated to animal rights groups, homeless shelters, Amnesty International, rain-forest preservation groups, and other social causes. Ben & Jerry's donates a percentage of its profits to help alleviate social and environmental problems. The company's corporate concept focuses on "caring capitalism," which involves the product as well as social and economic missions.

Marketing has had many other positive benefits for individuals and society. It has helped accelerate economic development and create new jobs. It has also contributed to technological progress and enhanced consumers' choices.

Importance of Marketing

Helps in Transfer, Exchange and Movement of Goods

Marketing is very helpful in transfer, exchange and movement of goods. Goods and services are made available to customers through various intermediaries' viz., wholesalers and retailers etc. Marketing is helpful to both producers and consumers.

To the former, it tells about the specific needs and preferences of consumers and to the latter about the products that manufacturers can offer. According to Prof. Haney Hansen "Marketing involves the design of the products acceptable to the consumers and the conduct of those activities which facilitate the transfer of ownership between seller and buyer."

Helpful in Raising and Maintaining the Standard of Living of the Community

Marketing is above all the giving of a standard of living to the community. Paul Mazur states, "Marketing is the delivery of standard of living". Professor Malcolm McNair has further added that "Marketing is the creation and delivery of standard of living to the society".

By making available the uninterrupted supply of goods and services to consumers at a reasonable price, marketing has played an important role in raising and maintaining living standards of the community. Community comprises of three classes of people i.e., rich, middle and poor. Everything which is used by these different classes of people is supplied by marketing.

In the modern times, with the emergence of latest marketing techniques even the poorer sections of society have attained a reasonable level of living standard. This is basically due to large scale production and lesser prices of commodities and services. Marketing has infact, revolutionised and modernised the living standard of people in modern times.

Creates Employment

Marketing is complex mechanism involving many people in one form or the other. The major marketing functions are buying, selling, financing, transport, warehousing, risk bearing and standardisation, etc. In each such function different activities are performed by a large number of individuals and bodies.

Thus, marketing gives employment to many people. It is estimated that about 40% of total population is directly or indirectly dependent upon marketing. In the modern era of large scale production and industrialisation, role of marketing has widened.

This enlarged role of marketing has created many employment opportunities for people. Converse, Huegy and Mitchell have rightly pointed out that "In order to have continuous production, there must be continuous marketing, only then employment can be sustained and high level of business activity can be continued".

Source of Income and Revenue

The performance of marketing function is all important, because it is the only way through which the concern could generate revenue or income and bring in profits. Buskirk has pointed out that, "Any activity connected with obtaining income is a marketing action. It is all too easy for the accountant, engineer, etc., to operate under the broad assumption that the Company will realise many dollars in total sales volume.

However, someone must actually go into the market place and obtain dollars from society in order to sustain the activities of the company, because without these funds the organisation will perish."

Marketing does provide many opportunities to earn profits in the process of buying and selling the goods, by creating time, place and possession utilities. This income and profit are reinvested in the concern, thereby earning more profits in future. Marketing should be given the greatest importance, since the very survival of the firm depends on the effectiveness of the marketing function.

Basis for Making Decisions

A businessman is confronted with many problems in the form of what, how, when, how much and for whom to produce. In the past problems was less on account of local markets. There was a direct link between producer and consumer. In modern times marketing has become a very complex and tedious task. Marketing has emerged as new specialised activity along with production.

As a result, producers are depending largely on the mechanism of marketing, to decide what to produce and sell. With the help of marketing techniques a producer can regulate his production accordingly.

Source of New Ideas

The concept of marketing is a dynamic concept. It has changed altogether with the passage of time. Such changes have far reaching effects on production and distribution. With the rapid change in tastes and preference of people, marketing has to come up with the same.

Marketing as an instrument of measurement, gives scope for understanding this new demand pattern and thereby produce and make available the goods accordingly.

Helpful in Development of an Economy

Adam Smith has remarked that "nothing happens in our country until somebody sells something". Marketing is the kingpin that sets the economy revolving. The marketing organisation, more scientifically organized, makes the economy strong and stable, the lesser the stress on the marketing function, the weaker will be the economy.

Marketing Management

Marketing management signifies an important functional area of business management responsible for the flow of goods and services from the producers to the consumers. It is accountable for planning, organizing, directing, coordinating, motivating and controlling the marketing activities. In effect, it is the demand management under customer oriented marketing philosophy.

Marketing management is the management of the crucial and creative task of delivering consumer satisfaction and thereby earning profits through consumer demand. It is the performance of managerial functions of planning, execution, coordination and control in relation to the marketing functions of marketing research, product-planning and development, pricing, advertising, selling and distribution with a view to satisfy the needs of consumer, business and society.

The above expressions bring home very clearly the very substance of marketing management as a matter of planning, implementing and controlling the marketing programmes. Marketing management is the marketing concept in action.

It includes all activities which are necessary to determine and satisfy the needs of consumers. To be very simple, marketing management sets marketing objectives, develops marketing plans, organizes marketing functions, puts marketing plans and strategies in action and monitors the marketing programmes in the final analysis.

Effective marketing management requires the ability and the skill of highest order. It warrants close appreciation of the consumer and an understanding of forces of change which are at work in the environment and which have deep-rooted impact on consumer buying habits and motives.

It calls for fertile imagination and creative skill in planning to meet the changing conditions of the market place; it also requires skills of coordinating and controlling the wide-spread and complex activities of a dynamic organisation.

The prime purpose of marketing management is to know the consumer so well that the firm is able to offer him or her products and services to which the consumer remains loyal and the new consumers keep on coming at increasing level.

Objectives of Marketing Management

The objectives of marketing management are derived from the overall objectives of business. The overall objectives of business are profit-making, growth and service of society among other things.

Marketing management can contribute towards the achievement of these objectives by developing and distributing products and services which satisfy the needs of customers and give profits to the business enterprise.

In brief, the objectives of marketing management are:

Creating Customers

A business firm is established to sell a product or service to customers. Therefore, the customer is the foundation of a business. It is the customer who provides revenue to business and determines what an enterprise will sell.

Creating customers means exploring and identifying the needs and requirements of customers. If a firm is to go and stay in business, it must create new customers. It should analyze and understand their wants.

Satisfying Customers Needs

Creating customer is not enough. Business should develop and distribute products and services which meet the requirements of customers to their satisfaction. If customers are not satisfied, the business will not be able to generate revenues to meet its costs and to earn a reasonable return on its capital. Satisfying customers does not simply mean matching products with customers' needs. It also requires regular supply of goods and services of reasonable quality at fair prices.

Types of Marketing 2

- **Direct Marketing**
- **Guerrilla Marketing**
- **Online Advertising**
- **Evangelism Marketing**
- **Multi-level Marketing**
- **Global Marketing**

Some of the common types of marketing are direct marketing, guerrilla marketing, online advertising, evangelism marketing, multi-level marketing and global marketing. The topics elaborated in this chapter will help in gaining a better perspective about these diverse types of marketing.

Direct Marketing

Direct marketing is a type of marketing where marketers communicate with their customer via various media such as phone, Whatsapp, brochures, flyers and targeted online advertisements. Often, potential customers are offered something tangible, such as a demo or other valuable content. It's a fairly aggressive form of marketing because customers are contacted without having requested this beforehand. Direct marketing is usually used by companies that focus on product and service sales, but also by non-profit organisations. While it's believed that mass marketing is slowly nearing its end, it's expected that direct marketing activities will increase. The most efficient way of direct marketing takes place when a direct and friction-less effort is made to reach the target group. This means that, in direct marketing, a specific call-to-action is often made, such as: 'call this number', or 'click this button to subscribe'. The advantage of this strategy is that, in such campaigns, efficiency can be measured directly given that the organisation can keep track of how many customers have responded via these calls-to-action.

Montgomery Ward started using direct marketing in the nineteenth century. Ward was a pioneer in the field of mail orders. He managed to remove the intermediary and directly serve his customers to keep prices low. However, the term was later invented by Lester Wunderman in 1967.

Wunderman is the man behind the free 1-800 number that's used in the United States and various customer loyalty programmes.

Effectiveness

Customers for whom direct marketing is highly suitable are those who are registered for mailing lists. For example, at the checkout of an online shopping cart, the user is often given the option to subscribe to a service, such as: 'send me information about promotions and offers in the future'. Such actions already show a customer's interest in a product or company.

Non-targeted mailing lists are also sent to lots of mail boxes and email accounts. Despite the fact that most people are frustrated by this 'spam', a relatively high percentage is converted into sales. These percentages are higher when emails are aimed at a certain group or community.

Due to this frustration, organisations must be creative with their direct marketing strategies. To stand out, they use unusual shapes such as 3D projects, pop-ups or they send large flyers with unusual shapes and colours. The type of direct marketing depends on the industry. A too aggressive or misleading form of marketing often leaves a bad impression of the company. Organisations must also adhere to privacy and contact regulations. Gathering email lists without users having registered beforehand, is punishable by law.

Responses and Profitability

As stated, the costs and responses when using direct marketing can be easily monitored because of the calls-to-action that are used. It's possible to measure whether the marketing strategy is effective. Successful marketers plan activities, determine objectives and demographics, implement strategies and test elements to make a campaign successful. Evaluating data is the key to success.

To evaluate the success of the direct marketing campaign, information is gathered about the fixed costs and variable costs regarding the number and type of pieces that are sent or the promotions that are offered. Subsequently, the arising generated income is tracked. Following this, a simple costs-benefit analysis can be used to calculate the profitability.

Examples of Direct Marketing

Foto Inc. is an organisation that specialises in developing photo editing software. The marketing team worked on a new direct marketing campaign where temporary free licenses are issued for the newest photo editing software. This demo is sent to 3,000 selected graphic designer agencies. To determine whether the campaign is successful and whether this could be continued in the future, Foto Inc. analyses the results with a simple costs-benefit analysis.

Beforehand, it's calculated that at least 65 of the total of 3,000 selected companies must purchase the software to make the campaign break even. For this reason, if Foto Inc. doesn't achieve a response percentage of 2.2% during the campaign period, no profit will be achieved and they will certainly not continue the campaign.

Challenges in Direct Marketing

Many marketers who use a direct marketing campaign acknowledge the financial advantages of increasing their product or service awareness by sending demos or sharing other valuable content with potential customers. Regardless, there are also direct marketing campaigns that use certain kinds of media that create leads of poor quality, with a low response percentage. This is a problem for both the consumer and marketer. Marketers don't want to waste money on communication and means for consumers who aren't interested in their products or services.

Undesired emails or postal mail also form a problem in direct marketing. This refers to unsolicited commercial advertisements that are delivered at the postal office or directly to the consumer's mailbox. Partly because of this, consumers have uttered their concern about the privacy implications of direct marketing.

Developing a Direct Marketing Campaign

A direct marketing campaign starts by gathering data of the demographic and categories of consumers that are thought to be interested in their product or service. For this purpose, lists are developed for making contact. These lists can be manually generated, but also through public or commercial sources. Commercial sources include those that people have actively registered for, such as a weekly newsletter.

Once lists have been created, the medium is selected. Various channels can be used, including email, phone, sending brochures or face-to-face contact. This depends on the type of organisation. A restaurant probably prefers to use flyers that are distributed door-to-door in the vicinity of the restaurant.

Each direct marketing campaign must contain a specific call-to-action. Often, the goal is an immediate purchase. 'Pick up your phone and order now', but it can also be something more subtle. In any case, a first step is taken here towards a new lead that could result in a sale.

Furthermore, each direct marketing campaign must implement a method of tracking responses. In the case of the restaurant, a specific phone number may be linked to the campaign, or alternatively, a unique online link or code the consumer can use to benefit from the promotion. Marketers use the response data to measure how effective a campaign was. These data are used to adjust the campaign if necessary, but are also combined with data of other campaigns to give the team a general idea of the demographics and effectiveness of the chosen marketing strategy.

Types of Direct Marketing

Direct Mail

Direct mail is posted mail that advertises your business and its products and services. There are several different types of direct mail (e.g. catalogues, postcards, envelope mailers). Direct mail campaigns are usually sent to all postal customers in an area or to all customers on a marketing list.

Telemarketing

Telemarketing involves contacting potential customers over the phone to sell products or services. It is capable of generating new customer prospects in large volumes and is also a useful tool for following up on direct marketing campaigns. However, a successful telemarketing involves planning and using accurate and well-researched customer data to match customer profiles to product profiles.

Email Marketing

Email marketing is a simple, cost-effective and measurable way of reaching your customers. It can include e-newsletters, promotional emails to generate new leads or offers for existing customers, or ads that can appear in other business's emails.

Text (SMS) Marketing

Text messaging allows businesses to reach individual customers and send messages to large groups of people at a low cost. You could use short message service (SMS) messaging to send customers sales alerts, links to website updates, appointment or delivery reminders, or personalised messaging.

Leaflet Marketing using Letterbox Drops and Handouts

Distributing well-designed leaflets or flyers through letterbox drops and handouts can work well for a local business whose products or services appeal to a broad audience. It is a simple, inexpensive and effective way of reaching customers, although it is a less targeted form of direct marketing.

Social Media Marketing

Social media can be used effectively as a marketing tool for business as it gives you the opportunity to interact directly with your customers and regularly share relevant product or service information. Social media platforms also make it very easy for your customers to share your content with their entire network, increasing your reach exponentially. Consider developing a profile for your business that allows you to promote your products and services while also encouraging customers to provide feedback by leaving comments.

Direct Selling

Direct selling is an effective way to grow a flexible, low-cost business. Direct selling involves an independent salesperson selling products or services directly to customers, often at a customer's home or workplace. Traditional direct selling methods include door-to-door sales, party plans and network marketing.

Guerrilla Marketing

Guerrilla marketing is an advertisement strategy in which a company uses surprise and/or unconventional interactions in order to promote a product or service. It is a type of publicity. The term was popularized by Jay Conrad Levinson's 1984 book *Guerrilla Marketing*.

Guerrilla marketing uses multiple techniques and practices in order to establish direct contact with the customers. One of the goals of this interaction is to cause an emotional reaction in the clients, and the ultimate goal of marketing is to get people to remember products or brands in a different way than they are accustomed to.

As traditional advertising media channels—such as print, radio, television, and direct mail—lose popularity, marketers and advertisers have to find new strategies to get their commercial messages to the consumer. Guerrilla marketing focuses on taking the consumer by surprise to make a big impression about the product or brand. This in turn creates buzz about the product being marketed. It is a way of advertising that increases consumers' engagement with the product or service, and is designed to create a memorable experience. By creating a memorable experience, it also increases the likelihood that a consumer, or someone who interacted with the campaign, will tell their friends about the product. Thus, via word of mouth, the product or service being advertised reaches more people than initially anticipated.

Guerrilla marketing is relatively inexpensive, and focuses more on reach rather than frequency. For guerrilla campaigns to be successful, companies don't need to spend large amounts, they just need to have imagination, energy and time. Therefore, it has the potential to be effective for small businesses, especially if they are competing against bigger companies.

The message to consumers is often designed to be clear and concise. This type of marketing also works on the unconscious mind,as purchasing decisions are often made by the unconscious mind. To keep the product or service in the unconscious mind requires repetition, so if a buzz is created around a product, and it is shared amongst friends, it enables repetition.

Types

Ambient Marketing

Ambient communication is advertising presented on elements of the environment, including nearly every available physical surface. It is a compilation of intelligence, flexibility, and effective use of the atmosphere. These kinds of ads can be found anywhere and everywhere from hand dryers in public bathrooms and petrol pumps through to bus hand straps and golf-hole cups.

Ambush Marketing

Ambush marketing is a form of associative marketing, used by an organization to capitalize upon the awareness, attention, goodwill, and other benefits, generated by having an association with an event or property, without that organization having an official or direct connection to that event or property.

It is typically seen at major events where rivals of official sponsors attempt to build an association with the event and increase awareness for their brands, sometimes covertly. For example, Nike during the 2012 London Olympics created 'find your Greatness' spots where they featured athletes from several locations called London (but without showing the real London or referring to the Olympic games) which was intended to build a strong association between London Olympics and Nike.

Stealth Marketing

Stealth marketing is a deliberate act of entering, operating in, or exiting a market in a furtive, secretive or imperceptible manner, or an attempt to do so.

Viral/Buzz Marketing

Viral marketing describes any strategy that encourages individuals to pass on a marketing message to others, creating the potential for exponential growth in the message's exposure and influence. Like viruses, such strategies take advantage of rapid multiplication to explode the message to thousands, to millions. Off the Internet, viral marketing has been referred to as "word-of-mouth", "creating a buzz", "leveraging the media", "network marketing", But on the Internet, for better or worse, it's called "viral marketing".

Similarly, buzz marketing uses high-profile media to encourage the public to discuss the brand or product. Buzz marketing works best when consumer's responses to a product or service and subsequent endorsements are genuine, without the company paying them. Buzz generated from buzz marketing campaigns is referred to as "amplified WOM" (word-of-mouth), and "organic WOM" is when buzz occurs naturally by the consumer.

Grassroots Marketing

Grassroots campaigns aim to win customers over on an individual basis. A successful grassroots campaign is not about the dissemination of the marketing message in the hope that possible consumers are paying attention, but rather highlights a personal connection between the consumer and the brand and builds a lasting relationship with the brand.

Astroturfing

Astroturfing is among the most controversial guerrilla marketing strategies, and has a high risk factor for the company marketing the product or service. Astroturfing derives from artificial "turf", often used in stadiums or tennis courts – also known as fake grass. Hence, fake endorsements, testimonials and recommendations are all products of Astroturfing in the public relations sector. Astroturfing involves generating an artificial hype around a particular product or company through a review or discussion on online blogs or forums by an individual who is paid to convey a positive view. This can have a negative and detrimental effect on a company, should the consumer suspect that the review or opinion is not authentic, damaging the company's reputation or even worse, resulting in litigation.

Street Marketing

Street marketing uses unconventional means of advertising or promoting products and brands in public areas. The main goal is to encourage consumers to remember and recall the brand or product marketed. As a division of guerrilla marketing, street marketing is specific to all marketing activities carried out in streets and public areas such as parks, streets, events etc. Street marketing also encompasses advertising outdoors, such as on shopping trolleys (shopping carts, in the US), public toilets, sides of cars or public transport, manhole covers, footpaths, rubbish bins, etc.

Street marketing isn't confined to fixed advertisements. It is common practice for organisations to use brand ambassadors who distribute product samples or discount vouchers, and answer queries about the product while emphasizing the brand. The brand ambassadors may be accompanied by a kiosk which contains the product samples or demonstration materials, or they may be wearing a "walking billboard". The physical interaction with consumers has a greater influencing power than traditional passive advertising.

Street marketing is understood as mobilizing not only the space of the streets but also the imagination of the street: that of street culture and street art. The Y-generation broadly consisting of young urbanites (15 – 30 years old), is often put forth as the most susceptible target for the campaigns due to its associations with the culture of the street.

According to Marcel Saucet and Bernard Cova, street marketing can be used as a general term encompassing six principal types of activities:

- Distribution of flyers or products:

  This activity is more traditional and is the most common form of street marketing employed by brands.

- Product animations:

  This consists of personalizing a high-traffic space using brand imagery. The idea is to create a micro-universe in order to promote a new product or service.

- Human animations:

  The goal of such actions is to create a space in which the brand's message is communicated through human activity.

- Road shows:

  This form of mobile presentation is based on the development of means of transport: Taxi, bike, Segway, etc.

- Uncovered actions:

  These activities involve the customization of street elements.

- Event actions:

  These activities take the form of spectacles, such as flash mobs or contests. The idea is to promote a product, service or brand value through organization of a public event.

Typical Procedure

First, enterprises identify the public places where the campaign can be developed such as beaches, cultural events, close to schools, sporting events and recreation areas for children. Next, companies have to develop a plan to get close to different media and the target market. In order to attract attention, street marketing events not only involve unusual activities, but use technology as part of the events. The purpose is to increase the value of the campaigns and get potential consumers' attention.

Besides, the plans that companies develop take into account that guerrilla or street marketing involves global communication and interaction not only with the customers or the media. They are also developed to identify opportunities and collect enough information about products, markets and competitors. For example, for business it is important that customers stay with them, instead of choosing the competitors' offers. They implement innovative strategies with which they will not lose position in the market, and they consider supplementation with other advertisement through other mediums, such as radio and television, when using street marketing.

There are various examples of strategies that are used in guerrilla marketing. One of them is to provide offers to increase sales. In many cases, businesses do not only supply their products or services to be recognized, but they also offer other things for free. Another instance is to present a fundraiser offer. The point of this strategy is to help other organizations, such as schools, by offering them money. Most companies implement this method not only to increase their sales, but to improve their reputation and image among the community. Finally, there is a strategy called "team selling" that consists of conforming groups of people, the majority of them young, who go knocking the doors of different houses in a neighborhood. They do this in order to help companies promoting and selling their products or services.

When doing guerrilla marketing or street marketing, organizations also consider focusing on the psychological approach. For many companies, this implies if they are having success or not. Street marketing focuses on some psychological aspects to know customers' behavior and preferences. For example, certain psychological areas study how people's brains are divided: 45% of people are left-brained, 45% are right brained, and 10% are balanced. Left-brained persons tend to be logical, right-brained ones tend to be emotional, and the rest combine the two. Then, according to the product or service that enterprises provide, and also the kind of customer, businesses decides the way they are going to manage their street marketing campaigns. Besides, almost all the enterprises base their street marketing campaigns on repeating the messages they spread among their customers. Repetition is related to the unconscious part of the mind. This is the one in charge of making decisions. It lets people know what they are going to choose, as well as what they are going to buy. Businesses follow the principle that establishes that, the more people paying attention to the campaign, the more possibilities that campaign has for being remembered.

When a company decides to do a guerrilla marketing campaign which could be anything out of viral, ambient, ambush, street or stealth, the focus for them is to meet the objectives. The main objectives for them are:

- To create enough buzz to serve in word-of-mouth, helping the brand to establish well with its products.
- To touch most of the five sensory identities of the customer/consumer enhancing personal experience with the brand and building good reputation.
- To reach the target successfully by taking the brand to them in their daily routine.

Through the experience and the ephemeral feelings shared between the company and the target, advertisers and agencies generate a feeling of intimacy that resonates beyond the encounter. This feeling of nearness becomes all the more lasting as the affected individuals relive this encounter on the internet through social media.

Strategy

Guerrilla marketers need to be creative in devising unconventional methods of promotion to maintain the public's interest in a product or service. Levinson writes that when implementing guerrilla marketing tactics, smaller organizations and entrepreneurs are actually at an advantage. Ultimately, however, guerrilla marketers must "deliver the goods." In order to sell a product or a service, a company must establish a relationship with the customer. It must build trust and support the customer's needs, and it must provide a product that delivers the promised benefits.

Online Guerilla Marketing

The web is rife with examples of guerrilla marketing, to the extent that many of us don't notice its presence - until a particularly successful campaign arises. The desire for instant gratification of internet users provides an avenue for guerrilla marketing by allowing businesses to combine wait marketing with guerrilla tactics. Simple examples consist of using 'loading' pages or image alt texts to display an entertaining or informative message to users waiting to access the content they were trying to get to. As users dislike waiting with no occupation on the web, it is essential, and easy, to capture their attention this way. Other website methods include interesting web features such as engaging landing pages.

Many online marketing strategies also use social media such as Facebook and LinkedIn to begin campaigns, share-able features and event host events. Other companies run competitions or discounts based on encouraging users to share or create content related to their product. Viral videos are an incredibly popular form of guerrilla marketing in which companies film entertaining or surprising videos that internet users are likely to share and enjoy, that subtly advertise their service or product. Some companies such as Google even create interactive elements like the themed Google logo games to spark interest and engagement. These dynamic guerrilla marketing tactics can become news globally and give businesses considerable publicity.

Examples:

There are various organizations who have implemented the guerrilla and street marketing strategies. The majority of them are small companies, but there are also big companies that have involved in the guerrilla and street marketing environment. Most of the examples of the strategies that both small and big enterprises have put into action include costumed persons, the distribution of tickets, people providing samples, among others. As stated before, one guerrilla marketing conventional method that is used by many businesses is to provide fliers. The goal is to create awareness on the customers about what the enterprise is doing. One example of this took place in Montpelier, Vermont, where the New England Culinary Institute (NECI) sent a group of students to a movie theatre to hand out 400 fliers. Those fliers had coupons in which NECI was inviting people to go to its monthly Theme Dinners. Another company, Boston's Kung-Fu Tai Chi Club, chose the option of disseminating fliers instead of placing its advertisements on the newspapers. The purpose of the fliers was to promote the company's self-defence classes for women.

Other businesses apply the technique of sending disguised people to promote things on the streets. For example, match.com organized a street marketing activity in the "Feria del Libro"

("Book Fair") in Madrid. It consisted of a man dressed like a prince who was walking among the crowd looking for his "real love". He had a glass slipper and even got to try the shoe on some people. A woman behind him was giving bookmarks to the people which contained messages such as "Times have changed; the way to find love, too" or "You have been reading love stories all your life; experience yours on Match.com". Also, in Madrid and Barcelona, Nokia developed a campaign called "Avestruz" ("Ostrich") to promote the 5500 and 5700 mobiles. In the campaign, a group of real-size ostrich puppets tried to interact with young people in order to let them know these mobiles provide a high-quality MP3 playback. The puppets were holding their own telephones and listening to the music. When a young person appeared, the puppet tried to catch his/her attention to show him/her the quality of the mobile. The reason why Nokia decided to use ostriches was that they are big animals, so people could easily look at them.

There are enterprises that disseminate passes or tickets to different events. For example, Sony invests on joining promoters and tells them that they have to infiltrate in public meetings. What they have to do is to distribute free tickets to concerts and other musical events sponsored by the company. Another instance is the Spanish company Clickair (an extension of Iberia airlines), that developed a campaign in which a group of five people had to walk through Barcelona streets dressed as Euros. The group was supplying approximately 3,000 tickets to promote different Clickair destinations. The people who first sent a text message with the required information would get free tickets to go on a trip. In the end, the company received a total of 3,390 messages. Along with these examples, there are other street marketing techniques that are even more unusual. Lee Jeans, a French company dedicated to the selling of jeans, promoted the opening of their new store in rue des Rosiers in Paris. The method they applied consisted of distributing denims, as well as denim accessories, on the different streets of the neighborhood. Furthermore, in Italy, the members of the company Nintendo put into action a campaign in which they used post-it's to promote the Wii console. They pasted several post-it with the shapes of some characters from different video games. Those images were placed as if they were billboards on the streets. "Wii not forget", the name of the campaign, and a brief explanation of it, were the words written on the post-its. In some cases, some street marketing may incite the ire of local authorities; such was the case in Houston, Texas, when BMW's ad agency (Street Factory Media in Minneapolis) attached a replication, made from Styrofoam, of a Mini-Cooper to the side of a downtown building. For the cost of a small city-issued fine, the company received front page advertising on the Houston Chronicle.

Sony Ericsson used an undercover campaign in 2002 when they hired 60 actors in ten major cities and had them accost strangers and ask them: "Would you mind taking my picture?" The actor then handed the target a brand new picture phone while talking about how cool the new device was. "And thus an act of civility was converted into a branding event.

Guerrilla marketing is not just exclusive to small companies. For big companies it is a high risk, high reward strategy. When successful it can capture even more market share, but if it fails it can damage the company's brand image. One successful guerrilla marketing campaign is the Coca-Cola 'Happiness Machine". In January 2010, Coca-Cola, with the help of Definition 6, filmed a reaction video of a Coke vending machine dispensing 'doses' of happiness to unsuspecting students in St. John's University. A seemingly normal vending machine surprised students by dispensing items that were more than they bargained for. The students received goodies ranging from extra coke, pizza, flowers, to even a twelve-foot hero sub. "Coke's goal to inspire consumers through small, surprise moments of happiness" said Paul Iannacchino Jr., Creative Director, Definition 6. With a budget of only $60,000, the video generated 500,000 views in the first week. It now has over 7 million views to date. The campaign was so popular that a 30-second edit of the footage was featured during American Idol's season finale. The Coca-Cola "Happiness Machine" also went on to receive the CLIO's prestigious Gold Interactive Award at the 51st annual awards dinner held in New York City. After the campaign's success, Coca-Cola decided to continue with the 'Happiness' theme and has released similar videos since then.

Strategic Risk

Because of the nature of guerrilla marketing, the message and objective must be clearly defined in order to avoid being misunderstood. Misinterpretation by the targeted audience of the message intended to be promoted is a risk. Word-of-mouth advertising does not always stay focused enough to present the intended message. The rumor-like spread of word-of-mouth marketing is uncontrollable once released, and can result in a misrepresentation of the message or confusion about a brand.

Another risk involves wrongly timed (or wrongly placed) events, which may actually be perceived to be against the interests of the consumer. For instance, in an ill-conceived promotion which took place on January 31, 2007, several magnetic circuit boards—each with an flashing LED cartoon figure—were attached to metal surfaces in and around Boston, Massachusetts to promote an animated series. The circuit boards were mistakenly taken for explosive devices. Several subway stations; bridges; and a portion of Interstate 93 were closed as police examined, removed, and (in some cases) destroyed the devices.

Some guerrilla marketing may incite the ire of local authorities. Then risks are assessed and may still be considered worthwhile. Such was the case in Houston, Texas, when BMW Auto's ad agency, Street Factory Media, attached a replica of a Mini-Cooper (made of Styrofoam), to the side of a downtown building in January 2013. For the small cost of a city-issued fine, the company received front page advertising in the Houston Chronicle.

Another problem presents itself if marketers fail to properly execute an undercover campaign. They run considerable risk of backlash. An example of this can be found in Sony Entertainment's on-line debacle with Zipatoni. The company attempted to promote Zipatoni through a stealth marketing campaign, which was quickly detected by the internet community, resulting in Sony immediately experiencing a backlash from video game enthusiasts.

Street art is thus a subversive activity, hijacking public places and inventing rather paradoxical forms of expression that reformulate ways of communicating, all of which inform street marketing practices. Thus marketing in the street, given that it is inspired by the work of such artists, brings with it constraints and statutory risks for which agencies and advertisers are generally not prepared. The main problem is that, by definition, street mobilization campaigns require the use of public space, and that use must be authorized by government authorities to be legal. This is just as true for simple operations like distributing flyers as it is for mobilizing products or people and, of course, for a disguised campaign.

The authorizations necessary to carry out such a campaign are often very difficult to obtain within the time allotted for bringing the plan to fruition. Numerous potential operations have failed to obtain authorization for safety reasons, and in certain urban areas it is even expressly forbidden to undertake a guerrilla marketing campaign. In such cases, many agencies and advertisers will simply go ahead with the operation, meaning that they choose to act without authorization. How is such a choice reached, and on what bases? How is it justified? What impact does this choice have on the performance and costs of the operation? What transformations does this choice bring to the agency–advertiser relationship? These are the main questions posed in the development of street marketing operations today.

Inexpensive Costs

In a declining economy, guerrilla marketing is an increasing solution to giving companies the comparative edge over others. During times where companies are downsizing and cutting costs, companies look to guerrilla marketing as a cheaper strategy than conventional marketing. Instead of investing money in the marketing process, guerrillas invest energy, time and creativity. If done successfully, companies will be able to reach conventional goals for profits and growth with a smaller marketing budget. One such example is the Blair Witch Project. A group of film students filmed an amateur horror movie. By setting up an internet campaign devoted to spreading rumors about the fictitious 'Blair Witch', it created a lot of interest for the film. With a budget of $50,000, the movie grossed $250 million worldwide.

According to Jay Levinson, guerrilla marketing emphasizes strongly on customer follow-up rather than ignoring customers after their purchase. Focusing on customer follow-up is a cheaper strategy because the cost of selling to a new customer is six times higher than selling to an existing customer. During a tough economy, it is important to focus on building relationships rather than sales, and aiming at individuals instead of groups. This promotes repeat sales, referrals and increased size of purchase. The use of telephone as a follow-up tool is helpful in improving customer relationships. Email is also another inexpensive tool for maintaining relationships. Emails can be used to direct people to the company website. The site can be then used to provide information and to advance sales.

Honesty is an important attribute when marketing to customers during tough times. When companies show that they are fully aware of the economic situation and why they have priced their products accordingly, this earns the customer's respect. Explaining the current situation and the risks and the steps the company is taking to the customers will give the customers assurance and also maintains their trust. One example is the Las Vegas tourism board. During the 2008 recession, Las Vegas was one of the cities hit the hardest. They released an ad campaign showing people they were fully aware of the recession, yet, in a dramatic way, showing 'that regular people are coming here and having a blast'. This piqued a lot of interest which led to an increase of tourism in Las Vegas during the recession.

Online Advertising

Online advertising, also called online marketing or Internet advertising or web advertising, is a form of marketing and advertising which uses the Internet to deliver promotional marketing messages to consumers. Many consumers find online advertising disruptive and have increasingly turned to ad blocking for a variety of reasons.

When software is used to do the purchasing, it is known as programmatic advertising.

Online advertising includes email marketing, search engine marketing (SEM), social media marketing, many types of display advertising (including web banner advertising), and mobile advertising. Like other advertising media, online advertising frequently involves a publisher, who integrates advertisements into its online content, and an advertiser, who provides the advertisements to be displayed on the publisher's content. Other potential participants include advertising agencies who help generate and place the ad copy, an ad server which technologically delivers the ad and tracks statistics, and advertising affiliates who do independent promotional work for the advertiser.

In 2016, Internet advertising revenues in the United States surpassed those of cable television and broadcast television. In 2017, Internet advertising revenues in the United States totaled $83.0 billion, a 14% increase over the $72.50 billion in revenues in 2016.

Many common online advertising practices are controversial and, as a result, have been increasingly subject to regulation. Online ad revenues also may not adequately replace other publishers' revenue streams. Declining ad revenue has led some publishers to place their content behind paywalls.

Delivery Methods

Display Advertising

Online Marketing.

Display advertising conveys its advertising message visually using text, logos, animations, videos, photographs, or other graphics. Display advertisers frequently target users with particular traits to increase the ads' effect. Online advertisers (typically through their ad servers) often use cookies, which are unique identifiers of specific computers, to decide which ads to serve to a particular consumer. Cookies can track whether a user left a page without buying anything, so the advertiser can later retarget the user with ads from the site the user visited.

As advertisers collect data across multiple external websites about a user's online activity, they can create a detailed profile of the user's interests to deliver even more targeted advertising. This aggregation of data is called behavioral targeting. Advertisers can also target their audience by using contextual to deliver display ads related to the content of the web page where the ads appear.

Retargeting, behavioral targeting, and contextual advertising all are designed to increase an advertiser's return on investment, or ROI, over untargeted ads.

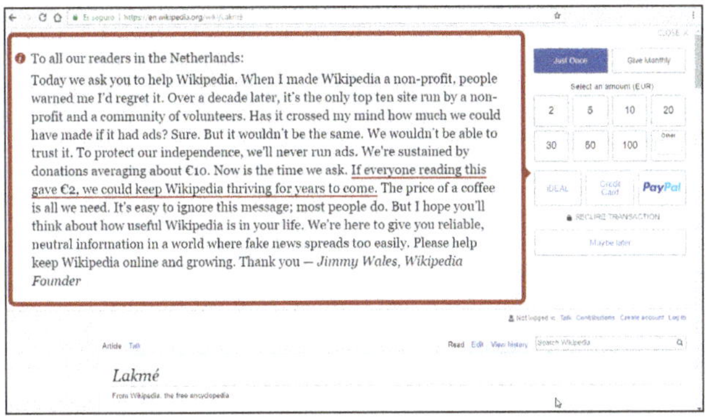

Example of *display advertising* featuring geotargeting.

Advertisers may also deliver ads based on a user's suspected geography through geotargeting. A user's IP address communicates some geographic information (at minimum, the user's country or general region). The geographic information from an IP can be supplemented and refined with other proxies or information to narrow the range of possible locations. For example, with mobile devices, advertisers can sometimes use a phone's GPS receiver or the location of nearby mobile towers. Cookies and other persistent data on a user's machine may provide help narrowing a user's location further.

Web Banner Advertising

Web banners or banner ads typically are graphical ads displayed within a web page. Many banner ads are delivered by a central ad server.

Banner ads can use rich media to incorporate video, audio, animations, buttons, forms, or other interactive elements using Java applets, HTML5, Adobe Flash, and other programs.

Frame Ad (Traditional Banner)

Frame ads were the first form of web banners. The colloquial usage of "banner ads" often refers to traditional frame ads. Website publishers incorporate frame ads by setting aside a particular space on the web page. The Interactive Advertising Bureau's Ad Unit Guidelines proposes standardized pixel dimensions for ad units.

Pop-ups/Pop-unders

A pop-up ad is displayed in a new web browser window that opens above a website visitor's initial browser window. A pop-under ad opens a new browser window under a website visitor's initial browser window. Pop-under ads and similar technologies are now advised against by online authorities such as Google, who state that they "do not condone this practice".

Floating Ad

A floating ad, or overlay ad, is a type of rich media advertisement that appears superimposed over the requested website's content. Floating ads may disappear or become less obtrusive after a preset time period.

Expanding Ad

An expanding ad is a rich media frame ad that changes dimensions upon a predefined condition, such as a preset amount of time a visitor spends on a webpage, the user's click on the ad, or the user's mouse movement over the ad. Expanding ads allow advertisers to fit more information into a restricted ad space.

Trick Banners

A trick banner is a banner ad where the ad copy imitates some screen element users commonly encounter, such as an operating system message or popular application message, to induce ad clicks. Trick banners typically do not mention the advertiser in the initial ad, and thus they are a form of bait-and-switch. Trick banners commonly attract a higher-than-average click-through rate, but tricked users may resent the advertiser for deceiving them.

News Feed Ads

"News Feed Ads", also called "Sponsored Stories", "Boosted Posts", typically exist on social media platforms that offer a steady stream of information updates ("news feed") in regulated formats (i.e. in similar sized small boxes with a uniform style). Those advertisements are intertwined with non-promoted news that the users are reading through. Those advertisements can be of any content, such as promoting a website, a fan page, an app, or a product.

Some examples are: Facebook's "Sponsored Stories", LinkedIn's "Sponsored Updates", and Twitter's "Promoted Tweets".

This display ads format falls into its own category because unlike banner ads which are quite distinguishable, News Feed Ads' format blends well into non-paid news updates. This format of online advertisement yields much higher click-through rates than traditional display ads.

Display Advertising Process

The process by which online advertising is displayed can involve many parties. In the simplest case, the website publisher selects and serves the ads. Publishers which operate their own advertising departments may use this method.

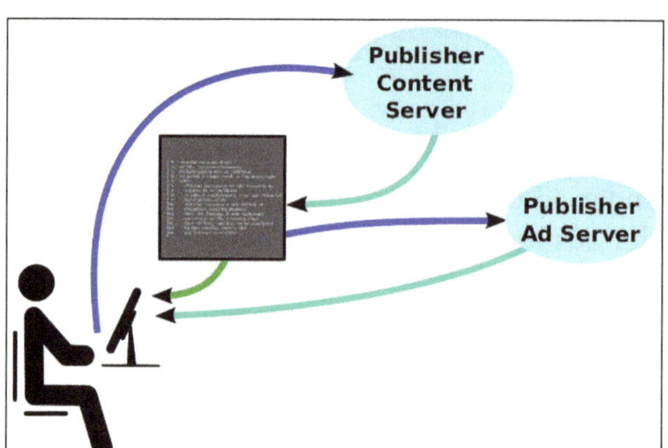

Online advertising serving process - simple publisher case.

The ads may be outsourced to an advertising agency under contract with the publisher, and served from the advertising agency's servers.

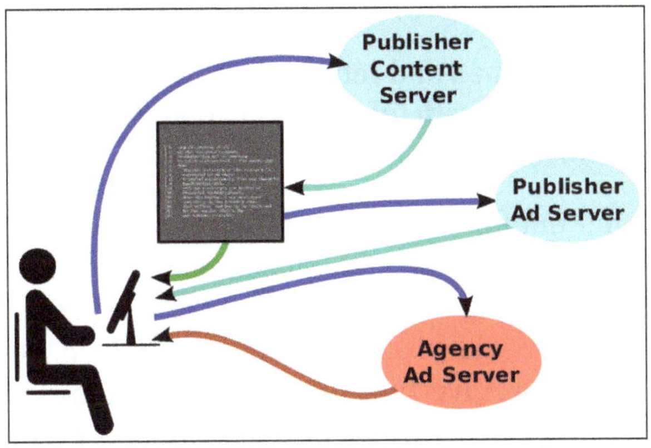

Online advertising serving process using an ad agency.

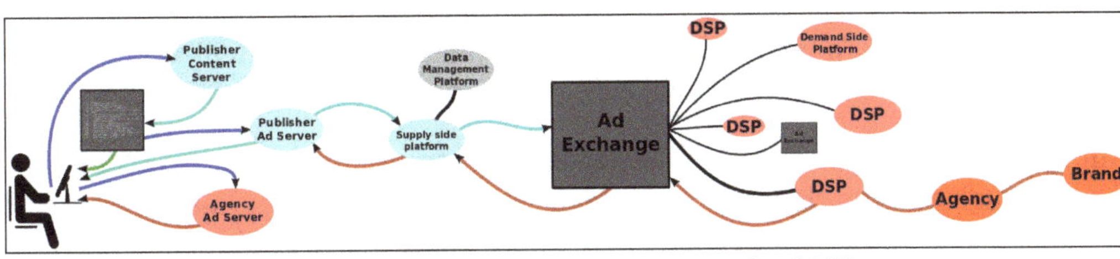

Online advertising serving process using online bidding.

Alternatively, ad space may be offered for sale in a bidding market using an ad exchange and real-time bidding. This involves many parties interacting automatically in real time. In response to a request from the user's browser, the publisher content server sends the web page content to the user's browser over the Internet. The page does not yet contain ads, but contains links which cause the user's browser to connect to the publisher ad server to request that the spaces left for ads be filled in with ads. Information identifying the user, such as cookies and the page being viewed, is transmitted to the publisher ad server.

The publisher ad server then communicates with a supply-side platform server. The publisher is offering ad space for sale, so they are considered the supplier. The supply side platform also receives the user's identifying information, which it sends to a data management platform. At the data management platform, the user's identifying information is used to look up demographic information, previous purchases, and other information of interest to advertisers.

Broadly speaking, there are three types of data obtained through such a data management platform:

1. First party data refers to the data retrieved from customer relationship management (CRM) platforms, in addition to website and paid media content or cross-platform data. This can include data from customer behaviors, actions or interests.
2. Second party data refers to an amalgamation of statistics related to cookie pools on external publications and platforms. The data is provided directly from the source (adservers, hosted solutions for social or an analytics platform). It is also possible to negotiate a deal with a particular publisher to secure specific data points or audiences.

3. Third party data is sourced from external providers and often aggregated from numerous websites. Businesses sell third-party data and are able to share this via an array of distribution avenues.

This customer information is combined and returned to the supply side platform, which can now package up the offer of ad space along with information about the user who will view it. The supply side platform sends that offer to an ad exchange.

The ad exchange puts the offer out for bid to demand-side platforms. Demand side platforms act on behalf of ad agencies, who sell ads which advertise brands. Demand side platforms thus have ads ready to display, and are searching for users to view them. Bidders get the information about the user ready to view the ad, and decide, based on that information, how much to offer to buy the ad space. According to the Internet Advertising Bureau, a demand side platform has 10 milliseconds to respond to an offer. The ad exchange picks the winning bid and informs both parties.

The ad exchange then passes the link to the ad back through the supply side platform and the publisher's ad server to the user's browser, which then requests the ad content from the agency's ad server. The ad agency can thus confirm that the ad was delivered to the browser.

This is simplified, according to the IAB. Exchanges may try to unload unsold ("remnant") space at low prices through other exchanges. Some agencies maintain semi-permanent pre-cached bids with ad exchanges, and those may be examined before going out to additional demand side platforms for bids. The process for mobile advertising is different and may involve mobile carriers and handset software manufacturers.

Interstitial Ads

An interstitial ad displays before a user can access requested content, sometimes while the user is waiting for the content to load. Interstitial ads are a form of interruption marketing.

Text Ads

A text ad displays text-based hyperlinks. Text-based ads may display separately from a web page's primary content, or they can be embedded by hyperlinking individual words or phrases to advertiser's websites. Text ads may also be delivered through email marketing or text message marketing. Text-based ads often render faster than graphical ads and can be harder for ad-blocking software to block.

Search Engine Marketing

Search engine marketing, or SEM, is designed to increase a website's visibility in search engine results pages (SERPs). Search engines provide sponsored results and organic (non-sponsored) results based on a web searcher's query. Search engines often employ visual cues to differentiate sponsored results from organic results. Search engine marketing includes all of an advertiser's actions to make a website's listing more prominent for topical keywords. The primary reason behind the rising popularity of Search Engine Marketing has been Google. There were a few companies that had its own PPC and Analytics tools. However, this concept was popularized by Google. Google Ad words was convenient for the advertisers to use and create campaigns. And, they realized that the tool did a fair job, by charging only for someone's click on the ad, which reported as the cost-per-click for which a penny was charged. This resulted in the advertisers monitoring the campaign by the number of clicks and were satisfied that the ads could be tracked.

Search Engine Optimization

Search engine optimization, or SEO, attempts to improve a website's organic search rankings in SERPs by increasing the website content's relevance to search terms. Search engines regularly update their algorithms to penalize poor quality sites that try to game their rankings, making optimization a moving target for advertisers. Many vendors offer SEO services.

Sponsored Search

Sponsored search (also called sponsored links, search ads, or paid search) allows advertisers to be included in the sponsored results of a search for selected keywords. Search ads are often sold via real-time auctions, where advertisers bid on keywords. In addition to setting a maximum price per keyword, bids may include time, language, geographical, and other constraints. Search engines originally sold listings in order of highest bids. Modern search engines rank sponsored listings based on a combination of bid price, expected click-through rate, keyword relevancy and site quality.

Social Media Marketing

Social media marketing is commercial promotion conducted through social media websites. Many companies promote their products by posting frequent updates and providing special offers through their social media profiles. Videos, interactive quizzes, and sponsored posts are all a part of this operation. Usually these ads are found on Facebook, Instagram, Twitter, and Snapchat.

Mobile Advertising

Mobile advertising is ad copy delivered through wireless mobile devices such as smartphones, feature phones, or tablet computers. Mobile advertising may take the form of static or rich media display ads, SMS (Short Message Service) or MMS (Multimedia Messaging Service) ads, mobile search ads, advertising within mobile websites, or ads within mobile applications or games (such as interstitial ads, "advergaming," or application sponsorship). Industry groups such as the Mobile Marketing Association have attempted to standardize mobile ad unit specifications, similar to the IAB's efforts for general online advertising.

Mobile advertising is growing rapidly for several reasons. There are more mobile devices in the field, connectivity speeds have improved (which, among other things, allows for richer media ads to be served quickly), screen resolutions have advanced, mobile publishers are becoming more sophisticated about incorporating ads, and consumers are using mobile devices more extensively. The Interactive Advertising Bureau predicts continued growth in mobile advertising with the adoption of location-based targeting and other technological features not available or relevant on personal computers. In July 2014 Facebook reported advertising revenue for the June 2014 quarter of $2.68 billion, an increase of 67 percent over the second quarter of 2013. Of that, mobile advertising revenue accounted for around 62 percent, an increase of 41 percent on the previous year.

Email Advertising

Email advertising is ad copy comprising an entire email or a portion of an email message. Email marketing may be unsolicited, in which case the sender may give the recipient an option to opt out of future emails, or it may be sent with the recipient's prior consent (opt-in). Businesses may ask for your email and send updates on new products or sales.

Chat Advertising

As opposed to static messaging, chat advertising refers to real time messages dropped to users on certain sites. This is done using live chat software or tracking applications installed within certain websites with the operating personnel behind the site often dropping adverts on the traffic surfing around the sites. In reality this is a subset of the email advertising but different because of its time window.

Online Classified Advertising

Online classified advertising is advertising posted online in a categorical listing of specific products or services. Examples include online job boards, online real estate listings, automotive listings, online yellow pages, and online auction-based listings. Craigslist and eBay are two prominent providers of online classified listings.

Adware

Adware is software that, once installed, automatically displays advertisements on a user's computer. The ads may appear in the software itself, integrated into web pages visited by the user, or in pop-ups/pop-unders. Adware installed without the user's permission is a type of malware.

Affiliate Marketing

Affiliate marketing occurs when advertisers organize third parties to generate potential customers for them. Third-party affiliates receive payment based on sales generated through their promotion. Affiliate marketers generate traffic to offers from affiliate networks, and when the desired action is taken by the visitor, the affiliate earns a commission. These desired actions can be an email submission, a phone call, filling out an online form, or an online order being completed.

Content Marketing

Content marketing is any marketing that involves the creation and sharing of media and publishing content in order to acquire and retain customers. This information can be presented in a variety of formats, including blogs, news, video, white papers, e-books, infographics, case studies, how-to guides and more.

Considering that most marketing involves some form of published media, it is almost (though not entirely) redundant to call 'content marketing' anything other than simply 'marketing'. There are, of course, other forms of marketing (in-person marketing, telephone-based marketing, word of mouth marketing, etc.) where the label is more useful for identifying the type of marketing.

However, even these are usually merely presenting content that they are marketing as information in a way that is different from traditional print, radio, TV, film, email, or web media.

Online Marketing Platform

Online marketing platform (OMP) is an integrated web-based platform that combines the benefits of a business directory, local search engine, search engine optimisation (SEO) tool, customer relationship management (CRM) package and content management system (CMS). Ebay and Amazon are used as online marketing and logistics management platforms. On Facebook, Twitter, YouTube, Pinterest, LinkedIn, and other Social Media, retail online marketing is also used. Online business marketing platforms such as Marketo, MarketBright and Pardot have been bought by major IT companies (Eloqua-Oracle, Neolane-Adobe and Unica-IBM).

Unlike television marketing in which Neilsen TV Ratings can be relied upon for viewing metrics, online advertisers do not have an independent party to verify viewing claims made by the big online platforms.

Compensation Methods

Advertisers and publishers use a wide range of payment calculation methods. In 2012, advertisers calculated 32% of online advertising transactions on a cost-per-impression basis, 66% on customer performance (e.g. cost per click or cost per acquisition), and 2% on hybrids of impression and performance methods.

CPM (Cost Per Mille)

Cost per mille, often abbreviated to CPM, means that advertisers pay for every thousand displays of their message to potential customers. In the online context, ad displays are usually called "impressions." Definitions of an "impression" vary among publishers, and some impressions may not be charged because they don't represent a new exposure to an actual customer. Advertisers can use technologies such as web bugs to verify if an impression is actually delivered.

Publishers use a variety of techniques to increase page views, such as dividing content across multiple pages, repurposing someone else's content, using sensational titles, or publishing tabloid or sexual content.

CPM advertising is susceptible to "impression fraud," and advertisers who want visitors to their sites may not find per-impression payments a good proxy for the results they desire.

CPC (Cost Per Click)

CPC (Cost Per Click) or PPC (Pay per click) means advertisers pay each time a user clicks on the ad. CPC advertising works well when advertisers want visitors to their sites, but it's a less accurate measurement for advertisers looking to build brand awareness. CPC's market share has grown each year since its introduction, eclipsing CPM to dominate two-thirds of all online advertising compensation methods.

Like impressions, not all recorded clicks are valuable to advertisers. GoldSpot Media reported that up to 50% of clicks on static mobile banner ads are accidental and resulted in redirected visitors leaving the new site immediately.

CPE (Cost Per Engagement)

Cost per engagement aims to track not just that an ad unit loaded on the page (i.e., an impression was served), but also that the viewer actually saw and/or interacted with the ad.

CPV (Cost Per View)

Cost per view video advertising. Both Google and TubeMogul endorsed this standardized CPV metric to the IAB's (Interactive Advertising Bureau) Digital Video Committee, and it's garnering a notable amount of industry support. CPV is the primary benchmark used in YouTube Advertising Campaigns, as part of Google's AdWords platform.

CPI (Cost Per Install)

The CPI compensation method is specific to mobile applications and mobile advertising. In CPI ad campaigns brands are charged a fixed of bid rate only when the application was installed.

Attribution of Ad Value

In marketing, "attribution" is the measurement of effectiveness of particular ads in a consumer's ultimate decision to purchase. Multiple ad impressions may lead to a consumer "click" or other action. A single action may lead to revenue being paid to multiple ad space sellers.

Other Performance-based Compensation

CPA (Cost Per Action or Cost Per Acquisition) or PPP (Pay Per Performance) advertising means the advertiser pays for the number of users who perform a desired activity, such as completing a purchase or filling out a registration form. Performance-based compensation can also incorporate revenue sharing, where publishers earn a percentage of the advertiser's profits made as a result of the ad. Performance-based compensation shifts the risk of failed advertising onto publishers.

Fixed Cost

Fixed cost compensation means advertisers pay a fixed cost for delivery of ads online, usually over a specified time period, irrespective of the ad's visibility or users' response to it. One examples is CPD (cost per day) where advertisers pay a fixed cost for publishing an ad for a day irrespective of impressions served or clicks.

Benefits of Online Advertising

Cost

The low costs of electronic communication reduce the cost of displaying online advertisements compared to offline ads. Online advertising, and in particular social media, provides a low-cost means for advertisers to engage with large established communities. Advertising online offers better returns than in other media.

Measurability

Online advertisers can collect data on their ads' effectiveness, such as the size of the potential audience or actual audience response, how a visitor reached their advertisement, whether the advertisement resulted in a sale, and whether an ad actually loaded within a visitor's view. This helps online advertisers improve their ad campaigns over time.

Formatting

Advertisers have a wide variety of ways of presenting their promotional messages, including the ability to convey images, video, audio, and links. Unlike many offline ads, online ads also can be interactive. For example, some ads let users input queries or let users follow the advertiser on social media. Online ads can even incorporate games.

Targeting

Publishers can offer advertisers the ability to reach customizable and narrow market segments for targeted advertising. Online advertising may use geo-targeting to display relevant advertisements to the user's geography. Advertisers can customize each individual ad to a particular user based on the user's previous preferences. Advertisers can also track whether a visitor has already seen a particular ad in order to reduce unwanted repetitious exposures and provide adequate time gaps between exposures.

Coverage

Online advertising can reach nearly every global market, and online advertising influences offline sales.

Speed

Once ad design is complete, online ads can be deployed immediately. The delivery of online ads does not need to be linked to the publisher's publication schedule. Furthermore, online advertisers can modify or replace ad copy more rapidly than their offline counterparts.

Concerns

Security Concerns

According to a US Senate investigation, the current state of online advertising endangers the security and privacy of users.

Banner Blindness

Eye-tracking studies have shown that Internet users often ignore web page zones likely to contain display ads (sometimes called "banner blindness"), and this problem is worse online than in offline media. On the other hand, studies suggest that even those ads "ignored" by the users may influence the user subconsciously.

Fraud on the Advertiser

There are numerous ways that advertisers can be overcharged for their advertising. For example, click fraud occurs when a publisher or third parties click (manually or through automated means) on a CPC ad with no legitimate buying intent. For example, click fraud can occur when a competitor clicks on ads to deplete its rival's advertising budget, or when publishers attempt to manufacture revenue.

Click fraud is especially associated with pornography sites. In 2011, certain scamming porn websites launched dozens of hidden pages on each visitor's computer, forcing the visitor's computer to click on hundreds of paid links without the visitor's knowledge.

As with offline publications, online impression fraud can occur when publishers overstate the number of ad impressions they have delivered to their advertisers. To combat impression fraud, several publishing and advertising industry associations are developing ways to count online impressions credibly.

Technological Variations

Heterogeneous Clients

Because users have different operating systems, web browsers and computer hardware (including mobile devices and different screen sizes), online ads may appear to users differently from how the advertiser intended, or the ads may not display properly at all. A study revealed that, on average, 31% of ads were not "in-view" when rendered, meaning they never had an opportunity to be seen. Rich media ads create even greater compatibility problems, as some developers may use competing (and exclusive) software to render the ads.

Furthermore, advertisers may encounter legal problems if legally required information doesn't actually display to users, even if that failure is due to technological heterogeneity. In the United States, the FTC has released a set of guidelines indicating that it's the advertisers' responsibility to ensure the ads display any required disclosures or disclaimers, irrespective of the users' technology.

Ad Blocking

Ad blocking, or ad filtering, means the ads do not appear to the user because the user uses technology to screen out ads. Many browsers block unsolicited pop-up ads by default. Other software programs or browser add-ons may also block the loading of ads, or block elements on a page with behaviors characteristic of ads (e.g. HTML autoplay of both audio and video). Approximately 9% of all online page views come from browsers with ad-blocking software installed, and some publishers have 40%+ of their visitors using ad-blockers.

Anti-targeting Technologies

Some web browsers offer privacy modes where users can hide information about themselves from publishers and advertisers. Among other consequences, advertisers can't use cookies to serve targeted ads to private browsers. Most major browsers have incorporated Do Not Track options into their browser headers, but the regulations currently are only enforced by the honor system.

Privacy Concerns

The collection of user information by publishers and advertisers has raised consumer concerns about their privacy. Sixty percent of Internet users would use Do Not Track technology to block all collection of information if given an opportunity. Over half of all Google and Facebook users are concerned about their privacy when using Google and Facebook.

Many consumers have reservations about online behavioral targeting. By tracking users' online activities, advertisers are able to understand consumers quite well. Advertisers often use technology, such as web bugs and respawning cookies, to maximize their abilities to track consumers. According to a 2011 survey conducted by Harris Interactive, over half of Internet users had a negative impression of online behavioral advertising, and forty percent feared that their personally-identifiable information had been shared with advertisers without their consent. Consumers can be especially troubled by advertisers targeting them based on sensitive information, such as financial or health status. Furthermore, some advertisers attach the MAC address of users' devices to their 'demographic profiles' so they can be retargeted (regardless of the accuracy of the profile) even if the user clears their cookies and browsing history.

Trustworthiness of Advertisers

Scammers can take advantage of consumers' difficulties verifying an online persona's identity, leading to artifices like phishing (where scam emails look identical to those from a well-known brand owner) and confidence schemes like the Nigerian "419" scam. The Internet Crime Complaint Center received 289,874 complaints in 2012, totaling over half a billion dollars in losses, most of which originated with scam ads.

Consumers also face malware risks, i.e. malvertising, when interacting with online advertising. Cisco's 2013 Annual Security Report revealed that clicking on ads was 182 times more likely to install a virus on a user's computer than surfing the Internet for porn. For example, in August 2014 Yahoo's advertising network reportedly saw cases of infection of a variant of Cryptolocker ransomware.

Spam

The Internet's low cost of disseminating advertising contributes to spam, especially by large-scale spammers. Numerous efforts have been undertaken to combat spam, ranging from blacklists to regulatorily-required labeling to content filters, but most of those efforts have adverse collateral effects, such as mistaken filtering.

Evangelism Marketing

Evangelism marketing is a type of word-of-mouth marketing where a company has a specific customer that believes in a product so much that he or she convinces others to buy it and use it.

Simply put, a customer loves the product so much they just have to spread the word to their friends and social networks. In the past, evangelism marketing often moved much slower through households, neighborhoods, and communities. Thanks to social media and other online platforms, every person has the potential to participate in evangelism marketing on a large scale.

According to a study by Zuberance, the average brand evangelist converts about three new customers. If every customer brought in three new ones, no business would fail. Don't underestimate the power of word-of-mouth; 92% of people trust a product recommendation from a friend compared to a 24% trust rating for an ad for the same company. Brand evangelists can be your key to significant revenue.

Examples of Evangelism Marketing

Every brand dreams of having powerful brand evangelists on their side. A brand evangelist is a true fan of your company that wants to talk about your brand, stay involved, and share your message.

What brands have you spread the word for? Whether it's telling your group of friends about a positive Costco experience or posting a video of your vacation on your GoPro, you are serving as a brand evangelist. Let's look at some real life examples.

LuLaRoe

A women's fashion brand, LuLaRoe, is a business built entirely on brand evangelism. Sellers join the company and sell a full line of dresses, shirts, tunics, and leggings for women and children.

The difference between LuLaRoe and other organizations is their massive brand evangelism that turns women into sellers. The leggings are known to be 'buttery soft' with some prints so in demand they sell for hundreds of dollars.

Women post photos with the tag #howdoyouroe, rave about the brand online, and also host pop-up events at their own homes for LuLaRoe sellers. This is a brand built on evangelism marketing.

Chubbies

This brand of men's shorts and swim trunks sells shorts with a shorter inseam than traditional men's shorts. According to Vert, "Chubbies co-founders make the customer the hero." They engage customers to take photos of themselves wearing their Chubbies.

In addition, the brand works to make sure customers are happy. For example, when a customer told the brand his shorts were stolen out of his gym locker, they replaced the shorts and gave the man a week of free karate lessons. The customer shared the story and became a brand evangelist.

Some ways to make evangelism work for industry:

1. Let it begin In-house: There is a saying that charity begins at home. Small and medium businesses should first get evangelism to work in-house. Employees, managers, and salespeople can carry the enthusiasm of the brand to its vendors and customers to win them over. When the company staff members itself become its evangelists that raises confidence among prospective customers.

2. It's not for big business but ideal for small and medium businesses too. When Apple tried out evangelism it was not a big player but a startup struggling to get a foothold in the market. Small retail business can create product evangelists from their own customers. They can try out the products, report on its quality and pass on the information to other prospective customers. Arizona based Buffalo Exchange, created a set of evangelists for its used clothes from among high school students interested in fashion design. The students dressed the display mannequins in their preferred styles and were rewarded with gift cards. This activity helped create a buzz around the product among their friends and classmates.

3. Go for Party time, not product demos or conferences: Party time creates feelings of happiness that can enable passing of product message to friends. Discovery Education created a party atmosphere for engaging educators and administrators to get prospects excited about their catalog. They, in turn, went back to school to spread the message of Discovery's products. This would not have been possible if it was done through a product demo or in the presentation in technology conferences.

4. Mainstream customers should be the focus: Early adopters of a product, especially for new technologies, would constitute only 2-3% of the market while the mass market constitutes the majority. If the new product is optimized for the minority, it's not going to help in the long run, according to Dorie Clark, marketing strategist and a teacher at Duke University.

5. Rely on big data: Unlike Steve Jobs of Apple, not all CEO's and marketing heads may be quite instinctive and they need to rely on market data to come up with the right evangelism marketing campaign. The best example is Amazon with its Kindle that grew on the basis of thousands of customer reviews. Alex Goldfayn, author of Evangelist Marketing: What Apple, Amazon, and Netflix Understand About Their Customers (That your Company probably Doesn't) opine that the cornerstone of a creating evangelist is a deep understanding of what the customers think, want and how they use your product or service.

6. Rely on Qualitative Research: It is not only in structured and unstructured data (big data) that customer preferences and wants the lie, but in direct interaction with customers and not internet surveys. Ideally, people should be sent to do a 20 or 30-minute interview with customers to understand what customers think and interact with your products.

7. Use social media to reach out to customers: According to Gerald Hanks of Demand Media, social media has emerged as an ideal medium for evangelism marketing examples. Even small businesses can employ Facebook, Twitter and YouTube to create a community around the lover of their products. In these platforms, the customers can express their likes, dislikes. Dominoes Pizza made several changes in their business after listening to conversations in online communities. This made the customers feel they are taken care of and naturally they become the evangelists for Dominoes.

8. Evangelize the right people, at right levels: Guy Kawasaki opines that marginally successful companies and start-ups turned out to be best Macintosh software developers and not established players as MS-DOS market leaders may have cared less whether Macintosh failed or succeeded as they had no motivation to do so.

   Similarly, in an organization, the right people to evangelize are not at the top of the organization as they only manage not do the real work. It could also annoy the real workers when they are bypassed and approached at the top. Johnny Carson sent a copy of his new book to NBC staffers who started to talk about it and soon it was noticed by the producer who in turn scheduled the program with Carson.

The company's employees are the people who directly interact with the customers. And if they are dissatisfied with the work environment, they will just do their job for a living but will not take the initiative to spread the good word about the brand- or preach. Therefore, it is important to increase job satisfaction and employee satisfaction level s in the company to get good evangelists in-house who will preach to customers and others about what the product, company, and the promoters stand for.

Employee satisfaction can be improved by providing performance led incentives, bonus, discounted movie tickets, company picnics, free lunch etc.

9. Blogging is effective for evangelism marketing: Aj Agrawal in a Forbes column feels blogging is a great way to go further in evangelism marketing. The blogs should be about what's happening behind the scenes in product development, release snippets of the product and get people to talk about it. Engagement is an essential part of a business blog. The best way to engage is to have a question at the end of the blog and once an answer is posted, a reply can be posted, tag them and put another question. This will create an atmosphere of interaction and soon more people will join the community as soon as it is shared on social media.
10. Understand your competitor/competing brands: Most often a start-up company may find it difficult to get a foothold in the market despite having a good product. It is very important to use market research to understand what is being offered by the competition. Why are people choosing those brands over our product and what do customers perceive of their service, product quality, brand value among others.

Advantages of Evangelism Marketing

1. Cost effective: Evangelism marketing is not for big businesses alone, it is most suitable for small and medium businesses as it is high on return on investment (ROI) and sales conversion is typically higher than the money spent as referrals are usually free. Evangelists support the cause of the product or brand with their money and word-of-mouth publicity which is much more valuable than a celebrity's endorsement of a product he or she may have never used at all.
2. Best way to brand your product: Unlike in mass media advertisement and hoardings, the goal of evangelist marketing is to find out how a brand fits into a customer's life and making that fit as easy as possible. The referrals come about when customers needs are satisfied with the product and the company's support in achieving it.
3. Evangelists are ordinary people: According to Guy Kawasaki, there is a myth that evangelists are people with special skills, dynamic personalities or charisma but very ordinary people. What makes them stand out is not their educational and career achievements but their passion for the cause. It is not that high achievers and gifted people can't become evangelists but often they end up selling themselves and not the cause. And the best way to find an evangelist is not to look for them at all, they'll find an opportunity and come.

4. In evangelism marketing, you are not selling the product, but a cause: Taliq Corporation in California produced liquid crystal technology in its glass products. This makes the office walls translucent for privacy or clear for a spacious feeling. It enables worked to remain cool in direct sunlight and yet allow customers to see inside the restaurant while picking up their orders. Taliq succeeded not because it sold LCDs in the glass but it sold the dream of comfort and privacy.
5. It breaks convention regarding product and solution: Many a time, the success formula in marketing is to find a need and fill it. In evangelism the opposite can happen, a solution can run in search of a need. Virtual reality was a concept in graphics lab of the University of North Carolina looking for a need.

Multi-level Marketing

Multi-level marketing (MLM), also called pyramid selling, network marketing, and referral marketing, is a marketing strategy for the sale of products or services where the revenue of the MLM company is derived from a non-salaried workforce selling the company's products/services, while the earnings of the participants are derived from a pyramid-shaped or binary compensation commission system.

Although each MLM company dictates its own specific financial compensation plan for the payout of any earnings to their respective participants, the common feature that is found across all MLMs is that the compensation plans theoretically pay out to participants only from two potential revenue streams. The first is paid out from commissions of sales made by the participants directly to their own retail customers. The second is paid out from commissions based upon the wholesale purchases made by other distributors below the participant who have recruited those other participants into the MLM; in the organizational hierarchy of MLMs, these participants are referred to as one's down line distributors.

MLM salespeople are, therefore, expected to sell products directly to end-user retail consumers by means of relationship referrals and word of mouth marketing, but most importantly they are incentivized to recruit others to join the company's distribution chain as fellow salespeople so that these can become down line distributors. According to a report that studied the business models of 350 MLMs, published on the Federal Trade Commission's website, at least 99% of people who join MLM companies lose money. Nonetheless, MLMs function because downline participants are encouraged to hold onto the belief that they can achieve large returns, while the statistical improbability of this is de-emphasised. MLMs have been made illegal or otherwise strictly regulated in some jurisdictions as a mere variation of the traditional pyramid scheme.

Business Model

Participant Profits and Losses

The overwhelming majority of MLM participants participate at either an insignificant or nil net profit. Indeed, the largest proportion of participants must operate at a net loss (after expenses are deducted) so that the few individuals in the uppermost level of the MLM pyramid can derive their significant earnings. Said earnings are then emphasized by the MLM company to all other participants to encourage their continued participation at a continuing financial loss.

Participant Financial Loss, Company Financial Gain

The end result of the MLM business model is, therefore, one of a company (the MLM company) selling its products and services through a non-salaried workforce ("partners") working for the MLM company on a commission-only basis while the partners simultaneously constitute the overwhelming majority of the very consumers of the MLM company's products and services that they, as participants of the MLM, are selling to each other in the hope of one day themselves being at the top of the pyramid. This creates great profit for the MLM company's actual owners and shareholders.

Many MLM companies do generate billions of dollars in annual revenue and hundreds of millions of dollars in annual profit. However, the profits of the MLM company are accrued at the detriment to the majority of the company's constituent workforce (the MLM participants). Only some of said profit is then significantly shared with individual participants at the top of the MLM distributorship pyramid. The earnings of those top few participants is emphasized and championed at company seminars and conferences, thus creating an illusion of how one can potentially become financially successful if they become a participant in the MLM. This is then advertised by the MLM company to recruit more distributors to participate in the MLM with a false anticipation of earning margins which are in reality merely theoretical and statistically improbable.

Although an MLM company holds out those few top individual participants as evidence of how participation in the MLM could lead to success, the reality is that the MLM business model depends on the failure of the overwhelming majority of all other participants, through the injecting of money from their own pockets, so that it can become the revenue and profit of the MLM company, of which the MLM company shares only a small proportion of it to a few individuals at the very top of the MLM participant pyramid. Participants, other than the few individuals at the top, provide nothing more than their own financial loss for the company's own profit and the profit of the top few individual participants.

Financial Independence

The main sales pitch of MLM companies to their participants and prospective participants is not the MLM company's products or services. The products/services are largely peripheral to the MLM model. Rather, the true sales pitch and emphasis is on a confidence given to participants of potential financial independence through participation in the MLM, luring with phrases like "the lifestyle you deserve" or "independent distributor." Erik German's memoir *My Father's Dream* documents the real life failures of German's father as he is lured into "get-rich-quick" schemes such as Amway. The memoir illustrates the multi-level marketing sales principle known as "selling the dream".

Although emphasis is always made on the potential of success and the positive life change that "might" or "could" (not "will" or "can") result, it is only in otherwise difficult to find disclosure statements (or at the very least, difficult to read and interpret disclosure statements), that MLM participants are given fine print disclaimers that they as participants should not rely on the earning results of other participants in the highest levels of the MLM participant pyramid as an indication of what they should expect to earn. MLMs very rarely emphasize the extreme likelihood of failure, or the extreme likelihood of financial loss, from participation in MLM. MLMs are also seldom forthcoming about the fact that any significant success of the few individuals at the top of the MLM participant pyramid is in fact dependent on the continued financial loss and failure of all other participants below them in the MLM pyramid.

Comparisons to Pyramid Schemes

MLMs have been made illegal in some jurisdictions as a mere variation of the traditional pyramid scheme, including in China. In jurisdictions where MLMs have not been made illegal, many illegal pyramid schemes attempt to present themselves as MLM businesses. Given that the overwhelming majority of MLM participants cannot realistically make a net profit, let alone a significant net profit, but instead overwhelmingly operate at net losses, some sources have defined all MLMs as a type of pyramid scheme, even if they have not been made illegal like traditional pyramid schemes through legislative statutes.

MLMs are designed to make profit for the owners/shareholders of the company, and a few individual participants at the top levels of the MLM pyramid of participants. According to the U.S. Federal Trade Commission (FTC), some MLM companies already constitute illegal pyramid schemes even by the narrower existing legislation, exploiting members of the organization.

Lawsuits

Companies that use the MLM business model have been a frequent subject of criticism and lawsuits. Legal claims against MLMs have included, among other things:

1. Their similarity to traditional illegal pyramid schemes,
2. Price fixing of products or services,
3. Collusion and racketeering in backroom deals where secret compensation packages are created between the MLM company and a few individual participants, to the detriment of others,
4. High initial entry costs (for marketing kit and first products),
5. Emphasis on recruitment of others over actual sales (especially sales to non-participants),
6. Encouraging if not requiring members to purchase and use the company's products,
7. Exploitation of personal relationships as both sales and recruiting targets,
8. Complex and exaggerated compensation schemes,
9. False product claims,
10. The company or leading distributors making major money off participant-attended conventions, training events and materials, advertising materials, and
11. Cult-like techniques which some groups use to enhance their members' enthusiasm and devotion.

Direct Selling versus Network Marketing

"Network marketing" and "multi-level marketing" (MLM) have been described by author Dominique Xardel as being synonymous, with it being a type of direct selling. Some sources emphasize that multi-level marketing is merely one form of direct selling, rather than being direct selling. Other terms that are sometimes used to describe multi-level marketing include "word-of-mouth marketing", "interactive distribution", and "relationship marketing". Critics have argued that the use of these and other different terms and "buzzwords" is an effort to distinguish multi-level marketing from illegal Ponzi schemes, chain letters, and consumer fraud scams.

The Direct Selling Association (DSA), a lobbying group for the MLM industry, reported that in 1990 only 25% of DSA members used the MLM business model. By 1999, this had grown to 77.3%. By 2009, 94.2% of DSA members were using MLM, accounting for 99.6% of sellers, and 97.1% of sales. Companies such as Avon, Electrolux, Tupperware, and Kirby were all originally single-level marketing companies, using that traditional and uncontroversial direct selling business model (distinct from MLM) to sell their goods. However, they later introduced multi-level compensation plans, becoming MLMs. The DSA has approximately 200 members while it is estimated there are over 1,000 firms using multi-level marketing in the United States alone.

Setup

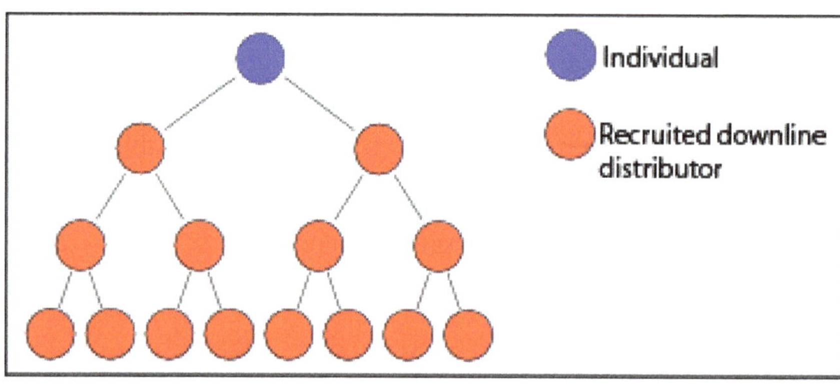

A typical Multi-level marketing MLM binary tree structure. The blue individual will receive compensation from the sales of the downline red members.

Independent non-salaried participants, referred to as distributors (variously called "associates", "independent business owners", "independent agents", etc.), are authorized to distribute the company's products or services. They are awarded their own immediate retail profit from customers plus commission from the company, not downlines, through a multi-level marketing compensation plan, which is based upon the volume of products sold through their own sales efforts as well as that of their downline organization.

Independent distributors develop their organizations by either building an active consumer network, who buy direct from the company, or by recruiting a downline of independent distributors who also build a consumer network base, thereby expanding the overall organization.

The combined number of recruits from these cycles are the sales force which is referred to as the salesperson's "downline". This "downline" is the pyramid in MLM's multiple level structure of compensation.

Assuming the blue individual recruits five, and those five recruit their own five, and so on, the maximum theoretical cycles of recruits possible in the "downline" of the blue individual is 14 cycles (5^{14} = 6.1 billion people), after which point the total human population is exceeded.

Global Marketing

Global marketing is defined as the process of adjusting the marketing strategies of your company to adapt to the conditions of other countries. Of course, global marketing is more than selling your product or service globally. It is the full process of planning, creating, positioning, and promoting your products in a global market.

Big businesses usually have offices abroad for countries they market to. Currently, with the proliferation of the internet, even small businesses can reach consumers anywhere in the world. If a business chooses not to extend internationally, it can face domestic competition from international companies that are extending their international presence. The presence of this competition almost makes it a requirement for many businesses to have an international presence.

There are many benfits of global marketing, when it is done right.

- First, it can improve the effectiveness of your product or service. This is because the more you grow, the more you learn, and the faster you learn, you become more effective at producing new product or service offerings.
- Second, you are able to have a strong competitive advantage. It is easy enough for companies to be competing in the local market. But there are very few companies who can do so on the worldwide arena. Hence, if you can compete in the worldwide market and your competitors cannot, you have become a strong force in your industry.
- Third, you increase consumer awareness of your brand and product or service. Through the internet, consumers can keep track of your progress in the world.
- Finally, global marketing can reduce your costs and increase your savings. In focusing on other markets, you can attain economies of scale and range by standardizing your processes – not to mention the savings that you get when you leverage the internet.

Companies evolving towards global marketing are actually quite gradual. The first stage has the company concentrating on the domestic side, with its activities focused on their home market. Stage two has the company still focusing domestically but has exports. By stage three, the company has realized that they need to adapt their marketing geared towards overseas. The concentration moves from multinational. Thus, adaption has become crucial. The fourth and last stage has the company creating value when it extends its programs and products to serve worldwide markets. Definitely, there are no definite time periods to this evolution process.

Global Marketing Strategies

Global marketing strategies are actually important parts of a global strategy. A good global marketing strategy incorporates all the countries from all regions of the world and coordinates their marketing efforts accordingly. Of course, this strategy does not always cover all the countries but should be applied for particular regions. For example, you can break down regions like North America, Latin America, Europe and the Middle East, Asia and the Pacific, and Africa.

Beyond its breakdown per country or region, a global marketing strategy almost always consists of several things: (1) uniform brand names; (2) identical packaging; (3) similar products; (4) standardized advertising messages; (5) synchronized pricing; (6) coordinated product launches; and (7) harmonious sales campaigns.

As a whole, these two are the most well known global marketing strategies used by companies expanding internationally:

- Create a consistent and strong brand culture. Creating a strong and consistent brand that always seems familiar to customers is a priority for companies growing internationally. With the ever-more rising and expanding internet, brand structure has become more of a brand culture. To be more specific, it has become more prevalent nowadays that the brand you support reflects your culture. It can be damaging if you compromise your brand culture. For example, Google found out the hard way when it launched a self-censored search engine in China, even though China subjects its new media to government blocks. Google's brand has been known to make the world access information at anytime.
- Market as if there were no borders. Due to the proliferation of digital platforms, brands cannot always adopt different strategies per country. In a way, due to the internet, companies have to adopt a marketing approach that is more or less unified.

Global Marketing Campaign Development

In order to develop your campaign globally, there are a few things you should keep in mind. You have to know the market, you have to create a marketing plan, you should tailor fit your approach to marketing, and you should localize your communications.

Know Your Market

As soon as your company decides to extend your marketing worldwide, you have to understand the context of where you will be working. Every region has various behaviors and norms as it deals with marketing messages; how people would like to be contacted; and what is appropriate for that place, and the like.

You have to make sure that you research how the market will respond to the marketing strategy you have, so you can get much leverage from your new market.

Create a Marketing Plan

Becoming successful worldwide is not merely altering your language. You have to make your global marketing plan consistent with your local efforts. Yet it still needs to be customized, according to your regional knowledge. Once you have an insight of the global environment, draft a marketing plan that details your actions.

First, identify your objectives and goals. As soon as that has been established, draw a map that covers the overall strategy and techniques to attain those objectives.

Tailor Fit your Approach

Keep in mind that what may have worked for your local audience may not translate as well to your foreign audience. Try to adapt your initiatives to your audience, giving them a tailor fit experience. Definitely, what works for one country may not work for another.

Localize your Communications

It is not only relevant to know the language and cultural hurdles and adjusting your communications for every market, it is also critical to know all the cultural references and relevant holidays and events. You need to create a more personalized experience. But make sure not to make international marketing mistakes when translating your brand message.

Global Marketing Issues and Mistakes

Companies, especially their marketing teams, often face the following issues and mistakes when expanding worldwide. These can become hurdles in achieving international success.

Non-specification of Countries

Many businesspersons usually think of foreign markets vaguely, like they want to shift to Asia or they want to increase their growth by offering their products to Europe. It is problematic to take things too simply. Europe can mean the European Union, Western Europe, Eastern Europe, and so on and so forth. Consumers always identify themselves at the local level and marketing teams have to remember that each country has its own norms, laws, payment types, and particular business practices.

By being specific in the start, companies can prioritize the markets they want to get into, generate a staffing plan, and allocate the budget. These are all important for a business to attain its global objectives.

No Focus on Internal Information

You have to conduct specialized and complicated market research when you are going to create a global market entry strategy. You would need to consider the potential opportunity in the market, how easy or hard it would be for your business to work in that market, and how successful you already are in the market.

There are a lot of companies that concentrated on outside data to help their decision-making, as described above. Nonetheless, you can simply use your own internal information to get the data, on whether there is a strong fit between your product or service and the market. Remember that data from third parties do not understand your company or even know your consumer. Only you have the best input on this.

Lack of Adaptation of Sales and Marketing Channels

Most Western companies think that they can go into new markets by doing the same things that brought them success domestically.

It is important to have brand consistency, but differing markets would like particular marketing approaches. Moreover, marketers have to consider at which channels it would be best to market, based on market behavior.

Case in point, for Brazil, marketing campaigns are more successful through Facebook because of its popularity there. However, in Latin America, you can draw in a bigger audience through Twitter. Hence, you may need to check which channels give you the best results through market research.

No Adaptation of Product Offerings

Business can only attain a fit between their product and the market one at a time. However, more often than not, businesses attempt to launch the same products in varying markets. In essence, they are ignoring that they are interacting with a different set of consumers.

Case in point, if a tech company sells a similar product abroad that it sells domestically and if the new customers do not know the advanced features of the product, the company could be in trouble. Alternatively, the company should begin with the basic version.

A market that is more advanced might need additional features than what the product already has.

Non-usage of Local Team Leads

Perhaps one of the usual mistakes companies make in global marketing is failing to consider the input of strong and competent employees in their foreign markets, especially when establishing strategic decisions.

These individuals are significant because they know their country and your company. Since one of the biggest issues businesses face when including local input is communication, the marketing team must have a system that guarantees that local perspectives are gathered and distributed often.

Lack of Knowledge on Global Logistics

Marketers often make use of software that allows them to publish website content, send email, publish updates on social media, and accomplish other marketing-related activities. However, these tools do not always support each market. For example, you have payment solutions only for a couple of countries, but your customer relationship management system has many contacts coming from a hundred countries.

Marketers have to guarantee that they could market to customers in the countries they are entering. They should consider how to display the local currency, how to email consumers in particular time zones, and how to support the languages of the consumers.

Examples of Global Marketing

If you are searching for inspiration on how to market your company successfully in the international arena, check out these examples from well known companies.

Airbnb

Airbnb is for people who book and list accommodations all over the world. Generally, it is a community marketplace that has more than a million listings in more than 34,000 cities in the world. Airbnb became very successful globally because of social media. In 2015, Airbnb began a social media campaign using the #OneLessStranger hashtag.

This social experiment had Airbnb asking its community to do random acts of hospitality for people they did not know and take a photograph or video with them and share by making use of the hashtag. In only 3 weeks after the campaign was launched, more than 3 million people created content, engaged, or talked about the campaign.

Coca-Cola

Even though Coca-Cola is a big corporation, it also concentrates on programs in small communities and infuses a lot of funds and time in small charities.

Case in point, Coco-Cola built 650 clean water installations in Beni, Suef in Egypt and sponsored meals (Ramadan) for children in the Middle East. Moreover, the brand goes with an emotion that everyone knows — happiness.

Domino's

Domino's positioned menu innovation in the forefront to increase its international awareness and interest. They have consistent items for the pizza in all markets like their sauce, bread, and cheese, where it works anywhere.

They just update the toppings for every market. If it is Asia, they have fish and seafood, for example.

Dunkin' Donuts

Did you know that Dunkin' Donuts China has seaweed and dry pork donuts? With thousands of stores in over 30 countries worldwide, Dunkin' Donuts updated its menus to satisfy its international consumers.

In Lebanon, they have the Mango Chocolate Donut; in South Korea, they have the Grapefruit Coolatta; and in Russia, they have Dunclairs.

H&M

H&M almost always increases its store openings by 10 to 15 percent each year. One of the secrets of their global expansion is maximizing their online experience.

Innocent Drinks

A leading smoothie company in the United Kingdom, Innocent Drinks can be found in 13 countries all over Europe. Even with its wide reach, they still maintain consistent branding.

Kentucky Fried Chicken

Kentucky Fried Chicken was able to do something quite interesting. In Japan, they were able to connect their products with Christmas. So every Christmas, Japanese line up at their nearest KFC for some chicken.

McDonald's

Even though McDonald's keeps its branding consistent, McDonald's tries to bring in some local flavor to particular menu items. McDonald's has the McArabia in the Middle East—this is a flatbread sandwich. It also introduced France to its macaroons and included the McSpaghetti in the Philippines. In Mexico, they have a green chili cheeseburger and in South Korea, they have bulgogi burgers.

Nike

Nike has evolved his international presence by carefully selecting international sponsorships. Even though spending for sponsorships is quite unpredictable, demand costs usually rise sharply because of triggers such as tournaments and championships. This has captured the attention of the international arena.

Red Bull

One of Red Bull's successful techniques is hosting extreme sports in the world. They have the Red Bull Air Race in the U.K., the Red Bull Soapbox Race in Jordan, and the Red Bull Indianapolis Grand Prix.

Starbucks

Starbucks adjusts its menu for local tastes. For Hong Kong, they have Dragon Dumplings, for example. The company has had a wide reputation for the engagement of local cultures.

Unger and Kowitt

Unger and Kowitt is a law firm that focuses on traffic tickets in Fort Lauderdale, Florida. Although its focus is in Florida, the business knows that the U.S. has many languages and cultures. So its website is translated to English, Portuguese, Spanish, and Creole.

World Wildlife Foundation

The World Wildlife Foundation or the WWF is known for its Earth Hour initiative and moved it to the mobile audience of Norway. Earth Hour is an international voluntary event wherein participants turn their lights off for 1 hour to show the ease of fighting climate change.

References

- Direct-marketin, marketing: toolshero.com, Retrieved 4 June, 2019
- Black; Neville (2009). "Fly-Posting: An Exploration of a 'Controversial' Medium". Journal of Marketing Communications. 15 (4): 209–226. Doi:10.1080/13527260802091022
- Direct-marketing, running-business, types, using, marketing-sales, marketing-promotion: business.qld.gov.au, Retrieved 5 July, 2019
- Gonzales, Niero (9 March 2013). "Half of Destructoid's readers block our ads. Now what?". Destructoid. Retrieved 14 June 2013
- Evangelism-marketing-definition-examples-strategy, lesson, academ: study.com, Retrieved 6 August, 2019
- Goldfarb, Avi; Tucker, Catherine E. (2011). "Privacy Regulation and Online Advertising". Management Science. 57(1): 57–71. Doi:10.1287/mnsc.1100.1246
- Evangelism-marketing: educba.com, Retrieved 7 January, 2019
- Josh Sanburn (2011-08-09). "The 25 Most Influential Business Management Books". Time. Retrieved April 12,2016
- Global-marketing-strategies: cleverism.com, Retrieved 8 February, 2019

Fundamental Concepts of Marketing

3

- Pricing
- Pricing Strategies in Marketing
- Marketing Mix
- Distribution
- Retail
- Brand Licensing
- Marketing Activation
- Social Marketing
- Social Marketing Process

There are numerous concepts which are studied and applied in the field of marketing. Some of them are pricing strategies, marketing mix, distribution, retail, brand licensing, marketing activation and social marketing. The topics elaborated in this chapter will help in gaining a better perspective about these fundamental concepts of marketing.

Pricing

Pricing is the method of determining the value a producer will get in the exchange of goods and services. Simply, pricing method is used to set the price of producer's offerings relevant to both the producer and the customer.

Every business operates with the primary objective of earning profits, and the same can be realized through the Pricing methods adopted by the firms.

While setting the price of a product or service the following points have to be kept in mind:

1. Nature of the product/service.

2. The price of similar product/service in the market.
3. Target audience i.e. for whom the product is manufactured (high, medium or lower class).
4. The cost of production viz. Labor cost, raw material cost, machinery cost, inventory cost, transit cost, etc.
5. External factors such as Economy, Government policies, Legal issues, etc.

Pricing Objectives

The objective once set gives the path to the business i.e. in which direction to go. The following are the pricing objectives that clears the purpose for which the business exists:

1. Survival: The foremost Pricing Objective of any firm is to set the price that is optimum and help the product or service to survive in the market. Each firm faces the danger of getting ruled out from the market because of the intense competition, a mature market or change in customer's tastes and preferences, etc. Thus, a firm must set the price covering the fixed and variable cost incurred without adding any profit margin to it. The survival should be the short term objective once the firm gets a hold in the market it must strive for the additional profits. The New Firms entering into the market adopts this type of pricing objective.
2. Maximizing the current profits: Many firms try to maximize their current profits by estimating the Demand and Supply of goods and services in the market. Pricing is done in line with the product's demand in the customers and the substitutes available to fulfill that demand. Higher the demand higher will be the price charged. Seasonal supply and demand of goods and services are the best examples that can be quoted here.
3. Capturing huge market share: Many firms charge low prices for their offerings to capture greater market share. The reason for keeping the price low is to have an increased sales resulting from the Economies of Scale. Higher sales volume lead to lower production cost and increased profits in the long run. This strategy of keeping the price low is also known as Market Penetration Pricing. This pricing method is generally used when competition is intense and customers are price sensitive. FMCG industry is the best example to supplement this.

4. Market Skimming: Market skimming means charging a high price for the product and services offered by the firms which are innovative, and uses modern technology. The prices are comparatively kept high due to the high cost of production incurred because of modern technology. Mobile phones, Electronic Gadgets are the best examples of skimming pricing that are launched at a very high cost and gets cheaper with the span of time.

5. Product–Quality Leadership: Many firms keep the price of their goods and services in accordance with the Quality Perceived by the customers. Generally, the luxury goods create their high quality, taste, and status image in the minds of customers for which they are willing to pay high prices. Luxury cars such as BMW, Mercedes, Jaguar, etc. create the high quality with high-status image among the customers.

Pricing Strategies in Marketing

The pricing of any product is extremely complex and intense as it is a result of a number of calculations, research work, risk taking ability and understanding of the market and the consumers. The management of the company considers everything before they price a product, this everything includes the segment of the product, the ability of a consumer to pay for the products, the conditions of the market, action of the competitor, the production and the raw material cost or you can say the cost of manufacturing, and of course the margin or the profit margins.

The main aim of the management of every organization is to maximize profits by effectively getting the products of the shelf; let's define and explain this better.

Pricing strategy is a way of finding a competitive price of a product or a service. This strategy is combined with the other marketing pricing strategies that are the 4P strategy (products, price, place and promotion) economic patterns, competition, market demand and finally product characteristic. This strategy comprises of one of the most significant ingredients of the mix of marketing as it is focused on generating and increasing the revenue for an organization, which ultimately becomes profit making for the company. Understanding the market conditions and the unmet desires of the consumers along with the price that the consumer is willing to pay to fulfill his unmet desires is the ultimate way of gaining success in the pricing strategy of a product or a service.

Do not forget the ultimate goal of the company is to maximize profit being in competition and sustaining the competitive market. However to maximize profits along with retaining your consumer you have to make sure you choose the right pricing strategy. The correct strategy will help you attain your objectives as an organization.

Penetration Pricing or Pricing to Gain Market Share

A few companies adopt these strategies in order to enter the market and to gain market share. Some companies either provide a few services for free or they keep a low price for their products for a limited period that is for a few months. This strategy is used by the companies only in order to set up their customer base in a particular market. For example France telecom gave away free telephone connections to consumers in order to grab or acquire maximum consumers in a given market. Similarly the Sky TV gave away their satellite dishes for free in order to set up a market for them. This gives the companies a start and a consumer base.

In the similar manner there are few companies that keep their product cost low as their introductory offer that is a way of introducing themselves in the market and creating a consumer base. Similarly when the companies want to promote a premier product or service they do raise the prices of the products and services for that particular time.

Economy pricing or No Frill Low Price

The pricing Strategies of these products are considered as no frill low prices where the promotion and the marketing cost of a product are kept to a minimum. Economy pricing is set for a certain time where the company does not spend more on promoting the product and service. For example the first few seats of the airlines are sold very cheap in budget airlines in order to fill in the airlines the seats sold in the middle are the economy seats where as the seats sold at the end are priced very high as that comes under the premium price strategy. This strategy sees more economy sales during the time of recession. Economy pricing can also be termed as or explained as budget pricing of a product or a service.

Use of Psychological Pricing Strategies

Psychological pricing Strategies is an approach of gathering the consumer's emotional respond instead of his rational respond. For example a company will price its product at Rs 99 instead of Rs 100. The price of the product is within Rs 100 this makes the customer feel that the product is not very expensive. For most consumers price is an indicating factor for buying or not buying a product. They do not analyze everything else that motivates the product. Even if the market is unknown to the consumer he will still use price as a purchase factor. For example if an ice cream weighted 100 gms for Rs 100 and a lesser quality ice cream weighted 200 gms is available at Rs 150, the consumer will buy the 200 gms ice cream for Rs 150 because he sees profit in buying the ice cream at lower cost ignoring the quality of the ice cream. Consumers are not aware price is also an indicator of quality.

Pricing Strategies of Product Line

Products line pricing is defined as pricing a single product or service and pricing a range of products.

Let us take and understand this with the help of an example. When you go for a car wash you have an option of choosing a car wash for Rs 200 or a car wash and a car wax for Rs 400 or the entire package including a service at Rs 600. This strategy reflects a strategic cost of making a product popular and consumed by the consumer with a fair increment over the range of the product or the service. In another example if you buy a pack of chips and chocolate separately you end up paying a separate price for each product; however of you buy a combo pack of the two you end up paying comparatively less price for both and if you buy a combo of both in a higher quantity you end up paying even lesser.

For the manufactures of the product manufacturing and marketing of larger pack is much more expensive as it does not fetch them good amount of profit, however they do the same to attract more consumers and keep them interest in their products. On the other hand manufacturing smaller packs and lesser quantity is more beneficial and fetches more profit for the manufacturer of the product.

Pricing Optional Products

It is a general approach, if the companies decrease the price of a product or a service they do increase their price for their other available optional services. Let's take a very simple and a common example of a budget airline. The prices of their airfare are low however they will charge you extra if you want to book a window seat, if you want to travel with your family and want to book an entire row together you might have to end up paying extra charges as per the their guidelines, in case you have too much of luggage to carry you will end up paying extra on the same, in fact you will end up paying extra charges even if you need extra leg space in a budget airlines. You can say that even if the price of the air fare is low you will end up paying more for the extra yet mandatory services that you will require as you travel.

Pricing of Captive Products

Captive products have products that compliment the products without which the main product is of no use or is useless. For example an inkjet printer is of no use without its cartridge it will not work and have no value and a plastic razor will have no value without its blades. If the company is manufacturing the inkjet printer it will have to manufacture its cartridges and if the company is manufacturing a plastic razor it will have to manufacture blades for the same. For a simple reason that any other company cartridge will not fit into the inkjet printer and neither will any other companies blade fit into the plastic razor. The consumer has no other option but to buy the complementary products from of the same company. This increases the sales and the profit margin of the company anyways.

Pricing for Promotions

Promotional pricing is very common these days. You will find it almost everywhere. Pricing for promoting a product is another very useful and helpful strategy. These promotion offers can include, discount offers, gift or money coupons or vouchers, buy one and get one free, etc. to promote new and even existing products companies do adopt such strategies where they roll out these offers to promote their products. An old strategy yet it is one of the most successful pricing strategies till date. Reason of its success is that the consumer considers buying the product and service for the offer that the consumer receives.

Pricing as Per Geographic Locations

For simple reasons such as the geographic location the companies do vary or change the price of the product. Why does location of the market affect the price of the product? The reasons can be many well some are scarcity of the product or the raw material of the product, the shipping cost of the product, taxes differ in a few countries, difference in the currency rate for products, etc.

Let's take a few pricing strategies examples, when a few fruits are not available in a country they are imported from another country, these fruits are exotic fruits, they are also scarce this increases their value in the country they are imported to, scarcity, the shipping cost of the imported product along with its quality increase its price, where as it is much cheaper where it is originally grown. Similarly the government implies heavy taxes on a few products such as petrol or petroleum products and alcohol to increase their revenue; hence such products are expensive in a few countries or part of the country compared to the other parts. Geographic location does create a huge impact on the pricing strategy of a product as the company has to consider every aspect before they price a product. Hence the price needs to be perfect and appropriate.

Value Pricing a Product

Let me first be clear about what value pricing means, value pricing is reducing the price of a product due to external factors that can affect the sales of the product for example competition and recession; value pricing does not mean that the company has added something or increased the value of a product. When the company is afraid of factors such as competition or recession affecting their sales and profits the company considers value pricing.

For example McDonalds the famous food chain has started value meals for their consumer since they have started facing competition with other fast food chains. They offer a meal or a combination of a few products as a lower price where the consumer feels emotionally content and continues to buy their products.

Pricing of Premium Products

Well this strategy works just the other way round. Premium products are priced higher due to their unique branding approach. A high price for premium products is an extensive competitive advantage to the manufacturer as the high price for these products assures them that they are safe in the market due to their relatively high price. Premium pricing can be charged for products and services such as precious jewelry, precious stones, luxurious services, cruses, luxurious hotel rooms, business air travel, etc. The higher the cost the more will be the value of the product amongst that class of audience.

Marketing Mix

Marketing Mix is a strategy which a company uses to formulate a product/service offering for its customers. Marketing mix strategy is created using the 4Ps of marketing - Product, Place, Price, Promotion and 7Ps in case of service- Physical Evidence, People, Process. The term Marketing Mix is attributed to Neil Bordon. The term is named marketing mix because it suggest how a marketer mixes various elements (Product, Price, Place, Promotion etc) in order to make a relevant/just right offering to the customer. The main objective of marketing mix strategy is to make the right product at correct price at the right place with right promotion.

This strategy has been one of the popular marketing topics in business. Let us talk more about the various elements in the marketing mix.

Product Marketing Mix

When a company is offering products or goods, it comes under the purview of the product marketing mix. It talks about the product strategies, pricing strategies, place where the products are distributed and promotional strategies. Elements of a product marketing mix can be explained in detail as below:

1. Product: It is the main part of the offering, the product itself. It is most important aspect of the mix. Product is something which has some functional value and can be used by the customer to achieve something. A marketer needs to define his product very carefully thinking about its value, its USP, features, competition etc.
2. Price: Pricing the second most important element in our marketing mix. This is value we will get in exchange for our product. This is what the customer will pay in return for the utility of the product. Pricing is mainly determined by the cost of the product and also how much the customer would be willing to pay. If we price it too high no one buys, if we price it too low, company makes losses. So we have to devise the right pricing strategy to make our marketing mix perfect.
3. Place: Also called the Distribution. If we are making a product as the right price, that is not enough, we need to make it available at the right place too. The customer mostly would not come to you until and unless our product and price is unbeatable. The product needs to be where customer is likely to buy. If we are soft drink manufacturer and the product is not available in grocery stores, supermarkets, restaurants etc then the first two elements of marketing mix are of no use and the offering fails.
4. Promotion: Also referred to as Communication about the product. This is the 4th element in marketing mix which means the communication done about the product to the customer. Advertising on TV, print and digital media would come under promotion.

Thus, the 4Ps or marketing mix is valid for every company, whether it is a product or a service company.

Service Marketing Mix

In case of a service brand like a restaurant, telecom service, hospitality etc, there are additional points apart from the 4Ps. The additional Ps i.e. physical evidence, people and processes are collectively known as the service marketing mix. These can be described as below:

1. Physical Evidence: A service is intangible but there has to be a reassurance to the customer that service happened. It can be a receipt of a service or may be an invoice. Physical evidence should be positive meaning that customer should be assured that service completed as expected.

2. People: These are the employees which help deliver the service e.g. delivery boy or a cab driver. They may become the face of the service hence are very important that is why very important to chose right people.
3. Process: The steps undertaken for completion/delivery of the service. The process is very crucial. The process should not only consist of the positive path but should also should consider the negative paths to address issues in the service delivery. e.g. Complain management, reverse supply chain etc.

All these help in understand the marketing mix for a service based business.

There is an alternative theory of 4 C's (Commodity, Cost, Communication, Channel) also which is similar to 4 Ps.

Importance of Marketing Mix

Marketing Mix is one of the most important marketing strategy used by companies. Marketing Mix is one of the first steps in the strategy. It lets companies decide on their formula for the four parameters-Product, Price, Place, Promotion. A marketer can use these four to adjust the product offering. Marketing mix along with other marketing techniques like segmentation, targeting, positioning, planning, research can lead to a successful marketing proposition.

Example of Marketing Mix

ABC ltd wants to launch a new Burger in menu. So as first element of marketing mix is product, we should be sure about the burger. The ingredients - bun, patty, vegetables, other elements like cheese and sauces should be well researched and thought upon. Once the approved burger is ready, we need to think about the Price as per the marketing mix. If ABC already has burgers in the menu, they can use comparative pricing along with the cost incurred to make a burger. They cannot afford to lose customers on the price.

In case of ABC, place can be the factory owned restaurants and franchise partners.

Being a fast food vendor, promotion becomes very important here. Promotions can be done through advertising on TV, radio, internet etc. Also in restaurants branding which would inform existing customers about the new product offering in the restaurants. Offers, promotional gifts can be included on every purchase of the new burger.

So Marketing Mix in simple terms is a tool which can be used to mix various elements in right proportions to make the best possible Product/Service Offering.

Distribution

Distribution is the activity of both selling and delivering products and services from manufacturer to customer. As businesses become more global it becomes important to improve distribution to ensure that customers and all members of the distribution channel are happy. Depending on the length of the distribution channel there can be many people involved in product distribution.

Differences Between Distributor and Wholesaler

There tends to be a bit of confusion between what a distributor is and how they differ to a wholesaler. In general, a distributor works closely with a manufacturer in order to sell more goods and gain better visibility on these goods. Distributors normally will find wholesalers who will resale their products. A wholesaler works more closely with retailers to match their needs through buying products in bulk at a discount. Therefore distribution is an important part of the distribution channel as it acts as the medium between the manufacturer and their customers.

Importance of Distribution

Distribution is an important element of operations as, without a role that tracks and improves the relationship between manufacturers and customers, a company cannot ensure the best possible service. If bottlenecks happen in distribution, deliveries fall short, customers, retailers and suppliers get angry, and trust is lost. For product distribution to be truly successful a continuous feedback loop needs to be implemented to ensure everyone is happy with the process and that any improvements that can be made, are made.

In terms of dropshipping and customers buying items online, merchants and customers do not get to try the product before they buy so they trust that the item will arrive just like in the pictures and descriptions. This means that the distribution channel needs to be efficient at providing responses and comments across the whole channel.

Distribution Management

Distribution management refers to the main activities of distributing a product, which includes:

1. Packaging: Providing adequate packaging for a product so it can be transported safely.
2. Inventory Management: Maintaining a good level of inventory is hugely important to distribution. Management of inventory is one of the main responsibilities for distribution management.
3. Order Processing: Once an order comes in from a customer, distribution management needs to plan for the delivery. This involves collecting the stock, loading it and delivering it in a timely manner. Approval needs to be sent and invoicing done for this step to be valid.
4. Logistics: Mode of transport is important to consider for all orders. If they require overseas shipping there must be agreements in place for permits to be approved quickly. Loading and handling need to be decided so that all equipment that could be needed is available onsite.
5. Communication: Clear communication is needed both on and offsite at distribution centers. This is to ensure that the correct products are shipped and customers know when they will receive their items. If a shipment is delayed, distribution management needs to notify all interested parties immediately.

E-Distribution

E-distribution is the electronic product distribution of things like software and digital downloads. Such items include video games, computer software, movies, music, and ebooks. Due to the ease of purchase and the immediate receipt of purchase this industry is fast moving and highly profitable. Different from physical distribution, e-distribution has to be immediate for it to be successful. Customers who do not achieve a download link within minutes of a purchase will reach out to suppliers to receive this.

The downside of this form of distribution is that it requires a constant internet connection to receive the goods and also file formats may lead to corrupt or usable downloads that cause dissatisfaction among customers.

Marketing Distribution

As slightly different from e-distribution and supply chain distribution, marketing distribution is how the marketing department makes products and services available to potential customers. Availability can be through the manufacturer, supplier, distributor, retailer, or wholesaler. From the perspective of the 4P's of the marketing mix, marketing distribution can be slotted into the place category. Examples of marketing distribution channels include:

1. A distributor can be employed by a manufacturer to reach out to suppliers or retailers to purchase their product,
2. A supplier can make their stock available on a marketplace for merchants to find and sell,
3. A retailer could stock a wide array of products strategically placed across their store to entice customers to buy,
4. A wholesaler can build a website so customers can order products straight from them.

Distribution Channel

The distribution channel is the path that a product or service takes in order to be sent from the manufacturer to the customer. If the customer bought the product or service straight from the manufacturer the distribution channel is a short one. If it includes a supplier, distributor, and retailer the distribution channel can be much longer. In general the longer the distribution channel from manufacturer to customer, the less profit the manufacturer will make as each intermediary or vendor charges for their services.

Functions of Distribution Channels

Distribution channels are important to businesses as they allow for the smooth delivery of goods or services to a customer. If a business does not source the best collection of businesses for this purpose, it can lead to unhappy customers and an inadequate provision of services. Creating an efficient process from warehouse to customer can make a huge difference in how customers view your business.

For example, if a business sources goods from a subpar manufacturer customer will receive unsatisfactory products. Or if a wholesaler is unreliable when delivering goods, customers will not receive their products on time.

Shorter distribution channels have fewer businesses involved in the process of delivery of goods meaning that there is more risk involved for the companies if products are not sold or delivered as promised. Therefore some businesses choose a longer distribution channel where less profit is made so that the risk and responsibility are lesser on each individual business.

Distribution Channel Strategy

A distribution channel strategy is normally designed by a retailer, or the business selling goods to a customer. This is so that they can source the product they aim to sell, they can reduce costs while making a nice profit themselves, and find the best way to deliver the product to the customer in the shortest time frame possible. This process will take some time to research suppliers, etc, and collect all the right information.

When a retailer is selling more than one type of product they may even require more than one distribution channel strategy where each business is different for them all. For instance, a shoe retailer may choose to start selling t-shirts online. As shoe manufacturers are different to t-shirt manufacturers the retailer has to find a t-shirt manufacturer or wholesaler to buy from. The wholesaler might not provide delivery but they are based in a different location to the shoe manufacturer so the retailer must then find a delivery option that makes sense to them.

Having many distribution channel strategies can become confusing and inefficient. That is why it is important to constantly improve relationships with businesses involved in this process and also to identify ways to improve efficiencies in the process.

Types of Distribution Channels

There are three main types of distribution models or channels that a business can fall into. It depends on the number of vendors used to distribute goods which model a business falls into.

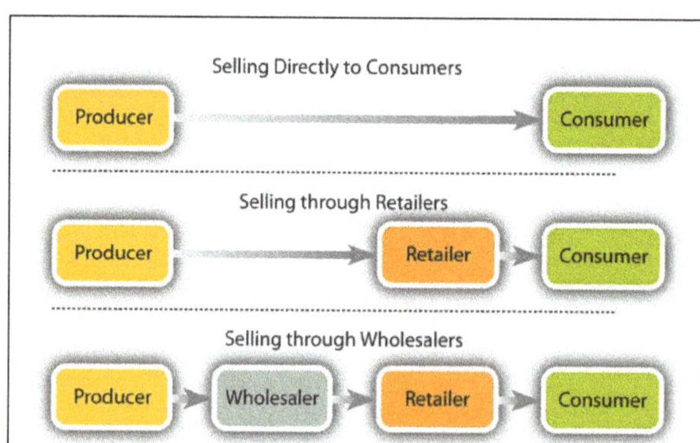

1. The first type of distribution channel is where the manufacturer sells straight to the customer. This channel is the shortest, most direct one. The manufacturer makes the most profit from the sale in this scenario as he does not have to share profits with other vendors.
2. The next channel is an indirect one, where an additional vendor is added between the manufacturer and the customer, like perhaps a retailer. Now the retailer will buy stock off a manufacturer and that retailer will sell the stock to the customer. A good example of this would be a supermarket which stocks many different types of goods which they have bought from the manufacturer, ready for the customer to buy and bring home.

3. The final channel or type of product distribution model is one where there is more than one vendor or intermediary. This could include a wholesaler, a producer, or even another retailer. A great example would be dropshipping, where manufacturers sell their products to a supplier who advertises their stock on marketplaces like AliExpress where a merchant opts to put the product on their website to sell to the customer. This distribution model can be a long one. The manufacturer makes less profit as more vendors get involved.

Retail

Retail is the process of selling consumer goods or services to customers through multiple channels of distribution to earn a profit. Retailers satisfy demand identified through a supply chain. The term "retailer" is typically applied where a service provider fills the small orders of a large number of individuals, who are end-users, rather than large orders of a small number of wholesale, corporate or government clientele. Shopping generally refers to the act of buying products. Sometimes this is done to obtain final goods, including necessities such as food and clothing; sometimes it takes place as a recreational activity. Recreational shopping often involves window shopping and browsing: it does not always result in a purchase.

Retail markets and shops have a very ancient history, dating back to antiquity. Some of the earliest retailers were itinerant peddlers. Over the centuries, retail shops were transformed from little more than "rude booths" to the sophisticated shopping malls of the modern era.

Most modern retailers typically make a variety of strategic level decisions including the type of store, the market to be served, the optimal product assortment, customer service, supporting services and the store's overall market positioning. Once the strategic retail plan is in place, retailers devise the retail mix which includes product, price, place, promotion, personnel and presentation. In the digital age, an increasing number of retailers are seeking to reach broader markets by selling through multiple channels, including both bricks and mortar and online retailing. Digital technologies are also changing the way that consumers pay for goods and services. Retailing support services may also include the provision of credit, delivery services, advisory services, stylist services and a range of other supporting services.

Retail shops occur in a diverse range of types and in many different contexts – from strip shopping centres in residential streets through to large, indoor shopping malls. Shopping streets may restrict traffic to pedestrians only. Sometimes a shopping street has a partial or full roof to create a more comfortable shopping environment – protecting customers from various types of weather conditions such as extreme temperatures, winds or precipitation. Forms of non-shop retailing include online retailing (a type of electronic-commerce used for business-to-consumer (B2C) transactions) and mail order.

Retail refers to the activity of selling goods or services directly to consumers or end-users. Some retailers may sell to business customers, and such sales are termed non-retail activity. In some jurisdictions or regions, legal definitions of retail specify that at least 80 percent of sales activity must be to end-users.

Retailing often occurs in retail stores or service establishments, but may also occur through direct selling such as through vending machines, door-to-door sales or electronic channels. Although the idea of retail is often associated with the purchase of goods, the term may be applied to service-providers that sell to consumers. Retail service providers include retail banking, tourism, insurance, private healthcare, private education, private security firms, legal firms, publishers, public transport and others. For example, a tourism provider might have a retail division that books travel and accommodation for consumers plus a wholesale division that purchases blocks of accommodation, hospitality, transport and sightseeing which are subsequently packaged into a holiday tour for sale to retail travel agents.

Some retailers badge their stores as "wholesale outlets" offering "wholesale prices." While this practice may encourage consumers to imagine that they have access to lower prices, while being prepared to trade-off reduced prices for cramped in-store environments, in a strictly legal sense, a store that sells the majority of its merchandise direct to consumers, is defined as a retailer rather than a wholesaler. Different jurisdictions set parameters for the ratio of consumer to business sales that define a retail business.

Retail Strategy

Retailers make many strategic decisions – store type, market served, product assortment and customer services.

The distinction between "strategic" and "managerial" decision-making is commonly used to distinguish "two phases having different goals and based on different conceptual tools. Strategic planning concerns the choice of policies aiming at improving the competitive position of the firm, taking account of challenges and opportunities proposed by the competitive environment. On the other hand, managerial decision-making is focused on the implementation of specific targets."

In retailing, the strategic plan is designed to set out the vision and provide guidance for retail decision-makers and provide an outline of how the product and service mix will optimize customer satisfaction. As part of the strategic planning process, it is customary for strategic planners to carry out a detailed environmental scan which seeks to identify trends and opportunities in the competitive environment, market environment, economic environment and statutory-political environment. The retail strategy is normally devised or reviewed every 3– 5 years by the chief executive officer.

The retailer also considers the overall strategic position and retail image.

The strategic retail analysis typically includes following elements:

1. Market analysis:

   Market size, stage of market, market competitiveness, market attractiveness, market trends.

2. Customer analysis:

   Market segmentation, demographic, geographic and psychographic profile, values and attitudes, shopping habits, brand preferences, analysis of needs and wants, media habits.

3. Internal analysis:

   Other capabilities e.g. human resource capability, technological capability, financial capability, ability to generate scale economies or economies of scope, trade relations, reputation, positioning, past performance.

4. Competition analysis:

   Availability of substitutes, competitor's strengths and weaknesses, perceptual mapping, competitive trends.

5. Review of product mix:

   Sales per square foot, stock-turnover rates, profitability per product line.

6. Review of distribution channels:

   Lead-times between placing order and delivery, cost of distribution, cost efficiency of intermediaries.

7. Evaluation of the economics of the strategy:

   Cost-benefit analysis of planned activities.

At the conclusion of the retail analysis, the retail marketers should have a clear idea of which groups of customers are to be the target of marketing activities. Retail research studies suggest that there is a strong relationship between a store's positioning and the socio-economic status of customers. In addition, the retail strategy, including service quality, has a significant and positive association with customer loyalty. A marketing strategy effectively outlines all key aspects of firms' targeted audience, demographics, preferences. In a highly competitive market, the retail strategy sets up long-term sustainability. It focuses on customer relationships, stressing the importance of added value, customer satisfaction and highlights how the store's market positioning appeals to targeted groups of customers.

Retail Marketing Mix

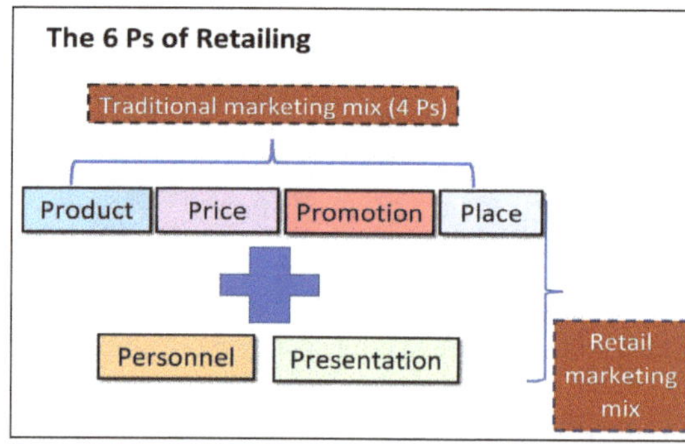

The retail marketing mix or the 6 Ps of retailing.

Once the strategic plan is in place, retail managers turn to the more managerial aspects of planning. A retail mix is devised for the purpose of coordinating day-to-day tactical decisions. The retail marketing mix typically consists of six broad decision layers including product decisions, place decisions, promotion, price, personnel and presentation (also known as physical evidence). The retail mix is loosely based on the marketing mix, but has been expanded and modified in line with the unique needs of the retail context. A number of scholars have argued for an expanded marketing, mix with the inclusion of two new Ps, namely, *Personnel* and *Presentation* since these contribute to the customer's unique retail experience and are the principal basis for retail differentiation. Yet other scholars argue that the *Retail Format* (i.e. retail formula) should be included. The modified retail marketing mix that is most commonly cited in textbooks is often called the *6 Ps of retailing*.

Product

Product Management

The primary product-related decisions facing the retailer are the product assortment (what product lines, how many lines and which brands to carry); the type of customer service (high contact through to self-service) and the availability of support services (e.g. credit terms, delivery services, after sales care). These decisions depend on careful analysis of the market, demand, competition as well as the retailer's skills and expertise.

Product Assortment

A typical supermarket carries an assortment of between 30,000 and 60,000 different products.

Assorted books.

The term product assortment refers to the combination of both product breadth and depth. The main characteristics of a company's product assortment are:

1. The length or number of products lines the number of different products carried by a store.
2. The breadth refers to the variety of product lines that a store offers. It is also known as product assortment width, merchandise breadth, and product line width.
3. Depth or number of product varieties within a product line the number of each item or particular styles carried by a store.
4. Consistency how products relate to each other in a retail environment.

For a retailer, finding the right balance between breadth and depth can be a key to success. An average supermarket might carry 30,000–60,000 different product lines (product length or assortment), but might carry up to 100 different types of toothpaste (product depth). Speciality retailers typically carry fewer product lines, perhaps as few as 20 lines, but will normally stock greater depth. Costco, for example, carries 5,000 different lines while Aldi carries just 1,400 lines per store.

Discount grocery retailer, Aldi, has successfully trimmed the number of product lines it carries to about 1,400.

Large assortments offer consumers many benefits, notably increased choice and the possibility that the consumer will be able to locate the ideal product. However, for the retailer, larger assortments incur costs in terms of record-keeping, managing inventory, pricing and risks associated with wastage due to spoiled, shopworn or unsold stock. Carrying more stock also exposes the retailer to higher risks in terms of slow-moving stock and lower sales per square foot of store space. On the other hand, reducing the number of product lines can generate cost savings through increased stock turnover by eliminating slow-moving lines, fewer stockouts, increased bargaining power with suppliers, reduced costs associated with wastage and carrying inventory, and higher sales per square foot which means more efficient space utilisation.

When determining the number of product lines to carry, the retailer must consider the store type, store's physical storage capacity, the perishability of items, expected turnover rates for each line and the customer's needs and expectations.

Customer Service and Supporting Services

Self-service is a more cost efficient way to deliver goods.

Customer service is the "sum of acts and elements that allow consumers to receive what they need or desire from the retail establishment." Retailers must decide whether to provide a full service outlet or minimal service outlet, such as no-service in the case of vending machines; self-service with only basic sales assistance or a full service operation as in many boutiques and speciality stores. In addition, the retailer needs to make decisions about sales support such as customer delivery and after sales customer care.

Retailing services may also include the provision of credit, delivery services, advisory services, exchange/return services, product demonstration, special orders, customer loyalty programs, limited-scale trial, advisory services and a range of other supporting services. Retail stores often seek to differentiate along customer service lines. For example, some department stores offer the services of a stylist; a fashion advisor, to assist customers selecting a fashionable wardrobe for the forthcoming season, while smaller boutiques may allow regular customers to take goods home on approval, enabling the customer to try out goods before making the final purchase. The variety of supporting services offered is known as the service type. At one end of the spectrum, self-service operators offer few basic support services. At the other end of the spectrum, full-service operators offer a broad range of highly personalised customer services to augment the retail experience.

When making decisions about customer service, the retailer must balance the customer's desire for full-service against the customer's willingness to pay for the cost of delivering supporting services. Self-service is a very cost efficient way of delivering services since the retailer harnesses the customers labour power to carry out many of the retail tasks. However, many customers appreciate full service and are willing to pay a premium for the benefits of full-service.

A sales assistant's role typically includes greeting customers, providing product and service-related information, providing advice about products available from current stock, answering customer questions, finalising customer transactions and if necessary, providing follow-up service necessary to ensure customer satisfaction. For retail store owners, it is extremely important to train personnel with the requisite skills necessary to deliver excellent customer service. Such skills may include product knowledge, inventory management, handling cash and credit transactions, handling product exchange and returns, dealing with difficult customers and of course, a detailed knowledge of store policies. The provision of excellent customer service creates more opportunities to build enduring customer relationships with the potential to turn customers into sources of referral or retail advocates. In the long term, excellent customer service provides businesses with an ongoing reputation and may lead to a competitive advantage. Customer service is essential for several reasons. Firstly, customer service contributes to the customer's overall retail experience. Secondly, evidence suggests that a retail organization which trains its employees in appropriate customer service benefits more than those who do not. Customer service training entails instructing personnel in the methods of servicing the customer that will benefit corporations and businesses. It is important to establish a bond amongst customers-employees known as Customer relationship management.

Counter service is associated with full service retail outlets and allows the salesperson to provide expert advice.

Types of Customer Service

There are several ways the retailer can deliver services to consumers:

1. Counter service, where goods are out of reach of buyers and must be obtained from the seller. This type of retail is common for small expensive items (e.g. jewellery) and controlled items like medicine and liquor.

2. Click and Commute, where products are ordered online and are picked up via a drive through.

3. Ship to Store, where products are ordered online and can be picked up at the retailer's main store.

4. Delivery, where goods are shipped directly to consumer's homes or workplaces.

5. Mail order from a printed catalogue was invented in 1744 and was common in the late 19th and early 20th centuries. Ordering by telephone was common in the 20th century, either from a catalog, newspaper, television advertisement or a local restaurant menu, for immediate service (especially for pizza delivery), remaining in common use for food orders. Internet shopping – a form of delivery – has eclipsed phone-ordering, and, in several sectors – such as books and music – all other forms of buying. There is increasing competitor pressure to deliver consumer goods – especially those offered online – in a more timely fashion. Large online retailers such as Amazon.com are continually innovating and as of 2015 offer one-hour delivery in certain areas. They are also working with drone technology to provide consumers with more efficient delivery options. Direct marketing, including telemarketing and television shopping channels, are also used to generate telephone orders. started gaining significant market share in developed countries in the 2000s.

6. Door-to-door sales, where the salesperson sometimes travels with the goods for sale.

7. Self-service, where goods may be handled and examined prior to purchase.

8. Digital delivery or Download, where intangible goods, such as music, film, and electronic books and subscriptions to magazines, are delivered directly to the consumer in the form of information transmitted either over wires or air-waves, and is reconstituted by a device which the consumer controls. The digital sale of models for 3D printing also fits here, as do the media leasing types of services, such as streaming.

Place

Place decisions are primarily concerned with consumer access and may involve location, space utilisation and operating hours.

Location

Perspective of large retail enterprises of supply chain relationship marketing is based on the theory of supply chain management in large retail enterprises of supply chain in the application of relationship marketing, it emphasizes that the suppliers, large-scale retail enterprises, customers form a chain of large retail enterprises and suppliers to form cooperative marketing, establish mutually beneficial long term good relationship with customers. Relationship marketing of huge retail enterprises from the perspective of supply chain mainly includes two relationship markets, supplier relationship and customer relationship market. Because the two stakeholders that have the greatest influence on the profits of retail enterprises are suppliers and customers. First, as the supplier of commodities to retail enterprises, it directly determines the procurement cost of commodities to retail enterprises, which is mainly reflected in the purchase price of commodities themselves, the cost incurred in the procurement process, and the loss cost caused by unstable supply of commodities. In addition, the good relationship with supplier interaction, large retail enterprises can also promote the suppliers timely grasp the market information, improved or innovative products according to customer demand, which contributed to the retail enterprises improve the market competitiveness of the goods are sold, so the retail enterprise's relationship with supplier directly affects the retail enterprises in the commodity market competitive. Second, due to the transfer of advantages between buyers and sellers, the retail industry has turned to the buyer's market, and consumers have become the key resources for major retailers to compete with each other. Therefore, it is very important to establish a good relationship with clients and improve customer loyalty.

Sellers of souvenirs are typically located in high traffic areas such as this London souvenir stand situated near a railway station on a busy street corner.

The relationship marketing of customer relationship market regards the transaction with clients as a long term activity. Retail enterprises should pursue long-term mutual benefit maximization rather than a single transaction sales profit maximization. This requires large retail enterprises to establish a customer-oriented trading relationship with the customer relationship market. Retail stores are typically located where market opportunities are optimal – high traffic areas, central business districts. Selecting the right site can be a major success factor. When evaluating potential sites, retailers often carry out a trade area analysis; a detailed analysis designed to approximate the potential patronage area. Techniques used in trade area analysis include: Radial (ring) studies; Gravity models and Drive time analyses.

In addition, retailers may consider a range of both qualitative and quantitative factors to evaluate to potential sites under consideration:

Macro Factors

Macro factors include market characteristics (demographic, economic and socio-cultural), demand, competition and infrastructure (e.g. the availability of power, roads, public transport systems).

Micro Factors

Micro factors include the size of the site (e.g. availability of parking), access for delivery vehicles.

Channels

A major retail trend has been the shift to multi-channel retailing. To counter the disruption caused by online retail, many bricks and mortar retailers have entered the online retail space, by setting up online catalogue sales and e-commerce websites. However, many retailers have noticed that consumers behave differently when shopping online. For instance, in terms of choice of online platform, shoppers tend to choose the online site of their preferred retailer initially, but as they gain more experience in online shopping, they become less loyal and more likely to switch to other retail sites. Online stores are usually available 24 hours a day, and many consumers in Western countries have Internet access both at work and at home.

Pricing Strategy and Tactics

A price tag is a highly visual and objective guide to value.

The broad pricing strategy is normally established in the company's overall strategic plan. In the case of chain stores, the pricing strategy would be set by head office. Broadly, there are six approaches to pricing strategy mentioned in the marketing literature:

1. Operations-oriented pricing: Where the objective is to optimise productive capacity, to achieve operational efficiencies or to match supply and demand through varying prices. In some cases, prices might be set to demarket.

2. Revenue-oriented pricing (also known as profit-oriented pricing or cost-based pricing): Where the marketer seeks to maximise the profits (i.e., the surplus income over costs) or simply to cover costs and break even.

3. Customer-oriented pricing: Where the objective is to maximise the number of customers; encourage cross-selling opportunities or to recognise different levels in the customer's ability to pay.

4. Value-based pricing (also known as image-based pricing): Occurs where the company uses prices to signal market value or associates price with the desired value position in the mind of the buyer. The aim of value-based pricing is to reinforce the overall positioning strategy e.g. premium pricing posture to pursue or maintain a luxury image.

5. Relationship-oriented pricing: Where the marketer sets prices in order to build or maintain relationships with existing or potential customers.

6. Socially-oriented pricing: Where the objective is to encourage or discourage specific social attitudes and behaviours. e.g. high tariffs on tobacco to discourage smoking.

Pricing Tactics

Retailers must also plan for mode of payment.

When decision-makers have determined the broad approach to pricing (i.e., the pricing strategy), they turn their attention to pricing tactics. Tactical pricing decisions are shorter term prices, designed to accomplish specific short-term goals. The tactical approach to pricing may vary from time to time, depending on a range of internal considerations (e.g. the need to clear surplus inventory) or external factors (e.g. a response to competitive pricing tactics). Accordingly, a number of different pricing tactics may be employed in the course of a single planning period or across a single year. Typically store managers have the necessary latitude to vary prices on individual lines provided that they operate within the parameters of the overall strategic approach.

Retailers must also plan for customer preferred payment modes – e.g. cash, credit, lay-by, Electronic Funds Transfer at Point-of-Sale (EFTPOS). All payment options require some type of handling and attract costs. If credit is to be offered, then credit terms will need to be determined. If lay-by is offered, then the retailer will need to take into account the storage and handling requirements. If cash is the dominant mode of payment, the retailer will need to consider small change requirements, the number of cash floats required, wages costs associated with handling large volumes of cash and the provision of secure storage for change floats. Large retailers, handling significant volumes of cash, may need to hire security service firms to carry the day's takings and deliver supplies of small change. A small, but increasing number of retailers are beginning to accept newer modes of payment including PayPal and Bitcoin. For example, Subway (US) recently announced that it would accept Bitcoin payments.

Contrary to common misconception, price is not the most important factor for consumers, when deciding to buy a product.

A discount is any form of reduction in price.

Discount Pricing

Discount pricing is where the marketer or retailer offers a reduced price. Discounts in a variety of forms – e.g. quantity discounts, loyalty rebates, seasonal discounts, periodic or random discounts etc.

Everyday Low Prices (EDLP)

Everyday Low Prices" are widely used in supermarkets
Everyday low prices (EDLP).

Everyday low prices refers to the practice of maintaining a regular low price-low price – in which consumers are not forced to wait for discounting or specials. This method is extensively used by supermarkets.

High-low Pricing

High-low pricing refers to the practice of offering goods at a high price for a period of time, followed by offering the same goods at a low price for a predetermined time. This practice is widely used by chain stores selling homewares. The main disadvantage of the high-low tactic is that consumers tend to become aware of the price cycles and time their purchases to coincide with a low-price cycle.

Loss Leader

A loss leader is a product that has a price set below the operating margin. Loss leadering is widely used in supermarkets and budget-priced retail outlets where it is intended to generate store traffic. The low price is widely promoted and the store is prepared to take a small loss on an individual item, with an expectation that it will recoup that loss when customers purchase other higher priced-higher margin items. In service industries, loss leadering may refer to the practice of charging a reduced price on the first order as an inducement and with anticipation of charging higher prices on subsequent orders.

Price Bundling

Price bundling (also known as product bundling) occurs where two or more products or services are priced as a package with a single price. There are several types of bundles: *pure bundles* where the goods can only be purchased as package or mixed bundles where the goods can be purchased individually or as a package. The prices of the bundle is typically less than when the two items are purchased separately. Price bundling is extensively used in the personal care sector to prices cosmetics and skincare.

Xbox price bundle price.

Price Lining

Price lining is the use of a limited number of prices for all product offered by a business. Price lining is a tradition started in the old five and dime stores in which everything cost either 5 or 10 cents. In price lining, the price remains constant but quality or extent of product or service adjusted to reflect changes in cost. The underlying rationale of this tactic is that these amounts are seen as suitable price points for a whole range of products by prospective customers. It has the advantage of ease of administering, but the disadvantage of inflexibility, particularly in times of inflation or unstable prices. Price lining continues to be widely used in department stores where customers often note racks of garments or accessories priced at predetermined price points e.g. separate racks of men's ties, where each rack is priced at $10, $20 and $40.

Promotional Pricing

Promotional pricing is a temporary measure that involves setting prices at levels lower than normally charged for a good or service. Promotional pricing is sometimes a reaction to unforeseen circumstances, as when a downturn in demand leaves a company with excess stocks; or when competitive activity is making inroads into market share or profits.

Psychological Pricing

Extensive use of the terminal digit 'nine' suggests that psychological pricing is at play.

Psychological pricing is a range of tactics designed to have a positive psychological impact. Price tags using the terminal digit "9", ($9.99, $19.99 or $199.99) can be used to signal price points and bring an item in at just under the consumer's reservation price. Psychological pricing is widely used in a variety of retail settings.

Personnel and Staffing

Because patronage at a retail outlet varies, flexibility in scheduling is desirable. Employee scheduling software is sold, which, using known patterns of customer patronage, more or less reliably predicts the need for staffing for various functions at times of the year, day of the month or week, and time of day. Usually needs vary widely. Conforming staff utilization to staffing needs requires a flexible workforce which is available when needed but does not have to be paid when they are not, part-time workers; as of 2012 70% of retail workers in the United States were part-time. This may result in financial problems for the workers, who while they are required to be available at all times if their work hours are to be maximized, may not have sufficient income to meet their family and other obligations.

Selling and Sales Techniques

One of the most well-known cross-selling sales scripts comes from McDonald's.

Retailers can employ different techniques to enhance sales volume and to improve the customer experience:

1. Add-on, Upsell or Cross-sell:

   Upselling and cross selling are sometimes known as *suggestive selling*. When the consumer has selected their main purchase, sales assistants can try to sell the customer on a premium brand or higher quality item (up-selling) or can suggest complementary purchases (cross-selling). For instance, if a customer purchases a non-stick frypan, the sales assistant might suggest plastic slicers that do not damage the non-stick surface.

2. Selling on Value:

   Skilled sales assistants find ways to focus on value rather than price. Selling on value often involves identifying a product's unique features. Adding value to goods or services such as a free gift or buy 1 get 1 free adds value to customers where as the store is gaining sales.

3. Know when to Close the Sale:

   Sales staff must learn to recognise when the customer is ready to make a purchase. If the sales person feels that the customer is ready, then they may seek to gain commitment and close the sale. Experienced sales staff soon learn to recognise specific verbal and non-verbal cues that signal the client's readiness to buy. For instance, if a customer begins to handle the merchandise, this may indicate a state of buyer interest. Clients also tend to employ different types of questions throughout the sales process. General questions such as, "Does it come in any other colours (or styles)?" indicate only a moderate level of interest. However, when clients begin to ask specific questions, such as "Do you have this model in black?" then this often indicates that the prospect is approaching readiness to buy. When the sales person believes that the prospective buyer is ready to make the purchase, a *trial close* might be used to test the waters. A trial close is simply any attempt to confirm the buyer's interest in finalising the sale. An example of a trial close, is "Would you be requiring our team to install the unit for you?" or "Would you be available to take delivery next Thursday?" If the sales person is unsure about the prospect's readiness to buy, they might consider using a 'trial close.' The salesperson can use several different techniques to close the sale; including the 'alternative close', the 'assumptive close', the 'summary close', or the 'special-offer close', among others.

Promotion

In the 1980s, the customary sales concept in the retail industry began to show many disadvantages. Many transactions cost too much, and the industry was unable to retain customers as it only paid attention to the process of a single transaction rather than to marketing for customer development and maintenance. The traditional marketing theory holds that transactions are one-time value exchange processes and the means of exchanging goods needed by both parties. Accordingly, when the transaction is completed, the relationship between the two parties will also end, so the theory is called "transactional marketing". Transactional marketing aims to find target consumers, then negotiate, trade, and finally end relationships to complete the transaction. In this one-time transaction process, both parties aim to maximize their own interests. As a result, transactional marketing raises follow-up problems such as poor after-sales service quality and a lack of feedback channels for both parties. In addition, because retail enterprises needed to redevelop client relationships for each transaction, marketing costs were high and customer retention was low. All these downsides to transactional marketing gradually pushed the retail industry towards establishing long-term cooperative relationships with customers. Through this lens, enterprises began to focus on the process from transaction to relationship. While expanding the sales market and attracting new customers is very important for the retail industry, it is also important to establish and maintain long term good relationships with previous customers, hence the name of the underlying concept, "relational marketing". Under this concept, retail enterprises value and attempt to improve relationships with customers, as customer relationships are conducive to maintaining stability in the current competitive retail market, and are also the future of retail enterprises.

One of the unique aspects of retail promotions is that two brands are often involved; the store brand and the brands that make up the retailer's product range. Retail promotions that focus on the store tend to be 'image' oriented, raising awareness of the store and creating a positive attitude towards the store and its services. Retail promotions that focus on the product range, are designed to cultivate a positive attitude to the brands stocked by the store, in order to indirectly encourage favourable attitudes towards the store itself. Some retail advertising and promotion is partially or wholly funded by brands and this is known as co-operative (or co-op) advertising.

Retailers make extensive use of advertising via newspapers, television and radio to encourage store preference. In order to up-sell or cross-sell, retailers also use a variety of in-store sales promotional techniques such as product demonstrations, samples, point-of-purchase displays, free trial, events, promotional packaging and promotional pricing. In grocery retail, shelf wobblers, trolley advertisements, taste tests and recipe cards are also used. Many retailers also use loyalty programs to encourage repeat patronage.

Presentation

The way that products are displayed is part of the store's presentation.

Presentation refers to the physical evidence that signals the retail image. Physical evidence may include a diverse range of elements – the store itself including premises, offices, exterior facade and interior layout, websites, delivery vans, warehouses, staff uniforms.

Designing Retail Spaces

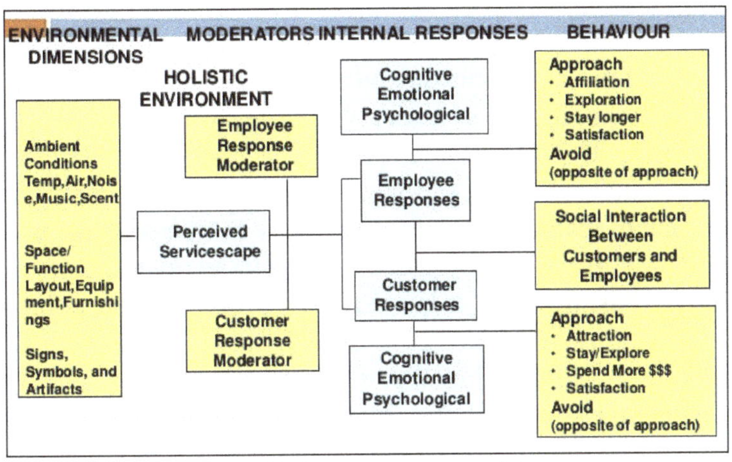

Simplified servicescapes model.

The environment in which the retail service encounter occurs is sometimes known as the *retail servicescape*. The store environment consists of many elements such as smells, the physical environment (furnishings, layout and functionality), ambient conditions (lighting, temperature, noise) as well as signs, symbols and artifacts (e.g. sales promotions, shelf space, sample stations, visual communications). Collectively, these elements contribute to the *perceived retail servicescape* or the overall *atmosphere* and can influence both the customer's cognitions, emotions and their behaviour within the retail space.

Relationship between market large retail enterprises of relationship marketing refers to a large retail enterprise with suppliers, customers, internal organization, channel distributors, market impact, and other competitors such as the interests of the enterprise marketing process related everything to establish and maintain good relations, thus maximizing the interests of the large retail enterprise in the long-term marketing activities, it was based on the relationship marketing concept as the core of innovation. Different from traditional marketing concepts, relationship marketing focuses on maintaining long-term good relations with relevant parties on marketing activities. The ultimate goal of relationship marketing is tantamount to maximize the long term interests of enterprises.

The marketing activities of large retail enterprises mainly have six relationship markets, which are supplier relationship market, customer relationship market, enterprise internal relationship market, intermediary relationship market at all levels, enterprise marketing activities influence relationship market and industry competitor relationship market. Among these six relational markets, supply relational market and customer relational market are the two markets that have the greatest influence on the relationship marketing of large retail enterprises. Substantial retail enterprises usually have two sources of profit. The principal source of profit is to reduce the purchase price from suppliers. The other is to develop new customers and keep old clients, so as to expand the market sales of goods. In addition, the extra four related markets have an indirect impact on the marketing activities of large retail enterprises. The internal relationship market of an enterprise can be divided into several different types of relationships according to distinct objects, such as employee relationship market, department relationship market, shareholder relationship market and the mutual relations among the relationship markets. The purpose of carrying out relationship marketing is to promote the cohesion and innovation ability of enterprises and maximize the long term interests of enterprises. Another relationship of relationship marketing middlemen is the relationship between market and intermediary in the process of corporate marketing is playing the intermediary role between suppliers and customers, in the current increasingly fierce market competition, more important distribution channels for enterprises, but for retail enterprises, too much sales levels will increase the cost of sales of the enterprise. Therefore, large retail enterprises should realize the simplification of sales channel level by reasonably selecting suppliers. Large-scale retail enterprises purchasing goods to suppliers with procurement scale advantage, can directly contact with the product manufacturing, with strong bargaining power, therefore, direct contact with the manufacturer is a large retail enterprise to take the main purchasing mode, it is a terminal to the starting point of zero level channel purchasing mode, therefore, the elimination of middlemen, so as to make the large retail enterprise in the marketing activity, the dealer relationship market is not so important. Then there is the enterprise influence relationship market, which is a relational marketing influence in the enterprise supply chain. It mainly guides and standardizes the advance direction of enterprises through formulating systems at the macro level. The relationship market mainly includes the relationship between the relevant government departments at all levels where the enterprise is located, the relationship with the industry association to which the enterprise belongs, and the relationship with all kinds of public organizations, etc., and the enterprise influence itself cannot directly affect the marketing activities of the enterprise. The final relational market is the industry's competitors, potential competitors, alternative competitors and so on. How to correctly deal with the relationship between competitors and the market has become a problem that large retail enterprises need to solve.

Retail designers pay close attention to the front of the store, which is known as the decompression *zone*. This is usually an open space in the entrance of the store to allow customers to adjust to their new environment. An open-plan floor design is effective in retail as it allows customers to see everything. In terms of the store's exterior, the side of the road cars normally travel, determines the way stores direct customers. New Zealand retail stores, for instance, would direct customers to the left.

In order to maximise the number of selling opportunities, retailers generally want customers to spend more time in a retail store. However, this must be balanced against customer expectations surrounding convenience, access and realistic waiting times. The overall aim of designing a retail environment is to have customers enter the store, and explore the totality of the physical environment engaging in a variety of retail experiences – from browsing through to sampling and ultimately to purchasing. The retail service environment plays an important role in affecting the customer's perceptions of the retail experience.

The retail environment not only affects quality perceptions, but can also impact on the way that customers navigate their way through the retail space during the retail service encounter. Layout, directional signage, the placement of furniture, shelves and display space along with the store's ambient conditions all affect patron's passage through the retail service system. Layout refers to how equipment, shelves and other furnishings are placed and the relationship between them. In a retail setting, accessibility is an important aspect of layout. For example, the grid layout used by supermarkets with long aisles and gondolas at the end displaying premium merchandise or promotional items, minimises the time customers spend in the environment and makes productive use of available space. The gondola, so favoured by supermarkets, is an example of a retail design feature known as a merchandise outpost and which refers to special displays, typically at or near the end of an aisle, whose purpose is to stimulate impulse purchasing or to complement other products in the vicinity. For example, the meat cabinet at the supermarket might use a merchandise outpost to suggest a range of marinades or spice rubs to complement particular cuts of meat. As a generalisation, merchandise outposts are updated regularly so that they maintain a sense of novelty.

The retail servicescape includes the appearance, equipment, display space, retail counters, signage, layout and functionality of a retail outlet.

According to Zicthaml et al., layout affects how easy or difficult it is to navigate through a system. Signs and symbols provide cues for directional navigation and also inform about appropriate behaviour within a store. Functionality refers to extent to which the equipment and layout meet the goals of the customer. For instance, in the case of supermarkets, the customer's goal may be to minimise the amount of time spent finding items and waiting at the check-out, while a customer in a retail mall may wish to spend more time exploring the range of stores and merchandise. With respect to functionality of layout, retail designers consider three key issues; circulation – design for traffic-flow and that encourages customers to traverse the entire store; coordination – design that combines goods and spaces in order to suggest customer needs and convenience – design that arranges items to create a degree of comfort and access for both customers and employees.

The way that brands are displayed is also part of the overall retail design. Where a product is placed on the shelves has implications for purchase likelihood as a result of visibility and access. Products placed too high or too low on the shelves may not turn over as quickly as those placed at eye level. With respect to access, store designers are increasingly giving consideration to access for disabled and elderly customers.

Through sensory stimulation retailers can engage maximum emotional impact between a brand and its consumers by relating to both profiles; the goal and experience. Purchasing behaviour can be influenced through the physical evidence detected by the senses of touch, smell, sight, taste and sound. Supermarkets offer taste testers to heighten the sensory experience of brands. Coffee shops allow the aroma of coffee to waft into streets so that passers-by can appreciate the smell and perhaps be lured inside. Clothing garments are placed at arms' reach, allowing customers to feel the different textures of clothing. Retailers understand that when customers interact with products or handle the merchandise, they are more likely to make a purchase.

Navigational floor signs are commonly used in complex environments such as shopping malls and department stores.

Within the retail environment, different spaces may be designed for different purposes. Hard floors, such as wooden floors, used in public areas, contrast with carpeted fitting rooms, which are designed to create a sense of homeliness when trying on garments. Peter Alexander, retailer of sleep ware, is renowned for using scented candles in retail stores.

Ambient conditions, such as lighting, temperature and music, are also part of the overall retail environment. It is common for a retail store to play music that relates to their target market. Studies have found that "positively valenced music will stimulate more thoughts and feeling than negatively valenced music", hence, positively valenced music will make the waiting time feel longer to the customer than negatively valenced music. In a retail store, for example, changing the background music to a quicker tempo may influence the consumer to move through the space at a quicker pace, thereby improving traffic flow. Evidence also suggests that playing music reduces the negative effects of waiting since it serves as a distraction. Jewellery stores like Michael Hill have dim lighting with a view to fostering a sense of intimacy.

The design of a retail store is critical when appealing to the intended market, as this is where first impressions are made. The overall servicescape can influence a consumer's perception of the quality of the store, communicating value in visual and symbolic ways. Certain techniques are used to create a consumer brand experience, which in the long run drives store loyalty.

Shopper Profiles

Two different strands of research have investigated shopper behaviour. One strand is primarily concerned with shopper motivations. Another stream of research seeks to segment shoppers according to common, shared characteristics. To some extent, these streams of research are inter-related, but each stream offers different types of insights into shopper behaviour.

Babin et al. carried out some of the earliest investigations into shopper motivations and identified two broad motives: utilitarian and hedonic. Utilitarian motivations are task-related and rational. For the shopper with utilitarian motives, purchasing is a work-related task that is to be accomplished in the most efficient and expedient manner. On the other hand, hedonic motives refer to pleasure. The shopper with hedonic motivations views shopping as a form of escapism where they are free to indulge fantasy and freedom. Hedonic shoppers are more involved in the shopping experience.

Many different shopper profiles can be identified. Retailers develop customised segmentation analyses for each unique outlet. However, it is possible to identify a number of broad shopper profiles. One of the most well-known and widely cited shopper typologies is that developed by Sproles and Kendal in the mid-1980s. Sproles and Kendall's consumer typology has been shown to be relatively consistent across time and across cultures. Their typology is based on the consumer's approach to making purchase decisions.

1. Quality conscious/Perfectionist: Quality-consciousness is characterised by a consumer's search for the very best quality in products; quality conscious consumers tend to shop systematically making more comparisons and shopping around.
2. Brand-conscious: Brand-consciousness is characterised by a tendency to buy expensive, well-known brands or designer labels. Those who score high on brand-consciousness tend to believe that the higher prices are an indicator of quality and exhibit a preference for department stores or top-tier retail outlets.
3. Recreation-conscious/Hedonistic: Recreational shopping is characterised by the consumer's engagement in the purchase process. Those who score high on recreation-consciousness regard shopping itself as a form of enjoyment.
4. Price-conscious: A consumer who exhibits price-and-value consciousness. Price-conscious shoppers carefully shop around seeking lower prices, sales or discounts and are motivated by obtaining the best value for money.
5. Novelty/fashion-conscious: characterised by a consumer's tendency to seek out new products or new experiences for the sake of excitement; who gain excitement from seeking new things; they like to keep up-to-date with fashions and trends, variety-seeking is associated with this dimension.
6. Impulsive: Impulsive consumers are somewhat careless in making purchase decisions, buy on the spur of the moment and are not overly concerned with expenditure levels or obtaining value. Those who score high on impulsive dimensions tend not to be engaged with the object at either a cognitive or emotional level.
7. Confused (by over-choice): characterised by a consumer's confusion caused by too many product choices, too many stores or an overload of product information; tend to experience information overload.
8. Habitual/brand loyal: characterised by a consumer's tendency to follow a routine purchase pattern on each purchase occasion; consumers have favourite brands or stores and have formed habits in choosing; the purchase decision does not involve much evaluation or shopping around.

Some researchers have adapted Sproles and Kendall's methodology for use in specific countries or cultural groups. Consumer decision styles are important for retailers and marketers because they describe behaviours that are relatively stable over time and for this reason, they are useful for market segmentation.

Retail Format: Types of Retail Outlet

The retail format (also known as the retail formula) influences the consumer's store choice and addresses the consumer's expectations. At its most basic level, a retail format is a simple marketplace, that is; a location where goods and services are exchanged. In some parts of the world, the retail sector is still dominated by small family-run stores, but large retail chains are increasingly dominating the sector, because they can exert considerable buying power and pass on the savings in the form of lower prices. Many of these large retail chains also produce their own private labels which compete alongside manufacturer brands. Considerable consolidation of retail stores has changed the retail landscape, transferring power away from wholesalers and into the hands of the large retail chains.

In Britain and Europe, the retail sale of goods is designated as a service activity. The European Service Directive applies to all retail trade including periodic markets, street traders and peddlers.

Retail Type by Product

Retail stores may be classified by the type of product carried:

Food Retailers

Retailers carrying highly perishable foodstuffs such as meat, dairy and fresh produce typically require cold storage facilities. Consumers purchase food products on a very regular purchase cycle – e.g. daily, weekly or monthly.

Softline Retailers

Softline retailers sell goods that are consumed after a single use, or have a limited life (typically under three years) in they are normally consumed. Soft goods include clothing, other fabrics, footwear, toiletries, cosmetics, medicines and stationery.

Grocery and Convenience Retail

Grocery stores, including supermarkets and hypermarkets, along with convenience stores carry a mix of food products and consumable household items such as detergents, cleansers, personal hygiene products. Consumer consumables are collectively known as fast-moving-consumer goods (FMCG) and represent the lines most often carried by supermarkets, grocers and convenience stores. For consumers, these are regular purchases and for the retailer, these products represent high turnover product lines. Grocery stores and convenience stores carry similar lines, but a convenience store (staffed or automated) is often open at times that suit its clientele and may be located for ease of access.

Hardline Retailers

Retailers selling consumer durables are sometimes known as hardline retailers – automobiles, appliances, electronics, furniture, sporting goods, lumber, etc., and parts for them. Goods that do not quickly wear out and provide utility over time. For the consumer, these items often represent major purchase decisions. Consumers purchase durables over longer purchase decision cycles. For instance, the typical consumer might replace their family car every 5 years, and their home computer every 4 years.

Specialist Retailers

Specialist retailers operate in many industries such as the arts e.g. green grocers, contemporary art galleries, bookstores, handicrafts, musical instruments, gift shops.

Types of retail outlet by product type

Food retailer.

Bookstore is another example of a specialist retailer.

An art gallery is a specialist retailer

Retail types by Marketing Strategy

Types of retail outlets (retail shops, retail stores) by marketing strategy include:

Arcade

A shopping arcade refers to a group of retail outlets operating under a covered walkway. Arcades are similar to shopping malls, although they typically comprise a smaller number of outlets. Shopping arcades were the evolutionary precursor to the shopping mall, and were very fashionable in the late 19th century. Stylish men and women would promenade around the arcade, stopping to window shop, making purchases and also taking light refreshments in one of the arcade's tea-rooms. Arcades offered fashionable men and women opportunities to 'be seen' and to socialise in a relatively safe environment. Arcades continue to exist as a distinct type of retail outlet. Historic 19th-century arcades have become popular tourist attractions in cities around the world. Amusement arcades, also known as penny arcades in the US, are more modern incarnation of the eighteenth and nineteenth century shopping arcade.

Anchor Store

An anchor store (also known as draw tenant or anchor tenant) is a larger store with a good reputation used by shopping mall management to attract a certain volume of shoppers to a precinct.

Bazaar

The term, 'bazaar' can have multiple meanings. It may refer to a Middle-Eastern market place while a 'penny bazaar' refers to a retail outlet that specialises in inexpensive or discounted merchandise. In the United States a bazaar can mean a "rummage sale" which describes a charity fundraising event held by a church or other community organization and in which either donated used goods are made available for sale.

Boutique

A Boutique is a small store offering a select range of fashionable goods or accessories. The term, 'boutique', in retail and services, appears to be taking on a broader meaning with popular references to retail goods and retail services such as boutique hotels, boutique beers (i.e. craft beers), boutique investments etc.

Category Killer

Australia's Officeworks is a category killer, retailing everything for the home office or small commercial office; stationery, furniture, electronics, communications devices, copying, printing and photography services, coffee, tea and light snacks.

By supplying a wide assortment in a single category for lower prices a category killer retailer can "kill" that category for other retailers. A category killer is a specialist store that dominates a given category. Toys "R" Us, established in 1957, is thought to be the first category killer, dominating the children's toys and games market. For a few categories, such as electronics, home hardware, office supplies and children's toys, the products are displayed at the centre of the store and a sales person will be available to address customer queries and give suggestions when required. Rival retail stores are forced to reduce their prices if a category killer enters the market in a given geographic area. Examples of category killers include Toys "R" Us and Australia's Bunnings (hardware, DIY and outdoor supplies) and Officeworks (stationery and supplies for the home office and small office). Some category killers redefine the category. For example, Australia's Bunnings began as a hardware outlet, but now supplies a broad range of goods for the home handyman or small tradesman, including kitchen cabinetry, craft supplies, gardening needs and outdoor furniture. Similarly Officeworks straddles the boundary between stationery supplies, office furniture and digital communications devices in its quest to provide for all the needs of the retail consumer and the small, home office.

Chain Store

Chain store is one of a series of stores owned by the same company and selling the same or similar merchandise. Chain stores aim to benefit from volume buying discounts (economies of scale) and achieve cost savings through economies of scope (e.g. centralised warehousing, marketing, promotion and administration) and pass on the cost savings in the form of lower prices.

Concept Store

Apple's concept stores include video walls, wi-fi and desks to provide an immersive customer experience.

Concept stores are similar to speciality stores in that they are very small in size, and only stock a limited range of brands or a single brand. They are typically operated by the brand that controls them. The limited size and offering of L'OCCITANE's stores is too small to be considered a speciality store. However, a concept store goes beyond merely selling products, and instead offers an immersive customer experience built around the way that a brand fits with the customer's lifestyle. Examples include Apple's concept stores, Kit Kat's concept store in Japan.

Co-operative Store

A co-operative store; also known as a co-op or coop, is a venture owned and operated by consumers to meet their social, economic and cultural needs.

Convenience Store

A convenience store provides limited amount of merchandise at above average prices with a speedy checkout. This store is ideal for emergency and immediate purchase consumables as it often operates with extended hours, stocking every day.

Department Store

Department stores are very large stores offering an extensive assortment of both "soft" and "hard" goods which often bear a resemblance to a collection of specialty stores. A retailer of such store carries a variety of categories and has a broad assortment of goods at moderate prices. They offer considerable customer service.

Destination Store

A destination store is one that customers will initiate a trip specifically to visit, sometimes over a large area. These stores are often used to "anchor" a shopping mall or plaza, generating foot traffic, which is capitalized upon by smaller retailers.

Demographic

Retailers that aim at one particular segment (e.g. high-end/ luxury retailers focusing on wealthy individuals or niche market).

Discount Store

Discount stores tend to offer a wide array of products and services, but they compete mainly on price. They offer extensive assortments of merchandise at prices lower than other retailers and are designed to be affordable for the market served. In the past, retailers sold less fashion-oriented brands. However, in more recent years companies such as TJX Companies (Own T.J. Maxx and Marshalls) and Ross Stores are discount store operations increasingly offering fashion-oriented brands on a larger scale.

E-tailer

The customer can shop and order through the internet and the merchandise is dropped at the customer's doorstep or an e-tailer. In some cases, e-retailers use drop shipping technique. They accept the payment for the product but the customer receives the product directly from the manufacturer or a wholesaler. This format is ideal for customers who do not want to travel to retail stores and are interested in home shopping.

General Merchandise Retailer

A general merchandise retailer stocks a variety of products in considerable depth. The types of product offerings vary across this category. Department stores, convenience stores, hypermarkets and warehouse clubs are all examples of general merchandise retailers.

General Store

A general store is a store that supplies the main needs of the local community and is often located in outback or rural areas with low population densities. In areas of very low population density, a general store may be the only retail outlet within hundreds of miles. The general store carries a very broad product assortment; from foodstuffs and pharmaceuticals through to hardware and fuel. In addition, a general store may provide essential services such as postal services, banking services, news agency services and may also act as an agent for farm equipment and stock-food suppliers.

A general store in Scarsdale, Victoria, Australia operates as a post-office, newsagent, petrol station, video hire, grocer and take-away food retailer.

Give-away Shop

As the name implies, a give-away shop provides goods for free. There are several different models of give-away shop in popular use. One is where goods are free to any shopper; an alternative is that shoppers must provide a product before they can take a product and a third variation is where consumers have the option of taking goods for free or paying any amount that they can afford. For example, Australia's restaurant group Lentil as Anything operates on a pay whatever you feel is right model.

Hawkers

Hawkers also known as a peddlers, costermongers or street vendors; refer to a vendor of merchandise that is readily portable. Hawkers typically operate in public places such as streets, squares, public parks or gardens or near the entrances of high traffic venues such as zoos, music and entertainment venues, but may also call on homes for door-to-door seling. Hawkers are a relatively common sight across Asia.

High Street Store

A high street store is a term used widely in the United Kingdom where more than 5,000 High Streets where a variety of stores congregate along a main road. Stores situated in the High Street provide for the needs of a local community, and often give a locality a unique identity.

Hypermarkets

A hypermarket (also known as hypermart) provides variety and huge volumes of exclusive merchandise at low margins. The operating cost is comparatively less than other retail formats; may be defined as "a combined supermarket and discount store, at least 200,000 square feet

(19,000 m²) or larger, that sells a wide variety of food and general merchandise at a low price."

Mall

A mall has a range of retail shops at a single building or outlet, arranged on a single level or multiple levels. A shopping mall typically includes one or more anchor stores. The retail mix in a mall may include outlets such as food and entertainment, grocery, electronics, furniture, gifts and fashion. Malls provide 7% of retail revenue in India, 10% in Vietnam, 25% in China, 28% in Indonesia, 39% in the Philippines, and 45% in Thailand. Malls are typically managed by a central management/ marketing authority which ensures that the mall attracts the right type of retailer and an appropriate retail mix.

Mom-and-pop Store

A small retail outlet owned and operated by an individual or family. Focuses on a relatively limited and selective set of products.

Pop-up Retail Store

UNIQLO Pop-Up store at Union Square station

A Pop-up retail store is a temporary retail space that opens for a short period of time, possibly opening to sell a specific run of merchandise or for a special occasion or holiday period. The key to the success of a pop-up is novelty in the merchandise.

Retail Marketplace

A Marketplace is defined as venue for the retail sales of all products, packed and unpacked where the sale is to end users. In practice, retail markets are most often associated with the sale of fresh produce, including fruit, vegetables, meat, fish and poultry, but may also sell small consumable household goods such as cleaning agents. Globally, different terms may be used to refer to a retail market. For instance, in the Middle East, a market place may be known as a bazaar or souq/souk.

Market Square

A market square is a city square where traders set up temporary stalls and buyers browse for purchases. In England, such markets operate on specific days of the week. This kind of market is very ancient, and countless such markets are still in operation around the world.

Speciality Store

A speciality store has a narrow marketing focus – either specializing on specific merchandise, such as toys, footwear, or clothing, or on a target audience, such as children, tourists, or plus-size women. Size of store varies – some speciality stores might be retail giants such as Toys "R" Us, Foot Locker, and The Body Shop, while others might be small, individual shops such as Nutters of Savile Row. Such stores, regardless of size, tend to have a greater depth of the specialist stock than general stores, and generally offer specialist product knowledge valued by the consumer. Pricing is usually not the priority when consumers are deciding upon a speciality store; factors such as branding image, selection choice, and purchasing assistance are seen as important. They differ from department stores and supermarkets which carry a wide range of merchandise.

Supermarket

A supermarket is a self-service store consisting mainly of grocery and limited products on non-food items. They may adopt a Hi-Lo or an EDLP strategy for pricing. The supermarkets can be anywhere between 20,000 square feet (1,900 m^2) and 40,000 square feet (3,700 m^2). Example: SPAR supermarket.

Variety Store

Variety stores offer extremely low-cost goods, with a vast array of selection. The downfall to this is that the items are not very high quality.

Vending Machine

Vending machines can be used to sell goods such as food and beverages as well as services such as tickets to events or public transport.

A vending machine is an automated piece of equipment wherein customers can drop the money in the machine which dispenses the customer's selection. The vending machine is a pure self-service option. Machines may carry a phone number which customers can call in the event of a fault.

Some stores take a no frills approach, while others are "mid-range" or "high end", depending on what income level they target.

Warehouse Club

Warehouse clubs are membership-based retailers that usually sell a wide variety of merchandise, in which customers may buy large, wholesale quantities of the store's products, which makes these clubs attractive to both bargain hunters and small business owners. The clubs are able to keep prices low due to the no-frills format of the stores. In addition, customers may be required to pay annual membership fees in order to shop.

Warehouse Store

Warehouse stores are retailers housed in warehouses, and offer low-cost, often high-quantity goods with minimal services, e.g. goods are piled on pallets or steel shelves. Shopping aisles are narrow and cramped, added-value services such as home delivery are non-existent.

Other Retail Types

Other types of retail store include:

1. Automated retail stores – self-service, robotic kiosks located in airports, malls and grocery stores. The stores accept credit cards and are usually open 24/7. Examples include ZoomShops and Redbox.
2. Big-box stores – encompass larger department, discount, general merchandise, and warehouse stores.
3. Second-hand retail – Some shops sell second-hand goods. In the case of a nonprofit shop, the public donates goods to the shop to be sold. In give-away shops goods can be taken free.

   Another form is the pawnshop, in which goods are sold that were used as collateral for loans. There are also "consignment" shops, which are where a person can place an item in a store and if it sells, the person gives the shop owner a percentage of the sale price. The advantage of selling an item this way is that the established shop gives the item exposure to more potential buyers. E-tailers like OLX and Quikr also offer second-hand goods.

Retailers can opt for a format as each provides different retail mix to its customers based on their customer demographics, lifestyle and purchase behaviour. An effective format will dtermine how products are display products, as well as how target customers are attracted.

Challenges

To achieve and maintain a foothold in an existing market, a prospective retail establishment must overcome the following hurdles:

1. Regulatory barriers including:
   a. Restrictions on real estate purchases, especially as imposed by local governments and against "big-box" chain retailers;

b. Restrictions on foreign investment in retailers, in terms of both absolute amount of financing provided and percentage share of voting stock (e.g. common stock) purchased;

2. Unfavourable taxation structures, especially those designed to penalize or keep out "big box" retailers;
3. Absence of developed supply chain and integrated IT management;
4. High competitiveness among existing market participants and resulting low profit margins, caused in part by
   a. Constant advances in product design resulting in constant threat of product obsolescence and price declines for existing inventory; and
5. Lack of properly educated and/or trained work force, often including management, caused in part by loss in Business.
   a. Lack of educational infrastructure enabling prospective market entrants to respond to the above challenges.

Retail trade provides 9% of all jobs in India and 14% of GDP.

Mergers and Acquisitions

Between 1985 and 2018 there have been 46,755 mergers or acquisitions conducted globally in the retail sector (either acquirer or target from the retail industry). These deals cumulate to an overall known value of around US$2,561 billion. The three major Retail M&A waves took place in 2000, 2007 and lately in 2017. However the all-time high in terms of number of deals was in 2016 with more than 2,700 deals. In terms of added value 2007 set the record with US$225 billion.

Consolidation

Among retailers and retails chains a lot of consolidation has appeared over the last couple of decades. Between 1988 and 2010, worldwide 40,788 mergers & acquisitions with a total known value of US$2.255 trillion have been announced. The largest transactions with involvement of retailers in/from the United States have been: the acquisition of Albertson's Inc. for 17 bil. USD in 2006, the merger between Federated Department Stores Inc with May Department Stores valued at 16.5 bil. USD in 2005 – now Macy's, and the merger between Kmart Holding Corp and Sears Roebuck & Co with a value of 10.9 bil. USD in 2004.

Goods displayed in the souq of Marrakech.

Macy's Herald Square, New York City.

A French itinerant vendor depicted selling medicine from a stage.

Brand Licensing

A licensing agreement allows a company (a licensee) which markets a product or service to rent a brand from a brand owner (a licensor). The responsibility of licensee's is to produce, promote and distribute the product while the licensor gets royalties for its brand.

After license branding, a licensee gets access to the logos and trademarks associated with the brands. Association with the brand gives marketing power to the licensee's products. It takes years of hard work, huge amount of money and luck to build a brand from scratch. Brand licensing is a shortcut way to gain immediate access to all the positive brand quality. It also enables companies to differentiate their product from competitors and communicate attributes of their products to consumers.

For example: Huge popularity of Reese's peanut butter cups created an immediate need for other peanut based chocolates. Reese's instead of manufacturing other peanut chocolates chose to go for brand licensing. Betty Crocker being a licensee handles the production, sales and distribution because of its experience and expertise in the market position. This partnership enabled Reese's to generate more revenue by extending its brand into an unfamiliar and unexplored area; in return Betty Crocker was able to increases its revenues by leveraging on Reese's brand which appealed to masses.

Brand Licensing Workflow

Brand licensing enables intellectual property owners to gain access to royalty income without the risks and business costs of manufacturing and distribution. Successfully establishing a profitable brand licensing program relies on a clear strategy with carefully devised operational segments.

Brand licensing workflow involves:

1. Detailed licensing program strategy;

2. Intellectual property protection;
3. Sales management;
4. Contracts, style guides;
5. Product development;
6. Brand assurance;
7. Marketing;
8. Financial management;
9. Operations;
10. Licensing management software.

Because brands risk damaging their image and potential financial loss by leasing their intellectual property, it is crucial for a licensor to oversee all aspects of property management and control.

In order to maintain a brand's reputation, steps must be taken to avoid oversights and errors. Implementing a strategic brand licensing workflow is essential for smooth and successful business transactions.

Good brand licensing workflows rely on the following framework:

1. Licensing Program Strategy
    a. Define intellectual property
    b. Define geographic markets
2. Intellectual Property Protection
    a. Determine the form of protection
    b. Confirm ownership
3. Sales Management
    a. Conduct market research
    b. Determine guidelines
    c. Evaluate licensee
4. Contracts
    a. Negotiate terms
    b. Exercise due diligence
    c. Create deal memo
    d. Draft NDA

5. Style Guides
    a. Provide images, logos, and graphics
6. Product Development and Brand Assurance
    a. Generate approvals
    b. Develop prototypes
7. Marketing
    a. Create promotional material
8. Financial Management
    a. Collect royalties
    b. Perform audits
9. Operations
    a. Supply work tools
    b. Monitor
10. Licensing Management Software
    a. Implement brand licensing software

Licensing Program Strategy

Brand licensing is an extremely successful and lucrative business strategy used across industries to broaden revenue sources and create brand awareness. Brands rely on third-parties to distribute products and reach markets they might not have access to.

Creating and implementing a new brand can be very time-consuming and success is not guaranteed. Producing licensed products from a reputable brand increases the chances of success for licensees and gives them access to markets and retailers they normally couldn't reach.

Avoiding common mistakes and implementing a solid brand licensing workflow helps all stakeholders reach their desired outcomes.

Before entering the licensing business, a brand should evaluate its intellectual property and build a licensing program strategy. The strategy should clearly define the intellectual property, identify targeted markets and end customer segments, create guidelines for preferred licensees, and evaluate the short and long term performance targets.

Failure to identify these elements in a brand licensing strategy can lead to over saturation of licensed products in a particular market or with certain retailers. This occurs when an error has been made estimating the supply and demand for a particular product and that the competition is too heavy.

Consistent revenue flow from licensing can typically achieved in around two years. The best partnerships are accomplished when all parties; licensor, agents, and licensees, reach a clear understanding of each others' strategies and objectives. Hiring an independent consultant to perform a market study may help make the licensors objectives more specific and clearly defined.

When a licensor targets a fandom for their products, there is a good chance that the goods will move faster and produce revenue within two years. Fashion goods like t-shirts with licensed video games have topped the list of successfully licensed products and can typically generate revenue much sooner than other categories. Celebrity-branded partnerships are also on the rise, with celebrities promoting beauty products, beverages, and an array of other items.

Intellectual Property Protection

Intellectual property refers to a work or invention that is the result of creativity, such as a manuscript or a design, to which one has rights and for which one may apply for a patent, copyright, trademark, etc. The image is usually very specific and is an essential part of brand awareness. Protecting intellectual property allows a brand to maintain their reputation and position the market.

In this context, we're discussing intellectual property as it refers to trademarks or copyrights that the licensor establishes when initiating the brand licensing program. The intellectual property is safeguarded against unauthorized use before the license is acquired. The licensor can give the right to use to a licensee, allowing them to use their intellectual property without transferring ownership.

Having intellectual property protection before pursuing brand licensing agreements is ideal but it can also be done during the planning phase of the brand licensing strategy. This allows the licensor to protect themself against possible infringement, and also reinforce a brand's credibility with the licensee during transactions.

Protections in this context means that the licensor owns everything related to the intellectual property that is being protected by trademark or copyright. Elements like logos, graphics, and designs are trademarked or and are owned by the licensor. Copyrights protect creative/artistic expression on a fixed medium (i.e. blog content). The licensor maintains complete control over the general image of the brand and licensees cannot infringe on this image. They must abide by the intellectual property rules, restrictions, and general appearance. No matter the product category being discussed, the intellectual property is protected to ensure quality items get launched and sold.

Trademarks

Trademarks are applied by category and can be time-consuming to obtain and quite expensive. They need to be filed and registered in each country the licensor intends to sell products. A trademark can protect words, brand names, character designs, symbols, phrases, and any combination of these elements. A conflict check should be performed before the actual filing of the trademark to make sure that the intellectual property is not being used by another brand on the market.

Trademark registration is good for 10 years and should be monitored closely and actively used during this time by the licensor. The trademark can be extended an unlimited number of times if you are able to provide proof that it is being used accurately.

Copyrights

Copyrights are easier and less expensive to obtain than trademarks. Copyright protection becomes valid upon creation of the work. The owner doesn't need to take any actions, as the intellectual property is automatically copyrighted when it is made. However, in order to take any legal action for infringement, the copyright must be registered.

It is recommended, however, that parties register the property with the copyright office, especially if the intellectual property will be used for brand licensing purposes. It's an extra way to protect the intellectual property that will be licensed. In additional, legal action for infringement or misuse cannot be taken unless copyright is registered.

The difference between a trademark and a copyright is that trademark only protects designs, logos, and images. Words, phrases and the written idea behind the creation of the intellectual property are not protected in the same way. Copyrights are the only way to ensure the protection of the ideas in a fixed form are safeguarded.

Once a copyright expires, it is considered public domain and can be used by anyone. Copyrights typically cover 70 years past the death of the intellectual property's creator.

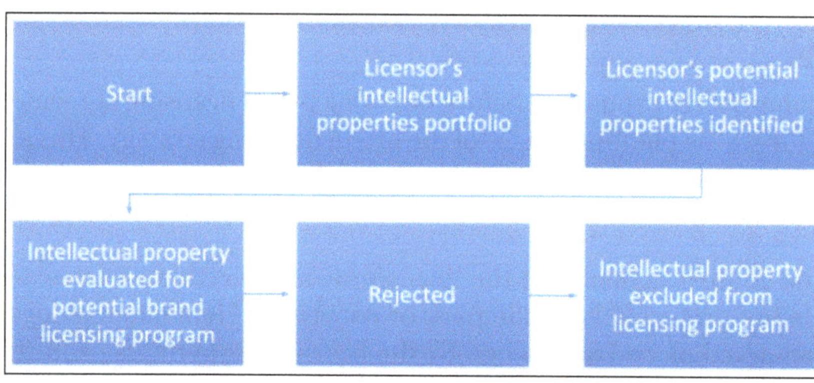

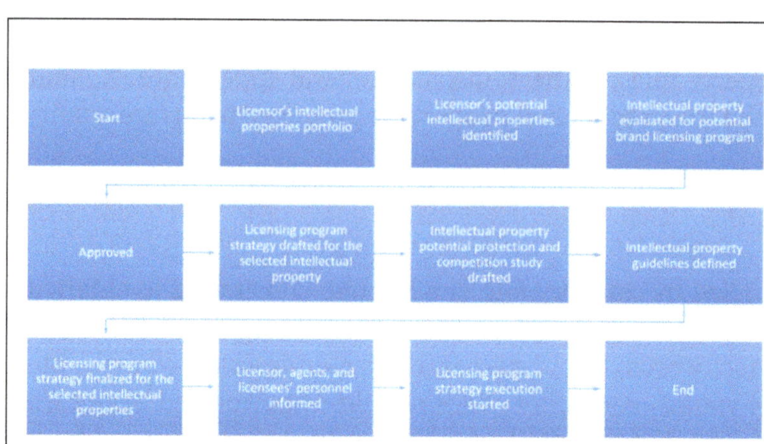

Brand Licensing Strategy Workflow.

Audits

In addition to protection through trademarks, copyrights, and close monitoring for counterfeits and licensing infringement, the licensor will conduct audits and execute regular checks.

The licensee is obligated to provide books, sales, and records that pertain to the licensed material. This can be performed by the licensor or by an audit team. During the audit, the obligations of both parties involved will be reviewed to make sure that all agreements are being respected.

Counterfeit products are a huge problem for licensors and licensees. Apart from restricting revenue to all parties involved in the brand licensing agreement, the reputation of the brand may also be compromised.

Infringement and piracy are different. Infringed products are produced by the licensee outside the terms of the contract while pirated or counterfeit products are unauthorized products manufactured by a company with no legal rights to the intellectual property.

One way to prevent piracy and counterfeits is to bring the quality branded products to the market in a timely manner. If the product enters the market quickly, the chances of the counterfeits reaching the market are greatly diminished. You saturate the market with your goods leaving limited need for consumers to seek out counterfeit products.

Sales Management

Once the intellectual property is protected by trademark or copyright and the licensing program has been implemented, the sales process can officially begin.

Before proceeding with a prospective licensee, market research should be conducted which includes market potential, due diligence, and confirmation of the brand protection. Licensee evaluation is essential to ensuring quality products are produced. Licensees will provide information regarding their viability as a business to show that they can actually embark on this endeavor.

Non-disclosure agreements should be signed with licensees in the very beginning to further ensure the privacy of the intellectual property. NDA's are not mandatory as the intellectual property is already protected, but it can be an extra precaution in case negotiations fail.

It's important to avoid licensee overlaps in the market. If two licensees end up on the same distribution path with the same category product they will conflict with each other. Double licensing should be avoided in order to keep the competition healthy. For this reason, evaluating and understanding the distribution possibilities and the licensee's market range and strategy is vital.

A deal memo is a deal-point memorandum that outlines the agreement terms and commercial details of the upcoming brand license. This is when the actual negotiations begin. Deal memos can save considerable production time and help assure on-time market launches, addressing important points without wasting time on unnecessary topics.

In order to sustain market demand, licensors must constantly update the core property and work with their licensees to create new product lines, promotional activities, marketing campaigns, and other programs to keep the intellectual property relevant in the eyes of the retailers and consumers.

Once all terms are negotiated and agreed upon, the brand licensing workflow goes into the contract administrative phase and the licensee will typically provide an advance payment at this point.

Contract Administration

Once all commercial details have been agreed upon, the actual contract administration process can begin. Usually, legal assistance is introduced at this point to make sure that the details are understood by all parties involved and to provide support if needed.

Each licensing agreement differs depending on the licensee which can present a challenge for the licensor. Negotiations are different for every licensee because this is a flexible and unique process with every new license distribution.

All parties involved want to get the best deal they possibly can in order to assure their own financial gain with the licensed product. Some negotiations with licensees may take longer than expected and therefore extend production schedules and market launches.

When the term of the licensing agreement is about to expire,, the licensee's performance is evaluated and if there is a valid business opportunity to continue operations, a renewal agreement is pursued. In cases where the contract is terminated or expires without renewal, the licensee is obligated to dispose of all the licensed inventory during an agreed period called a sell-off.

Style Guides and Assets

At this point in the brand licensing workflow, the licensor will develop and provide a graphic look with guidelines given to the licensees in the form of a style guide and possibly other materials.

Graphic assets and other design features for developing the licensed products are provided for the licensee to follow. The style guide will include guidelines for logos, representation, signatures, design variations, and packaging instructions. Licensees are obligated to follow this style guide for in all of the licensed products they will produce.

Ensuring a continuous development process of style guides is crucial y to stay relevant and fresh in the eyes of both retailers and consumers. This sometimes means developing seasonal products and changes in colorways and designs to reflect trends and guarantee satisfaction of market demands. This can be done by the licensor or by the licensee depending on the product.

Once the style guides and materials are reviewed and completely understood by the licensee, they can enter the product development stage where the items will be conceptualized and produced, under the regulations of the style guide and brand image.

Product Development and Brand Assurance

Licensors have the full control of their intellectual property usage in brand licensing by approving, denying or changing product development. The licensee is required to receive official approval from the licensor for each licensed product that will be manufactured before launch. The approval process is usually done in stages where the licensor approves each step before moving on to the next.

The drawings or concept sketches are first approved, then the prototypes are authorized. Finally, product samples are be reviewed and approved before they can be sent out to the market and to retailers.

The challenge in the brand licensing workflow at this point is to have the approvals completed by the launch dates and retail shipment dates. It is essential that every party in the process understands the style guide well and adheres to the instructions in order for the progression to go as smoothly as possible.

The main objective of the licensed products is to differentiate it from the non-licensed products. "Logo-slapping" should be avoided to ensure brand quality and reputation. The licensee needs an understanding of the intellectual property and must adhere to the brand's image and respect the brand's reputation in the marketplace. Understanding the brand's values is essential to produce products that reflect the brand properly.

The main challenges in the product development phase are the ability to control product quality and the dependency on the licensee's skills, abilities, and resources. The best results can be achieved by combining the licensor's expertise of the brand and licensee's knowledge of the product. This is why brands license their intellectual property to businesses that specialize in a particular kind of product. This provides entry to certain markets that the brand alone could not achieve. This is known as the "golden rule" of brand licensing.

Promotions and Marketing Campaigns

The most effective way to keep the product relevant in the market is to have continuous marketing and promotional programs to increase awareness, customer interest, and therefore sales. Marketing or promotional funds may be negotiated in the licensing agreement and collected as a marketing fee.

Both licensor and licensee should synchronize their marketing activation schedules for best outcomes. The responsibility of successfully launching a licensed product line is held by both licensor and licensee. As with the product development stage, all marketing and promotional materials will have to be approved by the licensor before unveiling.

A Common Marketing Fund (CMF) is a general practice for many in the industry and allows for the simultaneous promotion of multiple licensees. The funds are gathered from the licensees and used for common marketing strategies to be used by all licensees, no matter the market.

Financial Management

The most important financial key performance indicator (KPI) for licensors is the royalty percentage from every deal. Every licensing agreement is different, so the royalty payment accrued with each licensee will vary. This is usually calculated as a percentage of all net sales, gross sales, net profit, or fixed flat fee of licensed products. This payment method and percentage is determined and agreed upon during the negations and included in the licensing agreement contract.

The minimum guarantee (MG) serves to minimize the business risk for the licensor and to incentivize the licensee to sell actively during the contract term. All royalties usually accrue against the guarantee amount. The MG can take different forms and is worked out during the negotiation phase.

The main function of the licensing finance team is to collect royalty reports from the licensees on a monthly or quarterly basis and manage the invoicing process to assure that the royalty payments and guarantee instalments are paid in time.

Operations Management

During the brand licensing workflow, operations and licensing strategy will need to be closely monitored and managed. This ensures that program performance and progress and being regularly reviewed.

It is important to set up a workflow that assures that the licensee remains within the limit of the grant of rights and the transparency with different parties to work on their best performance with the tools needed.

A risk for the licensor is losing control on the intellectual property and damaging the brand's reputation. Everything from design details, product quality, sales, and distribution should be closely monitored by the operations team. It's important for the operations team to have the tools and capabilities needed to monitor all different licensing agreements during all stages of the licensing agreement.

Licensing Automation Software

The brand licensing workflow has been made easier thanks to the internet and digital tools that help improve efficiency. Brand licensing software can help the stakeholders exchange clear and consistent information throughout the production process.

Specialized royalty and licensing management software are helpful in the licensing workflow, but can sometimes take time to set up. Once implementation has been completed, the management of all departments and processes becomes easier and provides more efficiency in the work environment. Teams can stay connected and exchange valuable information much quicker and therefore avoid delays in production and deliveries.

The productivity of all parties and departments involved in the branded product creation and production is elevated with implemented brand licensing software. Design approvals reach every pertinent department in a timely manner and can be approved rapidly. Milestones can be closely monitored, so that nothing falls through the cracks. While As much as email is a good resource in business transactions, is it they are not the perfect answer to keep brand licensing agreements effective and running smoothly.

Negotiations can also be managed online, but human interface is strongly recommended, to perform the complete negotiations phase and to finalize licensing agreement paperwork.

Marketing Activation

Marketing activation is the execution of the marketing mix as part of the marketing process. The activation phase typically comes after the planning phase during which managers plan their marketing activities and is followed by a feedback phase in which results are evaluated with marketing analytics.

Depending on the business objective, two types of marketing activation can be used as part of a marketing strategy.

1. Brand activation, sometimes called brand engagement which focuses on building a longer term emotional connection between the brand and the customer.

2. Activation based on direct-response marketing will focus on generating immediate sales transactions.

Planning the Activation

Before executing its marketing activities, a firm will benefit from identifying which customer groups to target. By focusing on some fewer influencers only, activation can become more efficient and higher returns can be expected.

Customer data is a significant source of information for planning marketing activation. A common practice is to use customer relationship management tools and techniques to augment the impact of marketing activation because CRM provides an integrative framework in which marketing activation and customer activities collaborate to increase patronage

Challenges

A successful marketing activation will allow businesses to increase their profits and reach their strategic goals. There are however challenges that managers will face in putting in place a marketing activation program. One of the challenges is dealing with an ever-changing marketplace. Customer preferences and attitudes keep evolving and require managers to adapt rapidly. This poses a challenge because, for example, "direct marketing activation triggers that were accurate 6 months ago, may now be quite inappropriate."

Another challenge related to marketing activation has to do with reaching different target markets with culturally relevant propositions. McDonald's is said to be a good example of a company that can effectively reach a diverse audience. Among the techniques it uses, "it engages in unique marketing activation, including strong use of PR and events targeted at black, Asian, and Latino youth."

Data-driven Marketing Activation

Over the years, marketing activation has become more and more data-driven. This allows marketers to be more precise in their actions, measure results more effectively, and increase returns. This phenomenon has become more and more important because marketing activation usually entails a universal blast of information to all consumers. Often, only a small proportion of the consumers react positively to such activation, resulting to waste in marketing expenses. If a circle of influencers can be identified for certain events or phenomena, then such activities can be focused into a group of factors or individuals, thus, optimizing the outcomes.

Different types of data are used in marketing activation. For example, "video-based measurement provides visibility into shopper engagement and behaviour relative to exact marketing activation, enabling a holistic approach to shopper marketing."

CRM data and models are also used to improve the effectiveness of marketing activation. One of these models, the marketing funnel, is a key conceptual framework that is routinely used by practitioners to deconstruct the marketing activation and identify key issues.

Online Video

Marketing activation can be enriched with the use of online tools. The advent of online video has opened up many opportunities for marketers who use it to engage customers in more compelling ways with new forms of advertising. YouTube, for example, has given marketers a platform for celebrating and amplifying nearly every marketing activation.

Sports Marketing

Marketing activation techniques are commonly used in sports marketing. They are often associated with a brand sponsoring an athlete or an event in order to boost their brand awareness. It has been said that "with strong marketing activation and creativity, consumers should remember the sponsor's campaign."

Social Marketing

Social marketing has the primary goal of achieving "social good". Traditional commercial marketing aims are primarily financial, though they can have positive social affects as well. In the context of public health, social marketing would promote general health, raise awareness and induce changes in behaviour. Social marketing has been a large industry for some time now and was originally done with newspapers and billboards, but similar to commercial marketing has adapted to the modern world. The most common use of social marketing in today's society is through social media. However, to see social marketing as only the use of standard commercial marketing practices to achieve non-commercial goals is an oversimplified view.

Social marketing seeks to develop and integrate marketing concepts with other approaches to social change. Social marketing aims to influence behaviors that benefit individuals and communities for the greater social good. The goal is to deliver competition-sensitive and segmented social change programs that are effective, efficient, equitable and sustainable.

Increasingly, social marketing is described as having "two parents." The "social parent" uses social science and social policy approaches. The "marketing parent" uses commercial and public sector marketing approaches. Recent years have also witnessed a broader focus. Social marketing now goes beyond influencing individual behaviour. It promotes socio-cultural and structural change relevant to social issues. Consequently, social marketing scholars are beginning to advocate for a broader definition of social marketing: "social marketing is the application of marketing principles to enable individual and collective ideas and actions in the pursuit of effective, efficient, equitable, fair and sustained social transformation". The new emphasis gives equal weight to the effects (efficiency and effectiveness) and the process (equity, fairness and sustainability) of social marketing programs. Together with a new social marketing definition that focuses on social transformation, there is also an argument that "a systems approach is needed if social marketing is to address the increasingly complex and dynamic social issues facing contemporary societies."

Applications

The first documented evidence of the deliberate use of marketing to address a social issue comes from a 1963 reproductive health program led by K. T. Chandy at the Indian Institute of Management in Calcutta, India. Chandy and colleagues proposed, and subsequently implemented, a national family planning program with high quality, government brand condoms distributed and sold throughout the country at low cost. The program included an integrated consumer marketing campaign run with active point of sale promotion. Retailers were trained to sell the product aggressively, and a new organization was created to implement the program. In developing countries, the use of social marketing expanded to HIV prevention, control of childhood diarrhea (through the use of oral re-hydration therapies), malaria control and treatment, point-of-use water treatment, on-site sanitation methods and the provision of basic health services.

Health promotion campaigns began applying social marketing in practice in the 1980s. In the United States, The National High Blood Pressure Education Program and the community heart disease prevention studies in Pawtucket, Rhode Island and at Stanford University demonstrated the effectiveness of the approach to address population-based risk factor behaviour change. Notable early developments also took place in Australia. These included the Victoria Cancer Council developing its anti-tobacco campaign "Quit" (1988) and "SunSmart" (1988), its campaign against skin cancer which had the slogan "Slip! Slop! Slap!"

Since the 1980s, the field has rapidly expanded around the world to include active living communities, disaster preparedness and response, ecosystem and species conservation, environmental issues, development of volunteer or indigenous workforces, financial literacy, global threats of antibiotic resistance, government corruption, improving the quality of health care, injury prevention, landowner education, marine conservation and ocean sustainability, patient-centered health care, reducing health disparities, sustainable consumption, transportation demand management, water treatment and sanitation systems and youth gambling problems, among other social needs.

On a wider front, by 2007, government in the United Kingdom announced the development of its first social marketing strategy for all aspects of health. In 2010, the US national health objectives included increasing the number of state health departments that report using social marketing in health promotion and disease prevention programs and increasing the number of schools of public health that offer courses and workforce development activities in social marketing.

Two other public health applications include the CDC's CDCynergy training and software application and SMART (Social Marketing and Assessment Response Tool) in the U.S.

Social marketing theory and practice has been progressed in several countries such as the US, Canada, Australia, New Zealand and the UK, and in the latter a number of key government policy papers have adopted a strategic social marketing approach. Publications such as "Choosing Health" in 2004, "It's our health!" in 2006 and "Health Challenge England" in 2006, represent steps to achieve a strategic and operational use of social marketing. In India, AIDS controlling programs are largely using social marketing and social workers are largely working for it. Most of the social workers are professionally trained for this task.

A variation of social marketing has emerged as a systematic way to foster more sustainable behavior. Referred to as community-based social marketing (CBSM) by Canadian environmental psychologist Doug McKenzie-Mohr, CBSM strives to change the behavior of communities to reduce their impact on the environment. Realizing that simply providing information is usually not sufficient to initiate behavior change, CBSM uses tools and findings from social psychology to discover the perceived barriers to behavior change and ways of overcoming these barriers. Among the tools and techniques used by CBSM are focus groups and surveys (to discover barriers) and commitments, prompts, social norms, social diffusion, feedback and incentives (to change behavior). The tools of CBSM have been used to foster sustainable behavior in many areas, including energy conservation, environmental regulation, recycling and litter cleanup.

In recent years, the concept of strategic social marketing has emerged, which identifies that social change requires action at the individual, community, socio-cultural, political and environmental level, and that social marketing can and should influence policy, strategy and operational tactics to achieve pro-social outcomes.

Other social marketing can be aimed at products deemed, at least by proponents, as socially unacceptable. One of the most notable is People for the Ethical Treatment of Animals (PETA) which for many years has waged social marketing campaigns against the use of natural fur products. The campaigns' efficacy has been subject to dispute.

Not all social marketing campaigns are effective everywhere. For example, anti-smoking campaigns such as World No Tobacco Day while being successful (in concert with government tobacco controls) in curbing the demand for tobacco products in North America and in parts of Europe, have been less effective in other parts of the world such as China, India and Russia.

Types

Social marketing uses the benefits of doing social good to secure and maintain customer engagement. In social marketing the distinguishing feature is therefore its "primary focus on social good, and it is not a secondary outcome. Not all public sector and not-for-profit marketing is social marketing.

Public sector bodies can use standard marketing approaches to improve the promotion of their relevant services and organizational aims. This can be very important but should not be confused with social marketing where the focus is on achieving specific behavioral goals with specific audiences in relation to topics relevant to social good (e.g., health, sustainability, recycling, etc.). For example, a 3-month marketing campaign to encourage people to get a H1N1 vaccine is more tactical in nature and should not be considered social marketing. A campaign that promotes and reminds people to get regular check-ups and all of their vaccinations when they're supposed to encourages a long-term behavior change that benefits society. It can therefore be considered social marketing.

Social marketing can be confused with commercial marketing. A commercial marketer may only seek to influence a buyer to purchase a product. Social marketers have more difficult goals. They want to make potentially difficult and long-term behavior changes in target populations, which may or may not involve purchasing a product. For example, reducing cigarette smoking or encouraging use of condoms have difficult challenges to overcome that go beyond purchasing decisions.

Social marketing is sometimes seen as being restricted to a client base of non-profit organizations, health services groups, the government agency. However, the goal of inducing social change is not restricted to this narrow spectrum of organizations. Corporations, for example, can be clients. Public relations or social responsibility departments may champion social causes such funding for the arts, which would involve social marketing.

Social marketing should not be confused with the societal marketing concept which was a forerunner of sustainable marketing in integrating issues of social responsibility into commercial marketing strategies. In contrast to that, social marketing uses commercial marketing theories, tools and techniques to social issues.

Social marketing applies a "customer oriented" approach and uses the concepts and tools used by commercial marketers in pursuit of social goals like anti-smoking campaigns or fund raising for NGOs.

Social marketers must create competitive advantage by constantly adapting to and instigating change. With climate change in mind, adaptations to market changes are likely to be more successful if actions are guided by knowledge of the forces shaping market behaviours and insights that enable the development of sustainable competitive advantages.

Social Marketing Process

The social marketing process consists of five stages, each of which involves its own set of activities:

1. Formative evaluation and planning;
2. Message and materials development;
3. Pretesting and campaign adjustment;
4. Implementation and materials dissemination;
5. Impact evaluation and feedback.

Social Marketing Campaign Development

One of the key components of a social marketing campaign, and what sets it apart from a PSA trying to raise public awareness, is the formative research conducted prior to and during the creative production process. Collecting and analyzing quantitative and qualitative research data will help you better understand the problem and its context; the audience affected by the problem and its knowledge, attitudes, and beliefs; and develop more effective messaging and audience outreach tactics.

Quantitative research may be obtained through secondary research methods, such as reviewing academic articles, research studies, census data, and epidemiologic reports obtained from the health department. If a social marketing campaign is being implemented on a local level, it is also advised to distribute a survey directly to members of the target audience. Conducting your own primary quantitative research after reviewing the secondary research allows you to gather more specific information about the behaviors and needs of the precise people for whom the campaign is being developed.

As important as quantitative research is the qualitative research in the formative research stage of social marketing. If a campaign is local, it is beneficial to visit the communities you want to target to conduct ethnographic observation. This is the process of observing how the target audience behaves in their own community and how the behavior you are trying to change is valued in that community. Interviewing community stakeholders or key informants, such as a minister, bartender, or hair stylist, can help glean valuable insight into a community from people who know the community well. Hosting focus groups or town-hall meetings with members of the target audience can also be particularly insightful.

Audience Segmentation in Social Marketing

Following a robust analysis of the data collected from both quantitative and qualitative research, the final step before developing campaign messages and design elements is to segment the audience. Social marketing often fails because the audience is too broad. By segmenting your audience, you can identify the groups more reachable by the campaign and potentially create different messages and campaign elements for different subgroups of your target audience. Segments of your audience may also be based on geographic location, demographics, psychographics, and attitudes or beliefs.

References

- Pricing-in-marketing: businessjargons.com, Retrieved 9 March, 2019
- Casson, M. And Lee, J., "The Origin and Development of Markets: A Business History Perspective", Business History Review, Vol, 85, Spring 2011, doi:10.1017/S0007680511000018, p. 27
- Pricing-strategies-in-marketin: educba.com, Retrieved 10 April, 2019
- Anonymous (October 1, 2010). "What are the most crucial factors to effectively reach multicultural youth?". Prweek. Retrieved 18 August 2011
- Marketing-and-strategy-terms/3956-marketing-mix, business-concepts: mbaskool.com, Retrieved 11 May, 2019
- Jones, Brian D.G.; Shaw, Eric H. (2006). "A History of Marketing Thought", Handbook of Marketing. Weitz, Barton A.; Wensley, Robin (eds), Sage, p. 41, ISBN 1-4129-2120-1
- Distribution, ecommerce: oberlo.in, Retrieved 12 June, 2019
- Saunders, S. G.; Barrington, D. J. & Sridharan, S. (2015). "Redefining social marketing: beyond behavioural change". Journal of Social Marketing. 5 (2): 160–168. Doi:10.1108/JSOCM-03-2014-0021
- Distribution-channel, ecommerce: oberlo.in, Retrieved 13 July, 2019
- Townsend, Matt; Surane, Jenny; Orr, Emma; Cannon, Christopher (8 November 2017). "America's 'Retail Apocalypse' Is Really Just Beginning". Bloomberg. Retrieved 15 January 2018

- Brand-licensing-11121, marketing-and-strategy-terms, business-concepts: mbaskool.com, Retrieved 14 August, 2019
- Kotler, Philip, Ned Roberto and Nancy Lee. Social Marketing: Improving the Quality of Life, SAGE, 2002. (ISBN 0-7619-2434-5)
- Brand-licensing-workflow-101: flowhaven.com, Retrieved 15 January, 2019
- Truong, V. Dao; Saunders, Stephen Graham; Dong, X. Dam (8 April 2019). "Systems social marketing: a critical appraisal". Journal of Social Marketing. 9 (2): 180–203. Doi:10.1108/JSOCM-06-2018-0062
- Principles-of-social-marketing: frog-dog.com, Retrieved 16 February, 2019

Market Structure 4

- **Perfect Competition**
- **Imperfect Competition**
- **Monopsony**
- **Monopoly**
- **Oligopoly**
- **Monopolistic Competition**

The main types of market structure are perfect competition, imperfect competition, oligopoly, monopoly and monopsony. All the diverse principles and concepts related to these types of market structure such as monopsonistic competition and monopolistic competition have been carefully analyzed in this chapter.

Perfect Competition

Pure or perfect competition is a theoretical market structure in which the following criteria are met:

1. All firms sell an identical product (the product is a "commodity" or "homogeneous").
2. All firms are price takers (they cannot influence the market price of their product).
3. Market share has no influence on prices.
4. Buyers have complete or "perfect" information—in the past, present and future—about the product being sold and the prices charged by each firm.
5. Resources for such a labor are perfectly mobile.
6. Firms can enter or exit the market without cost.

This can be contrasted with the more realistic imperfect competition, which exists whenever a market, hypothetical or real, violates the abstract tenets of neoclassical pure or perfect competition.

Since all real markets exist outside of the plane of the perfect competition model, each can be classified as imperfect. The contemporary theory of imperfect versus perfect competition stems from the Cambridge tradition of post-classical economic thought.

How Perfect Competition Works

Perfect competition is a benchmark, or "ideal type," to which real-life market structures can be compared. Perfect competition is theoretically the opposite of a monopoly, in which only a single firm supplies a good or service and that firm can charge whatever price it wants since consumers have no alternatives and it is difficult for would-be competitors to enter the marketplace.

Under perfect competition, there are many buyers and sellers, and prices reflect supply and demand. Companies earn just enough profit to stay in business and no more. If they were to earn excess profits, other companies would enter the market and drive profits down.

Large and Homogeneous Market

There are a large number of buyers and sellers in a perfectly competitive market. The sellers are small firms, instead of large corporations capable of controlling prices through supply adjustments. They sell products with minimal differences in capabilities, features, and pricing. This ensures that buyers cannot distinguish between products based on physical attributes, such as size or color, or intangible values, such as branding.

A large population of both buyers and sellers ensures that supply and demand remain constant in this market. As such, buyers can easily substitute products made by one firm for another.

Perfect Information Availability

Information about the ecosystem and competition in an industry constitutes a significant advantage. For example, knowledge about component sourcing and supplier pricing can make or break the market for certain companies. In certain knowledge- and research-intensive industries, such as pharmaceuticals and technology, information about patents and research initiatives at competitors can help companies develop competitive strategies and build a moat around its products.

In a perfectly competitive market, however, such moats do not exist. Information is equally and freely available to all market participants. This ensures that each firm can produce its goods or services at exactly the same rate and with the same production techniques as another one in the market.

Absence of Controls

Governments play a vital role in market formation for products by imposing regulation and price controls. They can control the entry and exit of firms into a market by setting up rules to function in the market. For example, the pharmaceutical industry has to contend with a roster of rules pertaining to research, production, and sale of drugs.

In turn, these rules require big capital investments in the form of employees, such as lawyers and quality assurance personnel, and infrastructure, such as machinery to manufacture medicines.

The cumulative costs add up and make it extremely expensive for companies to bring a drug to the market. In comparison, the technology industry functions with relatively less oversight as compared to its pharma counterpart. Thus, entrepreneurs in this industry can start firms with less to zero capital, making it easy for individuals to start a company in the industry.

Such controls do not exist in a perfectly competitive market. The entry and exit of firms in such a market are unregulated, and this frees them up to spend on labor and capital assets without restrictions and adjust their output in relation to market demands.

Cheap and Efficient Transportation

Cheap and efficient transportation is another characteristic of perfect competition. In this type of market, companies do not incur significant costs to transport goods. This helps reduce the product's price and cuts back on delays in transporting goods.

Examples of Perfect Competition

As mentioned earlier, perfect competition is a theoretical construct and does not exist in reality. As such, it is difficult to find real-life examples of perfect competition but there are variants present in everyday society.

Consider the situation at a farmer's market, a place characterized by a large number of small sellers and buyers. Typically, there is little differentiation between products and their prices from one farmer's market to another. The provenance of the produce does not matter (unless they are classified as organic) in such cases and there is very little difference in the packaging or branding of products. Thus, even if one of the farms producing goods for the market goes out of business, it will not make a difference to average prices.

The situation may also be relatively similar in the case of two competing supermarkets, which stock their aisles from the same set of companies. Again, there is little to distinguish products from one another between both supermarkets and their pricing remains almost the same. Another example of perfect competition is the market for unbranded products, which features cheaper versions of well-known products.

Product knockoffs are generally priced similarly and there is little to differentiate them from one another. If one of the firms manufacturing such a product goes out of business, it is replaced by another one.

The development of new markets in the technology industry also resembles perfect competition to a certain degree. For example, there was a proliferation of sites offering similar services during the early days of social media networks. Some examples of such sites are Sixdegrees.com, Blackplanet.com, and Asianave.com. None of them had a dominant market share and the sites were mostly free. They constituted sellers in the market while consumers of such sites, who were mainly young people, were the buyers.

The startup costs for companies in this space were minimal, meaning that startups and companies can freely enter and exit these markets. Technologies, such as PHP and Java, were largely open-source and available to anyone. Capital costs, in the form of real estate and infrastructure, were not necessary.

Disadvantages of Perfect Competition Models

Perfect competition establishes an idealized framework for establishing a market. But that market is flawed and has a couple of disadvantages. The first one is the absence of innovation. The prospect of greater market share and setting themselves apart from the competition is an incentive for firms to innovate and make better products. But no firm possesses a dominant market share in perfect competition.

Profit margins are also fixed by demand and supply. Firms cannot thus set themselves apart by charging a premium for their product and services.

For example, it would be impossible for a company like Apple Inc. (AAPL) to exist in a perfectly competitive market because its phones are pricier as compared to competitors. The second disadvantage of perfect competition is the absence of economies of scale. Limited to zero profit margins means that companies will have less cash to invest in expanding their production capabilities.

An expansion of production capabilities could potentially bring down costs for consumers and increase profit margins for the firm. But the presence of several small firms cannibalizing the market for the same product prevents such an occurrence and ensures that the average firm size engaged in the market remains small.

Profits in a Perfectly Competitive Market

Profits may be possible for brief periods in perfectly competitive markets. But the market's dynamics cancel out the effects of positive or negative profits and bring them towards an equilibrium. Because there is no information asymmetry in the market, other firms will quickly ramp up their production or reduce their manufacturing costs to achieve parity with the firm which made profits.

The average revenue and marginal revenue for firms in a perfectly competitive market are equal to the product's price to the buyer. As a result, the perfectly competitive market's equilibrium, which had been disrupted earlier, will be restored. In the long run, an adjustment of supply and demand ensures all profits or losses in such markets tend towards zero.

Perfect Competition in the Real World

Real-world competition differs from this ideal primarily because of differentiation in production, marketing, and selling. For example, in agriculture, the owner of a small organic products shop can talk extensively about the grain fed to the cows that made the manure that fertilized the non-GMO soybeans—that's differentiation. Through marketing, companies seek to establish "brand value" around their differentiation and advertise to gain pricing power and market share.

Thus, the first two criteria—homogeneous products and price takers—are far from realistic. Yet, for the second two criteria—information and mobility—the global tech and trade transformation is improving information and resource flexibility. While the reality is far from this theoretical model, the model is still helpful because of its ability to explain many real-life behaviors.

Barriers to Entry Prohibit Perfect Competition

Many industries also have significant barriers to entry, such as high startup costs (as seen in the auto manufacturing industry) or strict government regulations (as seen in the utility industry), which limit the ability of firms to enter and exit such industries. And although consumer awareness has increased with the information age, there are still few industries where the buyer remains aware of all available products and prices.

As you can see, there are significant obstacles preventing perfect competition from appearing in today's economy. The agricultural industry probably comes closest to exhibiting perfect competition because it is characterized by many small producers with virtually no ability to alter the selling price of their products. The commercial buyers of agricultural commodities are generally very well-informed and, although agricultural production involves some barriers to entry, it is not particularly difficult to enter the marketplace as a producer.

Features of Perfect Competition

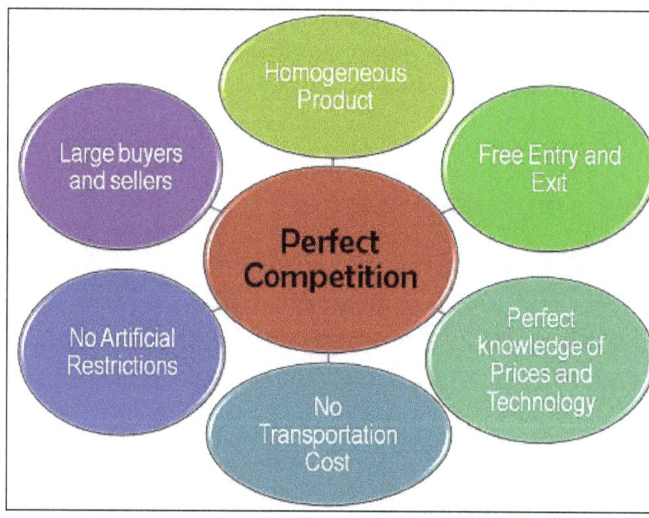

1. Large number of buyers and sellers: In perfect competition, the buyers and sellers are large enough, that no individual can influence the price and the output of the industry. An individual customer cannot influence the price of the product, as he is too small in relation to the whole market. Similarly, a single seller cannot influence the levels of output, who is too small in relation to the gamut of sellers operating in the market.

2. Homogeneous Product: Each competing firm offers the homogeneous product, such that no individual has a preference for a particular seller over the others. Salt, wheat, coal, etc. are some of the homogeneous products for which customers are indifferent and buy these from the one who charges a less price. Thus, an increase in the price would let the customer go to some other supplier.

3. Free Entry and Exit: Under the perfect competition, the firms are free to enter or exit the industry. This implies, If a firm suffers from a huge loss due to the intense competition in the industry, then it is free to leave that industry and begin its business operations in any of the industry, it wants. Thus, there is no restriction on the mobility of sellers.

4. Perfect knowledge of prices and technology: This implies, that both the buyers and sellers have complete knowledge of the market conditions such as the prices of products and the latest technology being used to produce it. Hence, they can buy or sell the products anywhere and anytime they want.

5. No transportation cost: There is an absence of transportation cost, i.e. incurred in carrying the goods from one market to another. This is an essential condition of the perfect competition since the homogeneous product should have the same price across the market and if the transportation cost is added to it, then the prices may differ.

6. Absence of Government and Artificial Restrictions: Under the perfect competition, both the buyers and sellers are free to buy and sell the goods and services. This means any customer can buy from any seller, and any seller can sell to any buyer. Thus, no restriction is imposed on either party. Also, the prices are liable to change freely as per the demand-supply conditions. In such a situation, no big producer and the government can intervene and control the demand, supply or price of the goods and services.

Thus, under the perfect competition, a seller is the price taker and cannot influence the market price.

Imperfect Competition

Imperfect competition exists whenever a market, hypothetical or real, violates the abstract tenets of neoclassical pure or perfect competition. Since all real markets exist outside of the plane of the perfect competition model, each can be classified as imperfect. The contemporary theory of imperfect versus perfect competition stems from the Cambridge tradition of post-classical economic thought.

The treatment of perfect competition models in economics, along with modern conceptions of monopoly, were founded by the French mathematician Augustin Cournot. His ideas were adopted and popularized by the Swiss economist Leon Walras, considered by many to be the founder of modern mathematical economics.

Prior to Walras and Cournot, mathematicians had a difficult time modeling economic relationships or creating reliable equations. The new perfect competition model simplified economic competition to a purely predictive and static state. This avoided many problems that exist in real markets, such as imperfect human knowledge, barriers to entry and monopoly.

The mathematical approach gained widespread academic acceptance, particularly in England. Any deviation from the new model of perfect competition was considered a troublesome violation of the new economic understanding.

Limitations of Imperfect Competition

The Cambridge school's wholesale devotion to creating a static and mathematically calculable economic science had its drawbacks. Ironically, a perfectly competitive market would require the absence of competition. All sellers in a perfect market must sell exactly similar goods at identical prices to the exact same consumers, all of whom possess the same perfect knowledge. There is no room for advertising, product differentiation, innovation, or brand identification in perfect competition.

No real market can or could attain the characteristics of a perfectly competitive market. The pure competition model ignores many factors, including the limited deployment of physical capital and capital investment, entrepreneurial activity, and changes in the availability of scarce resources. Other economists have adopted more flexible and less mathematically rigid theories of competition, such as the evenly rotating economy, though the language created by the Cambridge tradition still predominates the discipline.

Characteristics of Imperfect Competition

Under imperfect competition, there are large number of buyers and sellers. Each seller can follow its own price-output policy. Each producer produces the differentiated product, which are close substitutes of each other. Thus, the demand curve under monopolistic competition is highly elastic.

Large Number of Sellers and Buyers

There are large numbers of sellers in the market. All these firms are small sized. It means that each firm produces or sells such an insignificant portion of the total output or sale that it cannot influence the market price by its individual action. No firm can affect the sales of any other firm either by increasing or reducing its output; so there is no reaction from other firms. Every firm acts independently without bothering about the reactions of its rivals. There are a large number of buyers and none of them can affect price by his individual action.

Product Differentiation

Another important characteristic is product differentiation. The product of each seller may be similar to, but not identical with the product of other sellers in the industry. For example, a packet of Verka butter may be similar in kind to another packet of Vita butter, but because of the idea that there are differences, real or imaginary, in the quality of these two products, each buyer may have a definite preference for the one rather than for the other. As a result, each firm will have a group of buyers who prefer, for one reason or another, the product of that particular firm.

Selling Costs

Another important characteristic of the monopolistic competition is existence of selling costs. Since there is product differentiation and products are close substitutes, selling costs are important to persuade buyers to change their preferences, so as to raise their demand for a given article. Under monopolistic competition, advertisement is not only persuasive but also informatory because a large number of firms are operating in the market and buyer's knowledge about the market is not perfect.

Free Entry and Exit of Firms

Firms under monopolistic competition are free to join and leave the industry at any time they like to. The implication of this characteristic is that by entering freely into the market, the firms can produce close substitutes and increase the supply of commodity in the market. Similarly, the firm commands such a meager amount of resources that in the event of losses, they may easily quit the market.

Price-makers

In the monopolistic competitive market, each firm is a price-maker as it can determine the price of its own brand of the product.

Blend of Competition and Monopoly

In this market, each firm has a monopoly power over its product as it would not lose all customers if it raises the price as its product is not perfect substitute of other brands. At the same time, there is an element of competition because the consumers treat the different firms' products as close substitutes. Hence, if a firm raises the price of its brand, it would lose some customers to other brands.

Monopsony

Monopsony is a market in which a single buyer completely controls the demand for a good. While the market for any type of good, service, resource, or commodity could, in principle, function as monopsony, this form of market structure tends to be most pronounced for the exchange of factor services.

While the real world does not contain monopsony in its absolute purest form, labor markets in which a single large factory is the dominate employer in a small community comes as close as any.

Like a monopoly seller, a monopsony buyer is a price maker with complete market control. Monopsony is also comparable to monopoly in terms of inefficiency. Monopsony does not generate an efficient allocation of resources. The price paid by a monopsony is lower and the quantity exchanged is less than with the benchmark of perfect competition.

Characteristics

The three key characteristics of monopsony are: a single firm buying all output in a market, no alternative buyers, and restrictions on entry into the industry.

1. Single Buyer: First and foremost, a monopsony is a monopsony because it is the only buyer in the market. The word monopsony actually translates as "one buyer." As the only buyer, a monopsony controls the demand-side of the market completely. If anyone wants to sell the good, they must sell to the monopoly.
2. No Alternatives: A monopsony achieves single-buyer status because sellers have no alternative buyers for their goods. This is the key characteristics that usually prevents monopsony from existing in the real world in its pure, ideal form. Sellers almost always have alternatives.
3. Barriers to Entry: A monopsony often acquires and generally maintains single buyer status due to restrictions on the entry of other buyers into the market. The key barriers to entry

are much the same as those that exist for monopoly: government license or franchise, resource ownership, patents and copyrights, high start-up cost, and decreasing average total cost.

A Hypothetical Example

One example of a monopsony factor market is the hypothetical Natural Ned Lumber Company, which is a lumbering operation in the isolated Jagged Mountains region north of the greater Shady Valley metropolitan area. The Natural Ned Lumber Company is an expansive operation employing several thousand workers, all of whom reside in Lumber Town, which is adjacent to the Natural Ned Lumber Company lumbering operations. In fact, everyone living in Lumber Town works for the Natural Ned Lumber Company.

This makes the Natural Ned Lumber Company a monopsony employer. If anyone in Lumber Town seeks employment, then they must seek it with the Natural Ned Lumber Company. As such, the Natural Ned Lumber Company is a price maker when it comes to buying labor services. The Natural Ned Lumber Company can the determine of labor services desired, then charge the minimum factor price that sellers are willing and able to receive.

While the Natural Ned Lumber Company and Lumber Town is obviously a fictitious example of a monopsony, it does illustrate one of the more prevalent categories of monopsony that existed in the early history of the U.S. economy--the company town. During the early days of the U.S. industrial revolution, the late 1800s through the early 1900s, it was quite common for a large industrial facility (factory, mining operation, lumber company) to dominate employment in a given area. In some cases, the company literally built and owned the town in which the workers lived. Even those people who did not work directly in the primary activity (mining, lumber, etc.) worked in the company-owned store, hospital, school, or theater. Hence the term company town.

Modern Monopsony

Like other extreme market structures (perfect competition and monopoly) monopsony is only approximated in the real world. Achieving the status of "the only buyer" is not easy. Few if any buyers actually achieve this status. However, several have come close. In modern times a few examples of markets that come very close to monopsony come from the world of sports.

Should a talented quarterback wish to obtain a job as a professional football player, then "the" employer is the National Football League (NFL). Of course, the NFL is not absolutely the "only" employer. Employment as a professional football player can also be found with the Canadian Football League (CFL). However, sufficient difference exists between these two employers to give the NFL significant monopsony control.

Similar near monopsony status exists for other professional sports. A professional baseball player seeks employment with Major League Baseball (MLB), with minimal competition from Japan. A profession basketball player seeks employment with the National Basketball Association (NBA), with minimal competition from Europe. A professional hockey player seeks employment with the National Hockey League (NHL), again with some competition from Europe.

Other modern markets that exhibit varying degrees of monopsony status can be found in collegiate sports and the National Collegiate Athletic Association (NCAA) and the medical profession and the American Medical Association (AMA). Much like a professional football, baseball, basketball, or hockey player seeks employment in the "big leagues," a collegiate athlete seeks "employment" with a college affiliated with the NCAA. In a similar manner, a physician seeks "employment" through the AMA.

The reasons for quotation marks around employment for these two examples is that the monopsony employer does not technically employ these workers in a traditional sense. Monopsony status, however, is attributable to the ability to influence the factor market. In other words, a collegiate athlete who does not satisfy NCAA guidelines has difficulty "working" for a university, that is providing athletic entertainment services through the college in return for a scholarship. A physician who does not satisfy AMA guidelines also has difficulty working at a hospital or in private practice.

Supply and Cost

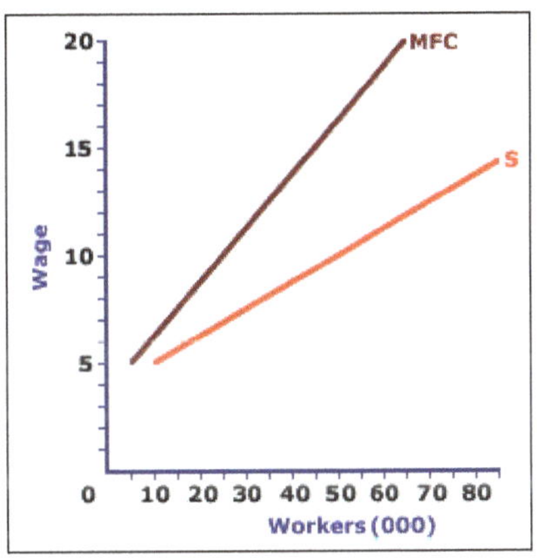

Single-buyer status means that monopsony faces a positively-sloped supply curve, such as the one displayed in the exhibit to the right. In fact, the supply curve facing the monopsony is the market supply curve for the product.

The far right curve in the exhibit is the red supply curve (S) facing the monopsony. The far left curve is the brown marginal factor cost curve (MFC). The marginal factor cost curve indicates the change in total factor cost incurred due to buying one additional unit of the good.

Because a monopsony is a price maker with extensive market control, it faces a positively-sloped supply curve. To buy a larger quantity of output, it must pay a higher price. For example, the monopsony can hire 10,000 workers for a wage of $5. However, if it wants to hire 20,000 workers, then it must raise the wage to $6.10.

For this reason, the marginal factor cost incurred from hiring extra workers is greater than the wage, or factor price. Suppose for example that the factor price needed to hire ten workers is $5 and the factor price needed to hire eleven workers is $5.10. The marginal factor cost incurred due to hiring the eleventh unit is $6.10. While the $6 factor price means the monopsony incurs a $5.10 factor cost from hiring this worker, this cost is compounded by an extra cost of $1 due to the higher wage paid to the first ten workers. The overall increase in cost, that is marginal factor cost, is thus $6.10 (= $5.10 + $1).

Profit Maximizing Employment

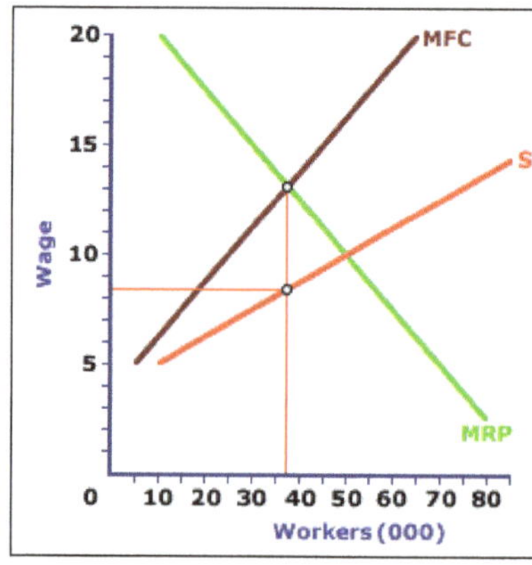

The exhibit to the right illustrates the profit-maximizing employment of a monopsony. This firm faces a positively-sloped supply curve, represented by the red supply curve (S). Because higher wages are needed to attract more labor, the positively-slope brown curve is the marginal factor cost curve (MFC). The third curve displayed in the exhibit is the green negatively-sloped marginal revenue product curve (MRP), which indicates the value of the extra production generated by each worker.

As a profit-maximizing firm, monopsony hires the quantity that equates marginal factor cost and marginal revenue product found at the intersection of the MFC and MRP curves. This quantity is 37,000 workers. The monopsony then pays each worker $8.40.

This price and quantity maximizes profit because the revenue generated from hiring the last worker (marginal revenue product) is exactly equal to the cost incurred from hiring the last worker (marginal factor cost). Because the extra revenue generated equals the extra cost incurred, there is no way to increase profit by hiring more or less of this input.

Monopsonistic Competition

Monopsonistic competition is a market in which a large number of relatively small buyers purchase goods (usually factor inputs) that are similar but not identical. While the market for any type of good, service, resource, or commodity can, in principle, function as monopsonistic competition, this form of market structure tends to be most pronounced for the exchange of factor services.

This market structure is the somewhat obscure and less noted buying counterpart of monopolistic competition. However, monopsonistic competition tends to be just as prevalent in the real world. In fact, firms operating as monopolistic competition in an output market often operate as monopsonistic competition in an input market.

In much the same way the monopolistic competition is a cross between perfect competition and monopoly, monopsonistic competition is a cross between perfect competition and monopsony. While each monopsonistically competitive buyer has very little market control, it does have some market control, each has its own little monopsony, each faces an input supply curve that is relatively elastic but not perfectly elastic.

Characteristics

The four characteristics of monopsonistic competition are much like those of monopolistic competition: (1) large number of small buyers, (2) similar, but not identical products, (3) relative, but not perfect resource mobility, and (4) extensive, but not perfect knowledge.

1. Large Number of Small Buyers: A monopsonistically competitive market contains a large number of small buyers, each of which is relatively small compared to the overall size of the market. This ensures that all buyers are relatively competitive with very little market control over price or quantity. In particular, each firm has hundreds or even thousands of potential competitors.
2. Similar Products: Each firm in a monopsonistically competitive market buys a similar, but not absolutely identical, product. The goods purchased by each of the buyers are close substitutes for one another, just not perfect substitutes. Most important, each good provides the same basic function, especially as productive inputs. The goods might have subtle but actual physical differences or they might only be perceived different by the buyers. Whatever the reason, buyers treat the goods as similar, but different.
3. Relative Resource Mobility: Monopsonistically competitive buyers are relatively free to enter and exit a market. There might be a few restrictions, but not many. These buyers are not "perfectly" mobile as with perfect competition, but they are relatively unrestricted by government rules and regulations, start-up cost, or other substantial barriers to entry.
4. Extensive Knowledge: In monopsonistic competition, buyers do not know everything, but that have relatively complete information about alternative prices. They also have relatively complete information about product or factor differences.

Real World (In)Efficiency

A monopsonistically competitive buyer generally purchases less output and pays a lower price than would be the case for perfect competition. In particular, the price paid by a monopsonistically competitive buyer is less than the marginal revenue product.

The inequality of price and marginal revenue product violates the key condition for efficiency. Resources are NOT being used to generate the highest possible level of satisfaction.

The reason for this inefficiency is found with market control. Because a monopsonistically competitive firm has control over a small slice of the market, it faces a positively-sloped supply curve and price is greater than marginal factor cost, which is set equal to marginal revenue product when maximizing profit.

While monopsonistic competition is technically inefficient, it tends to be less inefficient than other market structures on the buying side, especially monopsony. Even though price is less than marginal factor cost (and thus marginal revenue product), because the supply curve is relatively elastic, the difference is often relatively small.

For example, a monopsony that pays a $20 price while facing a marginal revenue product of $100 creates a serious inefficiency problem. In contrast, the inefficiency created by a monopsonistically competitive buyer that pays a $49.95 price while generating a marginal revenue product of $50 is substantially less.

The closer marginal factor cost is to factor price, the closer a monopsonistically competitive firm comes to allocating resources according to the efficiency benchmark established by perfect competition.

Monopsony Efficiency

Like any firm with market control, monopsony does not efficiently allocate resources. It violates the standard factor market efficiency criterion that factor price equal marginal revenue product. At the profit-maximizing quantity purchased by a monopsony, factor price is less than marginal revenue product.

The reason for monopsony inefficiency is found with market control. Because the monopsony firm is the market, the market supply curve is the supply curve for the monopsony's purchases. Because the supply curve is positively sloped, factor price is less than marginal factor cost. And because a profit maximizing firm equates marginal revenue product with marginal factor cost, the factor price paid by monopsony when it maximizes profit is less than marginal revenue product.

Profit Maximization

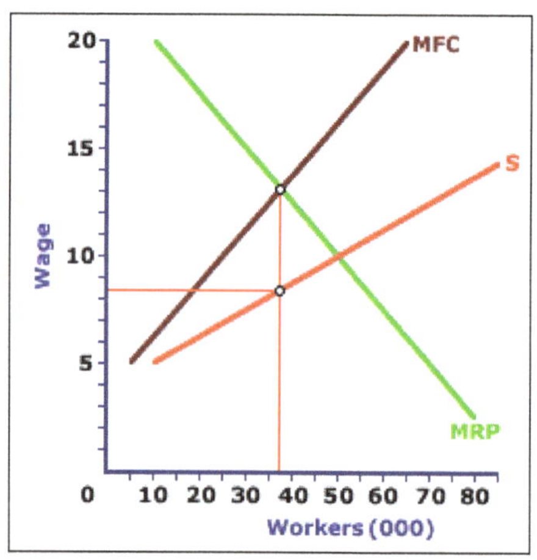

To illustrate the inefficiency of monopsony consider the Natural Ned Lumber Company, a hypothetical lumbering operation in the isolated Jagged Mountains region north of the greater Shady Valley metropolitan area. The Natural Ned Lumber Company is the only employer of labor located in nearby Lumber Town. This makes the Natural Ned Lumber Company a monopsony employer and a price maker when it comes to buying labor services from Lumber Town.

A typical profit-maximizing input hiring decision using the marginal revenue product and marginal factor cost is presented in this diagram. The three curves presented are the marginal revenue product curve (MRP), the market supply curve (S), and the corresponding marginal factor cost curve (MFC) for the monopsony.

A profit-maximizing monopsony produces the quantity of output that equates marginal revenue product with marginal factor cost, then pays the price sellers are willing and able to accept for that quantity. Natural Ned maximizes profit by hiring the number of workers that equates marginal revenue product and marginal factor cost, which is 37,000 workers in this example. The corresponding price paid is $8.40.

This profit-maximizing level of employment is not efficient. In particular, the factor price is $8.40, but the marginal revenue product is $13. Society is using labor to produce and consume a good that it values at $13 (marginal revenue product). However, in so doing, society is using resources that could have produced other goods valued at $8.40 (marginal factor cost). Society gives up $8.40 worth of value and receives $13.

This is a good thing. It is so good, that society should do more. However, the monopsony is not letting this happen. Natural Ned is not hiring as many labor resources that can be devoted to production as society would like.

Monopoly

A monopoly exists when a specific person or enterprise is the only supplier of a particular commodity. This contrasts with a monopsony which relates to a single entity's control of a market to purchase a good or service, and with oligopoly which consists of a few sellers dominating a market. Monopolies are thus characterized by a lack of economic competition to produce the good or service, a lack of viable substitute goods, and the possibility of a high monopoly price well above the seller's marginal cost that leads to a high monopoly profit. The verb monopolise or monopolize refers to the *process* by which a company gains the ability to raise prices or exclude competitors. In economics, a monopoly is a single seller. In law, a monopoly is a business entity that has significant market power, that is, the power to charge overly high prices. Although monopolies may be big businesses, size is not a characteristic of a monopoly. A small business may still have the power to raise prices in a small industry (or market).

A monopoly is distinguished from a monopsony, in which there is only one *buyer* of a product or service; a monopoly may also have monopsony control of a sector of a market. Likewise, a monopoly should be distinguished from a cartel (a form of oligopoly), in which several providers act together to coordinate services, prices or sale of goods. Monopolies, monopsonies and oligopolies are all situations in which one or a few entities have market power and therefore interact with their customers (monopoly or oligopoly), or suppliers (monopsony) in ways that distort the market.

Monopolies can be established by a government, form naturally, or form by integration. In many jurisdictions, competition laws restrict monopolies. Holding a dominant position or a monopoly in a market is often not illegal in itself, however certain categories of behavior can be considered abusive and therefore incur legal sanctions when business is dominant. A government-granted monopoly or legal monopoly, by contrast, is sanctioned by the state, often to provide an incentive to invest in a risky venture or enrich a domestic interest group. Patents, copyrights, and trademarks are sometimes used as examples of government-granted monopolies. The government may also reserve the venture for itself, thus forming a government monopoly.

Monopolies may be naturally occurring due to limited competition because the industry is resource intensive and requires substantial costs to operate.

Market Structures

In economics, the idea of monopoly is important in the study of management structures, which directly concerns normative aspects of economic competition, and provides the basis for topics such as industrial organization and economics of regulation. There are four basic types of market structures in traditional economic analysis: perfect competition, monopolistic competition, oligopoly and monopoly. A monopoly is a structure in which a single supplier produces and sells a given product. If there is a single seller in a certain market and there are no close substitutes for the product, then the market structure is that of a "pure monopoly". Sometimes, there are many sellers in an industry and/or there exist many close substitutes for the goods being produced, but nevertheless companies retain some market power. This is termed monopolistic competition, whereas in oligopoly the companies interact strategically.

In general, the main results from this theory compare price-fixing methods across market structures, analyze the effect of a certain structure on welfare, and vary technological/demand assumptions in order to assess the consequences for an abstract model of society. Most economic textbooks follow the practice of carefully explaining the perfect competition model, mainly because this helps to understand "departures" from it (the so-called imperfect competition models).

The boundaries of what constitutes a market and what does not are relevant distinctions to make in economic analysis. In a general equilibrium context, a good is a specific concept including geographical and time-related characteristics ("grapes sold during October 2009 in Moscow" is a different good from "grapes sold during October 2009 in New York"). Most studies of market structure relax a little their definition of a good, allowing for more flexibility in the identification of substitute goods.

Characteristics

1. Profit Maximizer: Maximizes profits.
2. Price Maker: Decides the price of the good or product to be sold, but does so by determining the quantity in order to demand the price desired by the firm.
3. High Barriers: Other sellers are unable to enter the market of the monopoly.
4. Single seller: In a monopoly, there is one seller of the good, who produces all the output. Therefore, the whole market is being served by a single company, and for practical purposes, the company is the same as the industry.
5. Price Discrimination: A monopolist can change the price or quantity of the product. He or she sells higher quantities at a lower price in a very elastic market, and sells lower quantities at a higher price in a less elastic market.

Sources of Monopoly Power

Monopolies derive their market power from barriers to entry – circumstances that prevent or greatly impede a potential competitor's ability to compete in a market. There are three major types of barriers to entry: economic, legal and deliberate.

1. Economic barriers: Economic barriers include economies of scale, capital requirements, cost advantages and technological superiority.

2. Economies of scale: Decreasing unit costs for larger volumes of production. Decreasing costs coupled with large initial costs, If for example the industry is large enough to support one company of minimum efficient scale then other companies entering the industry will operate at a size that is less than MES, and so cannot produce at an average cost that is competitive with the dominant company. Finally, if long-term average cost is constantly decreasing, the least cost method to provide a good or service is by a single company.

3. Capital requirements: Production processes that require large investments of capital, perhaps in the form of large research and development costs or substantial sunk costs, limit the number of companies in an industry: this is an example of economies of scale.

4. Technological superiority: A monopoly may be better able to acquire, integrate and use the best possible technology in producing its goods while entrants either do not have the expertise or are unable to meet the large fixed costs needed for the most efficient technology. Thus one large company can often produce goods cheaper than several small companies.

5. No substitute goods: A monopoly sells a good for which there is no close substitute. The absence of substitutes makes the demand for that good relatively inelastic, enabling monopolies to extract positive profits.

6. Control of natural resources: A prime source of monopoly power is the control of resources (such as raw materials) that are critical to the production of a final good.

7. Network externalities: The use of a product by a person can affect the value of that product to other people. This is the network effect. There is a direct relationship between the proportion of people using a product and the demand for that product. In other words, the more people who are using a product, the greater the probability that another individual will start to use the product. This reflects fads, fashion trends, social networks etc. It also can play a crucial role in the development or acquisition of market power. The most famous current example is the market dominance of the Microsoft office suite and operating system in personal computers.

8. Legal barriers: Legal rights can provide opportunity to monopolise the market in a good. Intellectual property rights, including patents and copyrights, give a monopolist exclusive control of the production and selling of certain goods. Property rights may give a company exclusive control of the materials necessary to produce a good.

9. Advertising- Advertising is most important to sell the product because of the single user they have to do it their own.

10. Manipulation: A company wanting to monopolise a market may engage in various types of deliberate action to exclude competitors or eliminate competition. Such actions include collusion, lobbying governmental authorities, and force.

In addition to barriers to entry and competition, barriers to exit may be a source of market power. Barriers to exit are market conditions that make it difficult or expensive for a company to end its involvement with a market. High liquidation costs are a primary barrier to exiting. Market exit and shutdown are sometimes separate events. The decision whether to shut down or operate is not affected by exit barriers. A company will shut down if price falls below minimum average variable costs.

Monopoly versus Competitive Markets

While monopoly and perfect competition mark the extremes of market structures there is some similarity. The cost functions are the same. Both monopolies and perfectly competitive (PC) companies minimize cost and maximize profit. The shutdown decisions are the same. Both are assumed to have perfectly competitive factors markets. There are distinctions, some of the most important distinctions are as follows:

1. Marginal revenue and price: In a perfectly competitive market, price equals marginal cost. In a monopolistic market, however, price is set above marginal cost.
2. Product differentiation: There is zero product differentiation in a perfectly competitive market. Every product is perfectly homogeneous and a perfect substitute for any other. With a monopoly, there is great to absolute product differentiation in the sense that there is no available substitute for a monopolized good. The monopolist is the sole supplier of the good in question. A customer either buys from the monopolizing entity on its terms or does without.
3. Number of competitors: PC markets are populated by an infinite number of buyers and sellers. Monopoly involves a single seller.
4. Barriers to Entry: Barriers to entry are factors and circumstances that prevent entry into market by would-be competitors and limit new companies from operating and expanding within the market. PC markets have free entry and exit. There are no barriers to entry, or exit competition. Monopolies have relatively high barriers to entry. The barriers must be strong enough to prevent or discourage any potential competitor from entering the market.
5. Elasticity of Demand: The price elasticity of demand is the percentage change of demand caused by a one percent change of relative price. A successful monopoly would have a relatively inelastic demand curve. A low coefficient of elasticity is indicative of effective barriers to entry. A PC company has a perfectly elastic demand curve. The coefficient of elasticity for a perfectly competitive demand curve is infinite.
6. Excess Profits: Excess or positive profits are profit more than the normal expected return on investment. A PC company can make excess profits in the short term but excess profits attract competitors, which can enter the market freely and decrease prices, eventually reducing excess profits to zero. A monopoly can preserve excess profits because barriers to entry prevent competitors from entering the market.
7. Profit Maximization: A PC company maximizes profits by producing such that price equals marginal costs. A monopoly maximises profits by producing where marginal revenue equals marginal costs. The rules are not equivalent. The demand curve for a PC company is perfectly

elastic – flat. The demand curve is identical to the average revenue curve and the price line. Since the average revenue curve is constant the marginal revenue curve is also constant and equals the demand curve, Average revenue is the same as price (AR = TR/Q = P x Q/Q = P). Thus the price line is also identical to the demand curve. In sum, D = AR = MR = P.

8. P-Max quantity, price and profit: If a monopolist obtains control of a formerly perfectly competitive industry, the monopolist would increase prices, reduce production, and realise positive economic profits.

9. Supply Curve: In a perfectly competitive market there is a well defined supply function with a one-to-one relationship between price and quantity supplied. In a monopolistic market no such supply relationship exists. A monopolist cannot trace a short term supply curve because for a given price there is not a unique quantity supplied. A change in demand "can lead to changes in prices with no change in output, changes in output with no change in price or both". Monopolies produce where marginal revenue equals marginal costs. For a specific demand curve the supply curve would be the price/quantity combination at the point where marginal revenue equals marginal cost. If the demand curve shifted the marginal revenue curve would shift as well and a new equilibrium and supply point would be established. The locus of these points would not be a supply curve in any conventional sense.

The most significant distinction between a PC company and a monopoly is that the monopoly has a downward-sloping demand curve rather than the "perceived" perfectly elastic curve of the PC company. Practically all the variations mentioned above relate to this fact. If there is a downward-sloping demand curve then by necessity there is a distinct marginal revenue curve. The implications of this fact are best made manifest with a linear demand curve. Assume that the inverse demand curve is of the form x = a – by. Then the total revenue curve is TR = ay – by2 and the marginal revenue curve is thus MR = a – 2by. From this several things are evident. First the marginal revenue curve has the same y intercept as the inverse demand curve. Second the slope of the marginal revenue curve is twice that of the inverse demand curve. Third the x intercept of the marginal revenue curve is half that of the inverse demand curve. What is not quite so evident is that the marginal revenue curve is below the inverse demand curve at all points. Since all companies maximise profits by equating MR and MC it must be the case that at the profit-maximizing quantity MR and MC are less than price, which further implies that a monopoly produces less quantity at a higher price than if the market were perfectly competitive.

The fact that a monopoly has a downward-sloping demand curve means that the relationship between total revenue and output for a monopoly is much different than that of competitive companies. Total revenue equals price times quantity. A competitive company has a perfectly elastic demand curve meaning that total revenue is proportional to output. Thus the total revenue curve for a competitive company is a ray with a slope equal to the market price. A competitive company can sell all the output it desires at the market price. For a monopoly to increase sales it must reduce price. Thus the total revenue curve for a monopoly is a parabola that begins at the origin and reaches a maximum value then continuously decreases until total revenue is again zero. Total revenue has its maximum value when the slope of the total revenue function is zero. The slope of the total revenue function is marginal revenue. So the revenue maximizing quantity and price occur when MR = 0. For example, assume that the monopoly's demand function is P = 50 – 2Q. The total revenue function would be TR = 50Q – 2Q² and marginal revenue would be 50 – 4Q. Setting marginal revenue equal to zero we have:

$$50-4Q=0$$

$$-4Q=-50$$

$$Q=12.5$$

So the revenue maximizing quantity for the monopoly is 12.5 units and the revenue maximizing price is 25.

A company with a monopoly does not experience price pressure from competitors, although it may experience pricing pressure from potential competition. If a company increases prices too much, then others may enter the market if they are able to provide the same good, or a substitute, at a lesser price. The idea that monopolies in markets with easy entry need not be regulated against is known as the "revolution in monopoly theory".

A monopolist can extract only one premium, and getting into complementary markets does not pay. That is, the total profits a monopolist could earn if it sought to leverage its monopoly in one market by monopolizing a complementary market are equal to the extra profits it could earn anyway by charging more for the monopoly product itself. However, the one monopoly profit theorem is not true if customers in the monopoly good are stranded or poorly informed, or if the tied good has high fixed costs.

A pure monopoly has the same economic rationality of perfectly competitive companies, i.e. to optimise a profit function given some constraints. By the assumptions of increasing marginal costs, exogenous inputs' prices, and control concentrated on a single agent or entrepreneur, the optimal decision is to equate the marginal cost and marginal revenue of production. Nonetheless, a pure monopoly can – unlike a competitive company – alter the market price for its own convenience: a decrease of production results in a higher price. In the economics' jargon, it is said that pure monopolies have "a downward-sloping demand". An important consequence of such behaviour is worth noticing: typically a monopoly selects a higher price and lesser quantity of output than a price-taking company; again, less is available at a higher price.

Inverse Elasticity Rule

A monopoly chooses that price that maximizes the difference between total revenue and total cost. The basic markup rule (as measured by the Lerner index) can be expressed as $\frac{P-MC}{P}=\frac{-1}{E_d}$, where E_d is the price elasticity of demand the firm faces. The markup rules indicate that the ratio between profit margin and the price is inversely proportional to the price elasticity of demand. The implication of the rule is that the more elastic the demand for the product the less pricing power the monopoly has.

Market Power

Market power is the ability to increase the product's price above marginal cost without losing all customers. Perfectly competitive (PC) companies have zero market power when it comes to setting prices. All companies of a PC market are price takers. The price is set by the interaction of demand and supply at the market or aggregate level. Individual companies simply take the price determined by the market and produce that quantity of output that maximizes the company's profits. If a PC company attempted to increase prices above the market level all its customers would abandon the company and purchase at the market price from other companies. A monopoly has considerable although not unlimited market power. A monopoly has the power to set prices or quantities although not both. A monopoly is a price maker. The monopoly is the market and prices are set by the monopolist based on their circumstances and not the interaction of demand and supply. The two primary factors determining monopoly market power are the company's demand curve and its cost structure.

Market power is the ability to affect the terms and conditions of exchange so that the price of a product is set by a single company (price is not imposed by the market as in perfect competition). Although a monopoly's market power is great it is still limited by the demand side of the market. A monopoly has a negatively sloped demand curve, not a perfectly inelastic curve. Consequently, any price increase will result in the loss of some customers.

Price Discrimination

Price discrimination allows a monopolist to increase its profit by charging higher prices for identical goods to those who are willing or able to pay more. For example, most economic textbooks cost more in the United States than in developing countries like Ethiopia. In this case, the publisher is using its government-granted copyright monopoly to price discriminate between the generally wealthier American economics students and the generally poorer Ethiopian economics students. Similarly, most patented medications cost more in the U.S. than in other countries with a (presumed) poorer customer base. Typically, a high general price is listed, and various market segments get varying discounts. This is an example of framing to make the process of charging some people higher prices more socially acceptable. Perfect price discrimination would allow the monopolist to charge each customer the exact maximum amount he would be willing to pay. This would allow the monopolist to extract all the consumer surplus of the market. While such perfect price discrimination is a theoretical construct, advances in information technology and micromarketing may bring it closer to the realm of possibility.

It is very important to realize that partial price discrimination can cause some customers who are inappropriately pooled with high price customers to be excluded from the market. For example, a poor student in the U.S. might be excluded from purchasing an economics textbook at the U.S. price, which the student may have been able to purchase at the Ethiopian price'. Similarly, a wealthy student in Ethiopia may be able to or willing to buy at the U.S. price, though naturally would hide such a fact from the monopolist so as to pay the reduced third world price. These are deadweight losses and decrease a monopolist's profits. As such, monopolists have substantial economic interest in improving their market information and market segmenting.

There is important information for one to remember when considering the monopoly model diagram displayed here. The result that monopoly prices are higher, and production output lesser, than a competitive company follow from a requirement that the monopoly not charge different prices for different customers. That is, the monopoly is restricted from engaging in price discrimination (this is termed first degree price discrimination, such that all customers are charged the same amount). If the monopoly were permitted to charge individualised prices (this is termed third degree price discrimination), the quantity produced, and the price charged to the marginal customer, would be identical to that of a competitive company, thus eliminating the deadweight loss; however, all gains from trade (social welfare) would accrue to the monopolist and none to the consumer. In essence, every consumer would be indifferent between going completely without the product or service and being able to purchase it from the monopolist.

As long as the price elasticity of demand for most customers is less than one in absolute value, it is advantageous for a company to increase its prices: it receives more money for fewer goods. With a price increase, price elasticity tends to increase, and in the optimum case above it will be greater than one for most customers.

A company maximizes profit by selling where marginal revenue equals marginal cost. A company that does not engage in price discrimination will charge the profit maximizing price, P*, to all its customers. In such circumstances there are customers who would be willing to pay a higher price than P* and those who will not pay P* but would buy at a lower price. A price discrimination strategy is to charge less price sensitive buyers a higher price and the more price sensitive buyers a lower price. Thus additional revenue is generated from two sources. The basic problem is to identify customers by their willingness to pay.

The purpose of price discrimination is to transfer consumer surplus to the producer. Consumer surplus is the difference between the value of a good to a consumer and the price the consumer must pay in the market to purchase it. Price discrimination is not limited to monopolies.

Market power is a company's ability to increase prices without losing all its customers. Any company that has market power can engage in price discrimination. Perfect competition is the only market form in which price discrimination would be impossible (a perfectly competitive company has a perfectly elastic demand curve and has zero market power).

There are three forms of price discrimination. First degree price discrimination charges each consumer the maximum price the consumer is willing to pay. Second degree price discrimination involves quantity discounts. Third degree price discrimination involves grouping consumers according to willingness to pay as measured by their price elasticities of demand and charging each group a different price. Third degree price discrimination is the most prevalent type.

There are three conditions that must be present for a company to engage in successful price discrimination. First, the company must have market power. Second, the company must be able to sort customers according to their willingness to pay for the good. Third, the firm must be able to prevent resell.

A company must have some degree of market power to practice price discrimination. Without market power a company cannot charge more than the market price. Any market structure characterized by a downward sloping demand curve has market power – monopoly, monopolistic competition and oligopoly. The only market structure that has no market power is perfect competition.

A company wishing to practice price discrimination must be able to prevent middlemen or brokers from acquiring the consumer surplus for themselves. The company accomplishes this by preventing or limiting resale. Many methods are used to prevent resale. For instance, persons are required to show photographic identification and a boarding pass before boarding an airplane. Most travelers assume that this practice is strictly a matter of security. However, a primary purpose in requesting photographic identification is to confirm that the ticket purchaser is the person about to board the airplane and not someone who has repurchased the ticket from a discount buyer.

The inability to prevent resale is the largest obstacle to successful price discrimination. Companies have however developed numerous methods to prevent resale. For example, universities require that students show identification before entering sporting events. Governments may make it illegal to resale tickets or products. In Boston, Red Sox baseball tickets can only be resold legally to the team.

The three basic forms of price discrimination are first, second and third degree price discrimination. In first degree price discrimination the company charges the maximum price each customer is willing to pay. The maximum price a consumer is willing to pay for a unit of the good is the reservation price. Thus for each unit the seller tries to set the price equal to the consumer's reservation price. Direct information about a consumer's willingness to pay is rarely available. Sellers tend to rely on secondary information such as where a person lives (postal codes); for example, catalog retailers can use mail high-priced catalogs to high-income postal codes. First degree price discrimination most frequently occurs in regard to professional services or in transactions involving direct buyer/seller negotiations. For example, an accountant who has prepared a consumer's tax return has information that can be used to charge customers based on an estimate of their ability to pay.

In second degree price discrimination or quantity discrimination customers are charged different prices based on how much they buy. There is a single price schedule for all consumers but the prices vary depending on the quantity of the good bought. The theory of second degree price discrimination is a consumer is willing to buy only a certain quantity of a good at a given price. Companies know that consumer's willingness to buy decreases as more units are purchased. The task for the seller is to identify these price points and to reduce the price once one is reached in the hope that a reduced price will trigger additional purchases from the consumer. For example, sell in unit blocks rather than individual units.

In third degree price discrimination or multi-market price discrimination the seller divides the consumers into different groups according to their willingness to pay as measured by their price elasticity of demand. Each group of consumers effectively becomes a separate market with its own demand curve and marginal revenue curve. The firm then attempts to maximize profits in each segment by equating MR and MC, Generally the company charges a higher price to the group with a more price inelastic demand and a relatively lesser price to the group with a more elastic demand. Examples of third degree price discrimination abound. Airlines charge higher prices to business travelers than to vacation travelers. The reasoning is that the demand curve for a vacation traveler is relatively elastic while the demand curve for a business traveler is relatively inelastic. Any determinant of price elasticity of demand can be used to segment markets. For example, seniors have a more elastic demand for movies than do young adults because they generally have more free time. Thus theaters will offer discount tickets to seniors.

Example:

Assume that by a uniform pricing system the monopolist would sell five units at a price of $10 per unit. Assume that his marginal cost is $5 per unit. Total revenue would be $50, total costs would be $25 and profits would be $25. If the monopolist practiced price discrimination he would sell the first unit for $50 the second unit for $40 and so on. Total revenue would be $150, his total cost would be $25 and his profit would be $125.00. Several things are worth noting. The monopolist acquires all the consumer surplus and eliminates practically all the deadweight loss because he is willing to sell to anyone who is willing to pay at least the marginal cost. Thus the price discrimination promotes efficiency. Secondly, by the pricing scheme price = average revenue and equals marginal revenue. That is the monopolist behaving like a perfectly competitive company. Thirdly, the discriminating monopolist produces a larger quantity than the monopolist operating by a uniform pricing scheme.

Qd	Price
1	50
2	40
3	30
4	20
5	10

Classifying Customers

Successful price discrimination requires that companies separate consumers according to their willingness to buy. Determining a customer's willingness to buy a good is difficult. Asking consumers directly is fruitless: consumers don't know, and to the extent they do they are reluctant to share that information with marketers. The two main methods for determining willingness to buy are observation of personal characteristics and consumer actions. As noted information about where a person lives (postal codes), how the person dresses, what kind of car he or she drives, occupation, and income and spending patterns can be helpful in classifying.

Monopoly and Efficiency

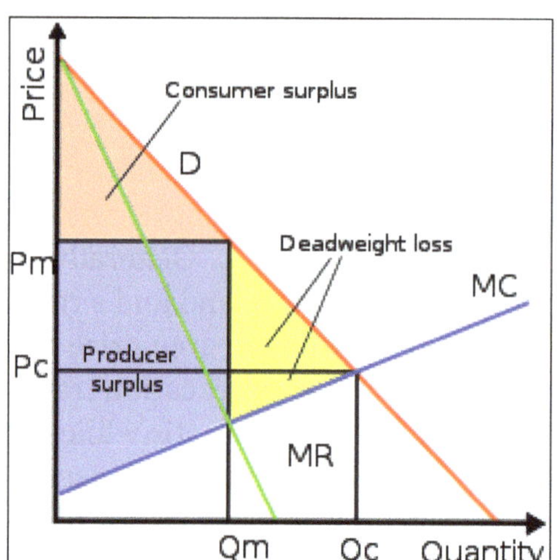

Surpluses and deadweight loss created by monopoly price setting.

Monopoly, besides, is a great enemy to good management. According to the standard model, in which a monopolist sets a single price for all consumers, the monopolist will sell a lesser quantity of goods at a higher price than would companies by perfect competition. Because the monopolist ultimately forgoes transactions with consumers who value the product or service more than its price, monopoly pricing creates a deadweight loss referring to potential gains that went neither to the monopolist nor to consumers. Given the presence of this deadweight loss, the combined surplus (or wealth) for the monopolist and consumers is necessarily less than the total surplus obtained by consumers by perfect competition. Where efficiency is defined by the total gains from trade, the monopoly setting is less efficient than perfect competition.

It is often argued that monopolies tend to become less efficient and less innovative over time, becoming "complacent", because they do not have to be efficient or innovative to compete in the marketplace. Sometimes this very loss of psychological efficiency can increase a potential competitor's value enough to overcome market entry barriers, or provide incentive for research and investment into new alternatives. The theory of contestable markets argues that in some circumstances (private) monopolies are forced to behave as if there were competition because of the risk of losing their monopoly to new entrants. This is likely to happen when a market's barriers to entry are low. It might also be because of the availability in the longer term of substitutes in other markets. For example, a canal monopoly, while worth a great deal during the late 18th century United Kingdom, was worth much less during the late 19th century because of the introduction of railways as a substitute.

Contrary to common misconception, monopolists do not try to sell items for the highest possible price, nor do they try to maximize profit per unit, but rather they try to maximize total profit.

Natural Monopoly

A natural monopoly is an organization that experiences increasing returns to scale over the relevant range of output and relatively high fixed costs. A natural monopoly occurs where the average cost of production "declines throughout the relevant range of product demand". The relevant range of product demand is where the average cost curve is below the demand curve. When this situation occurs, it is always cheaper for one large company to supply the market than multiple smaller companies; in fact, absent government intervention in such markets, will naturally evolve into a monopoly. An early market entrant that takes advantage of the cost structure and can expand rapidly can exclude smaller companies from entering and can drive or buy out other companies. A natural monopoly suffers from the same inefficiencies as any other monopoly. Left to its own devices, a profit-seeking natural monopoly will produce where marginal revenue equals marginal costs. Regulation of natural monopolies is problematic. Fragmenting such monopolies is by definition inefficient. The most frequently used methods dealing with natural monopolies are government regulations and public ownership. Government regulation generally consists of regulatory commissions charged with the principal duty of setting prices.

To reduce prices and increase output, regulators often use average cost pricing. By average cost pricing, the price and quantity are determined by the intersection of the average cost curve and the demand curve. This pricing scheme eliminates any positive economic profits since price equals average cost. Average-cost pricing is not perfect. Regulators must estimate average costs. Companies have a reduced incentive to lower costs. Regulation of this type has not been limited to natural monopolies. Average-cost pricing does also have some disadvantages. By setting price equal to the intersection of the demand curve and the average total cost curve, the firm's output is allocatively inefficient as the price is less than the marginal cost (which is the output quantity for a perfectly competitive and allocatively efficient market).

Government-granted Monopoly

A government-granted monopoly is a form of coercive monopoly, in which a government grants exclusive privilege to a private individual or company to be the sole provider of a commodity. Monopoly may be granted explicitly, as when potential competitors are excluded from the market by a specific law, or implicitly, such as when the requirements of an administrative regulation can only be fulfilled by a single market player, or through some other legal or procedural mechanism, such as patents, trademarks, and copyright.

Monopolist Shutdown Rule

A monopolist should shut down when price is less than average variable cost for every output level – in other words where the demand curve is entirely below the average variable cost curve. Under these circumstances at the profit maximum level of output (MR = MC) average revenue would be less than average variable costs and the monopolists would be better off shutting down in the short term.

Breaking up Monopolies

In a free market, monopolies can be ended at any time by new competition, breakaway businesses, or consumers seeking alternatives. In a highly regulated market environment a government will often either regulate the monopoly, convert it into a publicly owned monopoly environment, or forcibly fragment it. Public utilities, often being naturally efficient with only one operator and therefore less susceptible to efficient breakup, are often strongly regulated or publicly owned. American Telephone & Telegraph (AT&T) and Standard Oil are often cited as examples of the breakup of a private monopoly by government. Standard Oil never achieved monopoly status, a consequence of existing in a market open to competition for the duration of its existence. The Bell System, later AT&T, was protected from competition first by the Kingsbury Commitment, and later by a series of agreements between AT&T and the Federal Government. In 1984, decades after having been granted monopoly power by force of law, AT&T was broken up into various components, MCI, Sprint, who were able to compete effectively in the long distance phone market.

Law

The law regulating dominance in the European Union is governed by Article 102 of the Treaty on the Functioning of the European Union which aims at enhancing the consumer's welfare and also the efficiency of allocation of resources by protecting competition on the downstream market. The existence of a very high market share does not always mean consumers are paying excessive prices since the threat of new entrants to the market can restrain a high-market-share company's price increases. Competition law does not make merely having a monopoly illegal, but rather abusing the power a monopoly may confer, for instance through exclusionary practices (i.e. pricing high just because you are the only one around). It may also be noted that it is illegal to try to obtain a monopoly, by practices of buying out the competition, or equal practices. If one occurs naturally, such as a competitor going out of business, or lack of competition, it is not illegal until such time as the monopoly holder abuses the power.

Establishing Dominance

First it is necessary to determine whether a company is dominant, or whether it behaves "to an appreciable extent independently of its competitors, customers and ultimately of its consumer". Establishing dominance is a two-stage test. The first thing to consider is market definition which is one of the crucial factors of the test. It includes relevant product market and relevant geographic market.

Relevant Product Market

As the definition of the market is of a matter of interchangeability, if the goods or services are regarded as interchangeable then they are within the same product market. For example, in the case of United Brands v Commission, it was argued in this case that bananas and other fresh fruit were in the same product market and later on dominance was found because the special features of the banana made it could only be interchangeable with other fresh fruits in a limited extent and other and is only exposed to their competition in a way that is hardly perceptible. The demand substitutability of the goods and services will help in defining the product market and it can be access by the 'hypothetical monopolist' test or the 'SSNIP' test.

Relevant Geographic Market

It is necessary to define it because some goods can only be supplied within a narrow area due to technical, practical or legal reasons and this may help to indicate which undertakings impose a competitive constraint on the other undertakings in question. Since some goods are too expensive to transport where it might not be economic to sell them to distant markets in relation to their value, therefore the cost of transporting is a crucial factor here. Other factors might be legal controls which restricts an undertaking in a Member States from exporting goods or services to another.

Market definition may be difficult to measure but is important because if it is defined too broadly, the undertaking may be more likely to be found dominant and if it is defined too narrowly, the less likely that it will be found dominant.

Market Shares

As with collusive conduct, market shares are determined with reference to the particular market in which the company and product in question is sold. It does not in itself determine whether an undertaking is dominant but work as an indicator of the states of the existing competition within the market. The Herfindahl-Hirschman Index (HHI) is sometimes used to assess how competitive an industry is. It sums up the squares of the individual market shares of all of the competitors within the market. The lower the total, the less concentrated the market and the higher the total, the more concentrated the market. In the US, the merger guidelines state that a post-merger HHI below 1000 is viewed as not concentrated while HHIs above that will provoke further review.

By European Union law, very large market shares raise a presumption that a company is dominant, which may be rebuttable. A market share of 100% may be very rare but it is still possible to be found and in fact it has been identified in some cases, for instance the AAMS v Commission case. Undertakings possessing market share that is lower than 100% but over 90% had also been found dominant, for example, Microsoft v Commission case. In the AKZO v Commission case, the undertaking is presumed to be dominant if it has a market share of 50%. There are also findings of dominance that are below a market share of 50%, for instance, United Brands v Commission, it only possessed a market share of 40% to 45% and still to be found dominant with other factors. The lowest yet market share of a company considered "dominant" in the EU was 39.7%. If a company has a dominant position, then there is a special responsibility not to allow its conduct to impair competition on the common market however these will all falls away if it is not dominant.

When considering whether an undertaking is dominant, it involves a combination of factors. Each of them cannot be taken separately as if they are, they will not be as determinative as they are when they are combined together. Also, in cases where an undertaking has previously been found dominant, it is still necessary to redefine the market and make a whole new analysis of the conditions of competition based on the available evidence at the appropriate time.

Other Related Factors

According to the Guidance, there are three more issues that must be examined. They are actual competitors that relates to the market position of the dominant undertaking and its competitors, potential competitors that concerns the expansion and entry and lastly the countervailing buyer power.

1. Actual Competitors

   Market share may be a valuable source of information regarding the market structure and the market position when it comes to accessing it. The dynamics of the market and the extent to which the goods and services differentiated are relevant in this area.

2. Potential Competitors

   It concerns with the competition that would come from other undertakings which are not yet operating in the market but will enter it in the future. So, market shares may not be useful in accessing the competitive pressure that is exerted on an undertaking in this area. The potential entry by new firms and expansions by an undertaking must be taken into account, therefore the barriers to entry and barriers to expansion is an important factor here.

3. Countervailing Buyer Power

Competitive Constraints may not always come from actual or potential competitors. Sometimes, it may also come from powerful customers who have sufficient bargaining strength which come from its size or its commercial significance for a dominant firm.

Types of Abuses

There are three main types of abuses which are exploitative abuse, exclusionary abuse and single market abuse.

1. Exploitative Abuse

   It arises when a monopolist has such significant market power that it can restrict its output while increasing the price above the competitive level without losing customers. This type is less concerned by the Commission than other types.

2. Exclusionary Abuse

   This is most concerned about by the Commissions because it is capable of causing long-term consumer damage and is more likely to prevent the development of competition. An example of it is exclusive dealing agreements.

3. Single Market Abuse

   It arises when a dominant undertaking carrying out excess pricing which would not only have an exploitative effect but also prevent parallel imports and limits intra- brand competition.

Examples of Abuses

1. Limiting supply
2. Predatory pricing or undercutting
3. Price discrimination
4. Refusal to deal and exclusive dealing
5. Tying (commerce) and product bundling

Despite wide agreement that the above constitute abusive practices, there is some debate about whether there needs to be a causal connection between the dominant position of a company and its actual abusive conduct. Furthermore, there has been some consideration of what happens when a company merely attempts to abuse its dominant position.

Countering Monopolies

According to professor Milton Friedman, laws against monopolies cause more harm than good, but unnecessary monopolies should be countered by removing tariffs and other regulation that upholds monopolies.

> “A monopoly can seldom be established within a country without overt and covert government assistance in the form of a tariff or some other device. It is close to impossible to do so on a

world scale. The De Beers diamond monopoly is the only one we know of that appears to have succeeded. In a world of free trade, international cartels would disappear even more quickly."

However, professor Steve H. Hanke believes that although private monopolies are more efficient than public ones, often by a factor of two, sometimes private natural monopolies, such as local water distribution, should be regulated (not prohibited) by, e.g., price auctions.

Thomas DiLorenzo asserts, however, that during the early days of utility companies where there was little regulation, there were no natural monopolies and there was competition. Only when companies realized that they could gain power through government did monopolies begin to form.

Baten, Bianchi and Moser find historical evidence that monopolies which are protected by patent laws may have adverse effects on the creation of innovation in an economy. They argue that under certain circumstances, compulsory licensing – which allows governments to license patents without the consent of patent-owners – may be effective in promoting invention by increasing the threat of competition in fields with low pre-existing levels of competition.

Natural Monopoly

A natural monopoly is a monopoly in an industry in which high infrastructural costs and other barriers to entry relative to the size of the market give the largest supplier in an industry, often the first supplier in a market, an overwhelming advantage over potential competitors. This frequently occurs in industries where capital costs predominate, creating economies of scale that are large in relation to the size of the market; examples include public utilities such as water services and electricity. Natural monopolies were recognized as potential sources of market failure early as the 19th century; John Stuart Mill advocated government regulation to make them serve the public good.

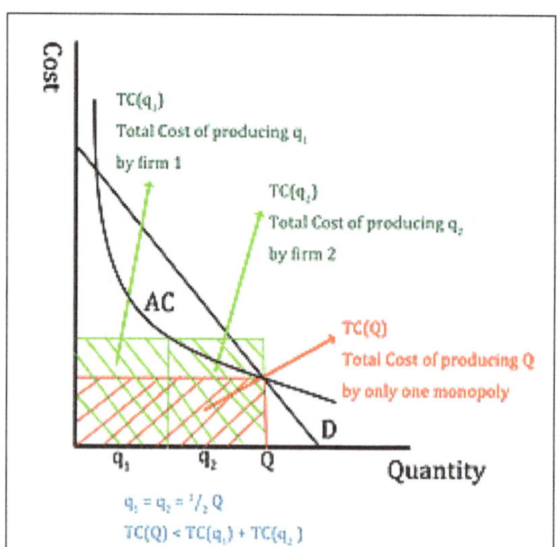

A graphical explanation of the inefficiencies of having several competitors in a naturally monopolistic market.

Two different types of cost are important in microeconomics: marginal cost, and fixed cost. The marginal cost is the cost to the company of serving one more customer. In an industry where a natural monopoly does not exist, the vast majority of industries, the marginal cost decreases with economies of scale, then increases as the company has growing pains (overworking its employees, bureaucracy, inefficiencies, etc.). Along with this, the average cost of its products decreases and increases. A natural monopoly has a very different cost structure. A natural monopoly has a high fixed cost for a product that does not depend on output, but its marginal cost of producing one more good is roughly constant, and small.

All industries have costs associated with entering them. Often, a large portion of these costs is required for investment. Larger industries, like utilities, require enormous initial investment. This barrier to entry reduces the number of possible entrants into the industry regardless of the earning of the corporations within. Natural monopolies arise where the largest supplier in an industry, often the first supplier in a market, has an overwhelming cost advantage over other actual or potential competitors; this tends to be the case in industries where fixed costs predominate, creating economies of scale that are large in relation to the size of the market, as is the case in water and electricity services. The fixed cost of constructing a competing transmission network is so high, and the marginal cost of transmission for the incumbent so low, that it effectively bars potential competitors from the monopolist's market, acting as a nearly insurmountable barrier to entry into the market place.

A firm with high fixed costs requires a large number of customers in order to have a meaningful return on investment. This is where economies of scale become important. Since each firm has large initial costs, as the firm gains market share and increases its output the fixed cost (what they initially invested) is divided among a larger number of customers. Therefore, in industries with large initial investment requirements, average total cost declines as output increases over a much larger range of output levels.

Companies that take advantage of economies of scale often run into problems of bureaucracy; these factors interact to produce an "ideal" size for a company, at which the company's average cost of production is minimized. If that ideal size is large enough to supply the whole market, then that market is a natural monopoly.

Once a natural monopoly has been established because of the large initial cost and that, according to the rule of economies of scale, the larger corporation (to a point) has lower average cost and therefore a huge advantage. With this knowledge, no firms attempt to enter the industry and an oligopoly or monopoly develops.

William Baumol provided the current formal definition of a natural monopoly where an industry in which multi-firm production is more costly than production by a monopoly. He linked the definition to the mathematical concept of subadditivity; specifically of the cost function. Baumol also noted that for a firm producing a single product, scale economies were a sufficient but not a necessary condition to prove subadditivity.

Government-granted Monopoly

In economics, a government-granted monopoly (also called a "de jure monopoly") and the monopoly to be served under government is a form of coercive monopoly by which a government grants exclusive privilege to a private individual or firm to be the sole provider of a good or service;

potential competitors are excluded from the market by law, regulation, or other mechanisms of government enforcement. As a form of coercive monopoly, government-granted monopoly is contrasted with a coercive monopoly or an efficiency monopoly, where there is no competition but it is not forcibly excluded.

Amongst forms of coercive monopoly it is distinguished from government monopoly or state monopoly (in which government agencies hold the legally enforced monopoly rather than private individuals or firms) and from government-sponsored cartels (in which the government forces several independent producers to partially coordinate their decisions through a centralized organization). Advocates for government-granted monopolies often claim that they ensure a degree of public control over essential industries, without having those industries actually run by the state. Opponents often criticize them as political favors to corporations. Government-granted monopolies may be opposed by those who would prefer free markets as well as by those who would prefer to replace private corporations with public ownership.

Patent

A patent is a set of exclusive rights granted by a state or national government to an inventor or his/her assignee for a limited period of time in exchange for a public disclosure of an invention.

The procedure for granting patents, the requirements placed on the patentee, and the extent of the exclusive rights vary widely between countries according to national laws and international agreements. Typically, however, a patent application must include one or more claims defining the invention which must be new, inventive, and useful or industrially applicable. In many countries, certain subject areas are excluded from patents, such as business methods and mental acts. The exclusive right granted to a patentee in most countries is the right to prevent others from making, using, selling, or distributing the patented invention without permission.

Copyright

Copyright is a legal right created by the law of a country that grants the creator of an original work exclusive rights for its use and distribution. This is usually only for a limited time. The exclusive rights are not absolute but limited by limitations and exceptions to copyright law, including fair use. A major limitation on copyright is that copyright protects only the original expression of ideas, and not the underlying ideas themselves.

Trademark

A trademark or trade mark is a distinctive sign or indicator used by an individual, business organization, or other legal entity to identify that the products or services to consumers with which the trademark appears originate from a unique source, and to distinguish its products or services from those of other entities.

Trademarks can act as a form of consumer protection that lowers the transaction costs between a buyer and seller who are not personally acquainted.

Directly Mandated

Governments have granted monopolies to forms of copy prevention. In the Digital Millennium Copyright Act, for example, the proprietary Macrovision copy prevention technology is required for analog video recorders. Though other forms of copy prevention aren't prohibited, requiring Macrovision effectively gives it a monopoly and prevents more effective copy prevention methods from being developed.

Role of Government

The theory of rent seeking - that is, artificially created socially harmful competition for scarcity due to scarcity - can be caused by monopolies, foreign trade restrictions and state subsidies. Governments can also create monopolies in order to reduce inefficiency of market as: scarcity of resources, reduced wealth-creation, lost government revenue, heightened income inequality, incomplete markets. The reason also can be simply as economies of scale, as well as the government can use its power to gather influence on the market by regulation.

Companies can also cause rent seeking: a company has a monopoly power – there is no other competitor on the market – then the company can limit the amount produced, so creating scarcity. Therefore it can raise the price in principle, so it can earn more than its costs, or what other factors could make. While monopolies, for example, can be considered a market failure as prices rise and output falls, monopoly creation is not always a strict market phenomena. Costs of government policies sometimes exceed benefits. This may occur because of incentives facing voters, government officials, and government employees, because of actions by special interest groups that can impose costs on the general public, or because social goals other than economic efficiency are being pursued. Government granted monopolies comprise a fair portion of monopolized industries.

Natural Monopolies

A natural monopoly is when a company can serve the market most efficient way. This is usually due to fixed costs and variable costs. If the fixed costs are very high, it will result in it not being effective for more than one company on the market. For example, if we consider the electricity supply of a city, it is not worthwhile for anyone to build a second tram network. Since the (fixed) cost of network construction is too high, the expected return is not worth the investment. (Of course, if not only one company can supply the wires but anyone, then the fixed cost will disappear and competition can be realized.) It follows from a significant proportion of fixed costs that, in the case of a natural monopoly, the company provides a declining phase of the average cost curve.

According to Arnold Harberger the loss of deadweight from monopolies in the US manufacturing industry is only 0.1% of GNP, so the real problem is not the existence of monopoly. The real problem is the social costs. These are not only the amount of deadweight loss and the cost of lobbying companies, but also the efforts that consumers make to prevent this. Indirect costs that are caused by rent seeking in other markets should also be taken into account. For example, if there is a need for more economists because of lobbying activities, the cost of not having many other professions or the cost of competing in offices for bribes. Interestingly, however, bribes alone are not a social cost, just a transfer from certain groups (renters) to other groups (clerks).

In the case of natural monopolies in private hands, regulation can be introduced to break monopolies. The government can regulate prices in certain sectors where natural monopolies develop. This can be done directly by setting the price (for example, the price of rail or gas) or by regulating the return (for example, in the case of telephone services). Whatever method is used, the goal is to lower prices to cost levels. By reducing the price, the rent seeking and the deadweight loss are also reduced or eliminated. In addition to natural monopolies, there are monopolies created by companies themselves through acquisitions and mergers. They do it due to the fact that in addition to decreasing average costs (economies of scale), there may be other reasons for this. There is no rent seeking in the race because the companies offer each other until the prices exceed the costs. Their purpose is to agree on a higher price, thus dividing the annuity. However, they cannot trust each other either - in such a cartel, in the short term, each company has the interest of reducing the price, acquiring the customers of others, and thus getting close to all annuities. This is the easiest way for companies to solve this distrust when they unite and then share the annuity in proportion to the shares. Preventing such cases is a competition policy that prohibits the creation of price cartels and only allows mergers if it does not entail the risk of a monopoly power.

Oligopoly

An oligopoly is a market form wherein a market or industry is dominated by a small number of large sellers (oligopolists). Oligopolies can result from various forms of collusion which reduce competition and lead to higher prices for consumers. Oligopolies have their own market structure.

With few sellers, each oligopolist is likely to be aware of the actions of the others. According to game theory, the decisions of one firm therefore influence and are influenced by decisions of other firms. Strategic planning by oligopolists needs to take into account the likely responses of the other market. Entry barriers include high investment requirements, strong consumer loyalty for existing brands and economies of scale. In developed economies oligopolies dominate the economy as the perfectly competitive model is of negligible importance for consumers. Oligopolies differ from price takers in that they do not have a supply curve. Instead, they search for the best price-output combination.

Oligopoly is a common market form where a number of firms are in competition. As a quantitative description of oligopoly, the four-firm concentration ratio is often utilized. This measure expresses, as a percentage, the market share of the four largest firms in any particular industry. For example, as of fourth quarter 2008, if we combine total market share of Verizon Wireless, AT&T, Sprint, and T-Mobile, we see that these firms, together, control 97% of the U.S. cellular telephone market.

Oligopolistic competition can give rise to both wide-ranging and diverse outcomes. In some situations, particular companies may employ restrictive trade practices (collusion, market sharing etc.) in order to inflate prices and restrict production in much the same way that a monopoly does. Whenever there is a formal agreement for such collusion, between companies that usually compete with one another, this practice is known as a cartel. A prime example of such a cartel is OPEC, which has a profound influence on the international price of oil.

Firms often collude in an attempt to stabilize unstable markets, so as to reduce the risks inherent in these markets for investment and product development. There are legal restrictions on such collusion in most countries. There does not have to be a formal agreement for collusion to take place (although for the act to be illegal there must be actual communication between companies)–for example, in some industries there may be an acknowledged market leader which informally sets prices to which other producers respond, known as price leadership.

In other situations, competition between sellers in an oligopoly can be fierce, with relatively low prices and high production. This could lead to an efficient outcome approaching perfect competition. The competition in an oligopoly can be greater when there are more firms in an industry than if, for example, the firms were only regionally based and did not compete directly with each other.

Thus the welfare analysis of oligopolies is sensitive to the parameter values used to define the market's structure. In particular, the level of dead weight loss is hard to measure. The study of product differentiation indicates that oligopolies might also create excessive levels of differentiation in order to stifle competition.

Oligopoly theory makes heavy use of game theory to model the behavior of oligopolies:

1. Stackelberg's duopoly. In this model, the firms move sequentially.
2. Cournot's duopoly. In this model, the firms simultaneously choose quantities.
3. Bertrand's oligopoly. In this model, the firms simultaneously choose prices.

Characteristics

1. Profit maximization conditions:

   An oligopoly maximizes profits.

2. Ability to set price:

   Oligopolies are price setters rather than price takers.

3. Entry and exit:

   Barriers to entry are high. The most important barriers are government licenses, economies of scale, patents, access to expensive and complex technology, and strategic actions by incumbent firms designed to discourage or destroy nascent firms. Additional sources of barriers to entry often result from government regulation favoring existing firms making it difficult for new firms to enter the market.

4. Number of firms:

   "Few" – a "handful" of sellers. There are so few firms that the actions of one firm can influence the actions of the other firms.

5. Long run profits:

   Oligopolies can retain long run abnormal profits. High barriers of entry prevent sideline firms from entering market to capture excess profits.

6. Product differentiation:

   Product may be homogeneous (steel) or differentiated (automobiles).

7. Perfect knowledge:

   Assumptions about perfect knowledge vary but the knowledge of various economic factors can be generally described as selective. Oligopolies have perfect knowledge of their own cost and demand functions but their inter-firm information may be incomplete. Buyers have only imperfect knowledge as to price, cost and product quality.

8. Interdependence:

   The distinctive feature of an oligopoly is interdependence. Oligopolies are typically composed of a few large firms. Each firm is so large that its actions affect market conditions. Therefore, the competing firms will be aware of a firm's market actions and will respond appropriately. This means that in contemplating a market action, a firm must take into consideration the possible reactions of all competing firms and the firms' countermoves. It is very much like a game of chess, in which a player must anticipate a whole sequence of moves and countermoves in order to determine how to achieve his or her objectives; this is known as game theory. For example, an oligopoly considering a price reduction may wish to estimate the likelihood that competing firms would also lower their prices and possibly trigger a ruinous price war. Or if the firm is considering a price increase, it may want to know whether other firms will also increase prices or hold existing prices constant. This anticipation leads to price rigidity, as firms will only be willing to adjust their prices and quantity of output in accordance with a "price leader" in the market. This high degree of interdependence and need to be aware of what other firms are doing or might do stands in contrast with the lack of interdependence in other market structures. In a perfectly competitive (PC) market there is zero interdependence because no firm is large enough to affect market price. All firms in a *PC* market are price takers, as current market selling price can be followed predictably to maximize short-term profits. In a monopoly, there are no competitors to be concerned about. In a monopolistically-competitive market, each firm's effects on market conditions is so negligible as to be safely ignored by competitors.

9. Non-Price Competition:

   Oligopolies tend to compete on terms other than price. Loyalty schemes, advertisement, and product differentiation are all examples of non-price competition.

Oligopolies in Countries with Competition Laws

Oligopolies become "mature" when they realise they can profit maximise through joint profit maximising. As a result of operating in countries with enforced competition laws, the Oligopolists will operate under tacit collusion, which is collusion through an understanding that if all the competitors in the market raise their prices, then collectively all the competitors can achieve economic profits close to a monopolist, without evidence of breaching government market regulations. Hence, the kinked demand curve for a joint profit maximising Oligopoly industry can model the behaviours of oligopolists pricing decisions other than that of the price leader (the price leader being the firm that all other firms follow in terms of pricing decisions). This is because if a firm unilaterally raises the prices of their good/service, and other competitors do not follow then, the firm that raised their price will then lose a significant market as they face the elastic upper segment of the demand curve. As the joint profit maximising achieves greater economic profits for all the firms, there is an incentive for an individual firm to "cheat" by expanding output to gain greater market share and profit. In Oligopolist cheating, and the incumbent firm discovering this breach in collusion, the other firms in the market will retaliate by matching or dropping prices lower than the original drop. Hence, the market share that the firm that dropped the price gained, will have that gain minimised or eliminated. This is why on the kinked demand curve model the lower segment of the demand curve is inelastic. As a result, price rigidity prevails in such markets.

Modeling

There is no single model describing the operation of an oligopolistic market. The variety and complexity of the models exist because you can have two to 10 firms competing on the basis of price, quantity, technological innovations, marketing, and reputation. However, there are a series of simplified models that attempt to describe market behavior by considering certain circumstances. Some of the better-known models are the dominant firm model, the Cournot–Nash model, the Bertrand model and the kinked demand model.

Cournot–Nash Model

The Cournot–Nash model is the simplest oligopoly model. The model assumes that there are two "equally positioned firms"; the firms compete on the basis of quantity rather than price and each firm makes an "output of decision assuming that the other firm's behavior is fixed." The market demand curve is assumed to be linear and marginal costs are constant. To find the Cournot–Nash equilibrium one determines how each firm reacts to a change in the output of the other firm. The path to equilibrium is a series of actions and reactions. The pattern continues until a point is reached where neither firm desires "to change what it is doing, given how it believes the other firm will react to any change." The equilibrium is the intersection of the two firm's reaction functions. The reaction function shows how one firm reacts to the quantity choice of the other firm. For example, assume that the firm 1's demand function is $P = (M - Q_2) - Q_1$ where Q_2 is the quantity produced by the other firm and Q_1 is the amount produced by firm 1, and M=60 is the market. Assume that marginal cost is C_M=12. Firm 1 wants to know its maximizing quantity and price. Firm 1 begins the process by following the profit maximization rule of equating marginal revenue to marginal costs. Firm 1's total revenue function is $R_T = Q_1 P = Q_1(M - Q_2 - Q_1) = MQ_1 - Q_1 Q_2 - Q_1^2$. The marginal revenue function is:

$$R_M = \frac{\partial R_T}{\partial Q_1} = M - Q_2 - 2Q_1 .$$

$$R_M = C_M$$

$$M - Q_2 - 2Q_1 = C_M$$

$$2Q_1 = (M - C_M) - Q_2$$

$$Q_1 = (M - C_M)/2 - Q_2/2 = 24 - 0.5\, Q_2$$

$$Q_2 = 2(M - C_M) - 2Q_1 = 96 - 2\, Q_1$$

Equation $Q_1 = (M - C_M)/2 - Q_2/2 = 24 - 0.5\, Q_2$ is the reaction function for firm 1. Equation $Q_2 = 2(M - C_M) - 2Q_1 = 96 - 2\, Q_1$ is the reaction function for firm 2.

To determine the Cournot–Nash equilibrium you can solve the equations simultaneously. The equilibrium quantities can also be determined graphically. The equilibrium solution would be at the intersection of the two reaction functions. Note that if you graph the functions the axes represent quantities. The reaction functions are not necessarily symmetric. The firms may face differing cost functions in which case the reaction functions would not be identical nor would the equilibrium quantities.

Bertrand Model

The Bertrand model is essentially the Cournot–Nash model except the strategic variable is price rather than quantity.

The model assumptions are:

1. There are two firms in the market.
2. They produce a homogeneous product.
3. They produce at a constant marginal cost.
4. Firms choose prices P_A and P_B simultaneously.
5. Firms outputs are perfect substitutes.
6. Sales are split evenly if $P_A = P_B$.

The only Nash equilibrium is $P_A = P_B = MC$.

Neither firm has any reason to change strategy. If the firm raises prices it will lose all its customers. If the firm lowers price $P < MC$ then it will be losing money on every unit sold.

The Bertrand equilibrium is the same as the competitive result. Each firm will produce where P = marginal costs and there will be zero profits. A generalization of the Bertrand model is the Bertrand–Edgeworth model that allows for capacity constraints and more general cost functions.

Oligopolistic Market: Kinked Demand Curve Model

According to this model, each firm faces a demand curve kinked at the existing price. The conjectural assumptions of the model are; if the firm raises its price above the current existing price, competitors will not follow and the acting firm will lose market share and second if a firm lowers prices below the existing price then their competitors will follow to retain their market share and the firm's output will increase only marginally.

If the assumptions hold then:

1. The firm's marginal revenue curve is discontinuous (or rather, not differentiable), and has a gap at the kink.

2. For prices above the prevailing price the curve is relatively elastic.
3. For prices below the point the curve is relatively inelastic.

The gap in the marginal revenue curve means that marginal costs can fluctuate without changing equilibrium price and quantity. Thus prices tend to be rigid.

Examples:

In industrialized economies, barriers to entry have resulted in oligopolies forming in many sectors, with unprecedented levels of competition fueled by increasing globalization. Market shares in an oligopoly are typically determined by product development and advertising. For example, there are now only a small number of manufacturers of civil passenger aircraft, though Brazil (Embraer) and Canada (Bombardier) have participated in the small passenger aircraft market sector. Oligopolies have also arisen in heavily-regulated markets such as wireless communications: in some areas only two or three providers are licensed to operate.

World Wide

Aircraft

1. Boeing and Airbus have a duopoly over the airliner market.
2. General Electric, Pratt and Whitney and Rolls-Royce plc own more than 50% of the marketshare in the airliner engine market.
3. Aircraft tires is dominated by a four-firm oligopoly that controls 85% of market share, these firms are Goodyear, Michelin, Dunlop, and Bridgestone.

Finance

1. Three credit rating agencies (Standard & Poor's, Moody's, and Fitch Group) dominate their market and extend their crucial importance into the financial sector.
2. The accountancy market is dominated by PriceWaterhouseCoopers, KPMG, Deloitte Touche Tohmatsu, and Ernst & Young (commonly known as the Big Four).
3. Credit card processing is dominated by Visa and Mastercard.

Food

1. Three leading food processing companies, Kraft Foods, PepsiCo and Nestlé, together achieve a large proportion of global processed food sales. These three companies are often used as an example of "Rule of three", which states that markets often become an oligopoly of three large firms.
2. Nestlé, The Hershey Company and Mars, Incorporated together make most of the confectionery made worldwide.

Technology

1. Intel and AMD are the only two major players in desktop CPU market worldwide.

2. Microsoft, Sony, Valve, and Nintendo dominate the video game platform market.
3. Nvidia and AMD together make most of the chips for discrete graphics.
4. Apple and Microsoft's desktop operating systems run on the majority of the worlds PC's.
5. Apple and Google's mobile operating systems run on the majority of the worlds smartphones.

Australia

1. Most print and online media outlets are owned either by News Corporation or by Fairfax Media.
2. 60 per cent of grocery revenue goes to Coles Group and Woolworths.
3. Banking is dominated by ANZ, Westpac, NAB, and Commonwealth Bank. To an extent this oligopoly is enshrined in law in what is known as the "Four pillars policy", in order to ensure the stability of Australia's banking system.
4. Fixed line telecommunications products in Australia are primarily delivered by Telstra, Optus, TPG or increasingly NBN Co. Other brands are virtual network operators (VNO). In the mobile market there are three main operators, Telstra, Optus and Vodafone Hutchison Australia with other mobile virtual network operators (MVNO) selling access to those three networks.

Canada

Media

1. Torstar and Postmedia Network dominate the newspaper industry.
2. Bell Media, Rogers Media, and Corus Entertainment dominate English-language television broadcasting.
3. Bell Media Radio, Newcap Radio, Rogers Media, and Corus Entertainment dominate the English-language radio industry.
4. Loblaw Companies, Metro Inc., and Sobeys control the majority of the supermarket industry.

Other

1. Five companies dominate the banking industry: Royal Bank of Canada, Toronto Dominion Bank, Bank of Nova Scotia, Bank of Montreal, and Canadian Imperial Bank of Commerce.
2. As of 2008 Rogers Wireless, Bell Mobility and Telus Mobility control a combined 94% of Canada's wireless telecommunications market.
3. Rogers Communications, Bell Canada, Telus, and Shaw Communications dominate the internet service provider market.

4. Husky Energy, Imperial Oil, Nexen, Shell Canada, Suncor Energy, Syncrude, Canadian Natural Resources and Repsol Oil & Gas Canada dominate the oil and gas sector.
5. Air Canada and Westjet dominate the domestic airline market.

India

1. The petroleum and gas industry is dominated by Indian Oil, Bharat Petroleum, Hindustan Petroleum, and Reliance Petroleum.
2. Most of the telecommunication in India is dominated by Airtel, Vodafone, BSNL and Reliance Jio.

European Union

1. The VHF Data Link market as air-ground part of aeronautical communications is controlled by ARINC and SITA, commonly known as the organisations providing communication services for the exchange of data between air-ground applications in the Commission Regulation (EC) No 29/2009.

United Kingdom

1. Five banks (Barclays, Halifax, HSBC, Lloyds TSB and NatWest) dominate the UK banking sector, they were accused of being an oligopoly by the relative newcomer Virgin Money.
2. Four companies (Tesco, Sainsbury's, Asda and Morrisons) share 74.4% of the grocery market.
3. The detergent market is dominated by two players, Unilever and Procter & Gamble.
4. Six utilities (EDF Energy, Centrica, RWE npower, E.on, Scottish Power and Scottish and Southern Energy) share 95% of the retail electricity market.
5. Four mobile phone networks. Virtual mobile networks like Tesco Mobile have attempted to broaden the market, but there are still just four core network providers in EE, Vodafone, O2 and 3 Mobile.
6. Big Four Accounting Firms- (KPMG, PWC, Ernst and Young and Deloitte) These four firms audit 99% of the companies in the FTSE100 and 96% of the companies in the FTSE 250 Index.

United States

Media

1. Five movie studios (Walt Disney Pictures, Sony Pictures, Universal Pictures, Paramount Pictures, Warner Bros. Entertainment) receive almost 87% of American film revenues.
2. The television and high speed internet industry is mostly an oligopoly of seven companies: The Walt Disney Company, CBS Corporation, Viacom, Comcast, Hearst Corporation, Time Warner, and News Corporation (now 21st Century Fox and News Corp).
3. In March 2012, the United States Department of Justice announced that it would sue six

major publishers for price fixing in the sale of electronic books. The accused publishers are Apple, Simon & Schuster Inc, Hachette Book Group, Penguin Group, Macmillan, and HarperCollins Publishers.

Other

1. Four wireless providers (AT&T Mobility, Verizon Wireless, T-Mobile, Sprint Corporation) control 89% of the cellular telephone service market. This is cellular telephone manufacturing, an integral portion of the cellular telephone market as a whole.
2. Healthcare insurance in the United States consists of very few insurance companies controlling major market share in most states. For example, California's insured population of 20 million is the most competitive in the nation and 44% of that market is dominated by two insurance companies, Anthem and Kaiser Permanente.
3. Mergers among airlines have left the industry in the United States dominated by four main entities – Delta Air Lines, United Airlines, Southwest Airlines and American Airlines – which purposely do not compete on some air travel routes.
4. Transcontinental freight lines are vastly controlled by two railroads: Union Pacific Railroad and BNSF Railroad.
5. The big box retail industry in the U.S. is dominated by Walmart, Target, and Costco.
6. Walgreens and CVS Pharmacy take up 86% of the U.S. pharmacy market.

Demand Curve

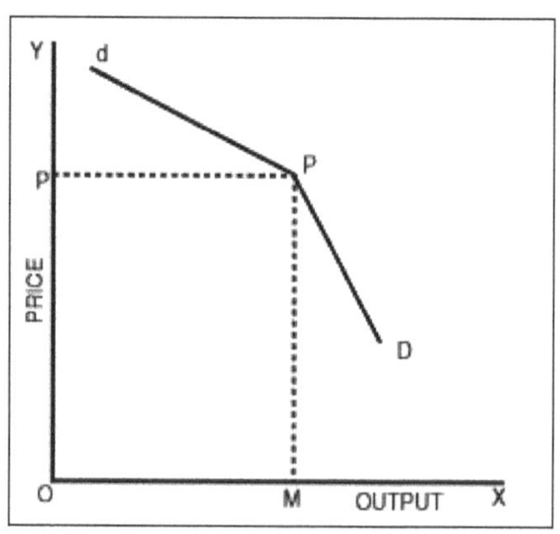

Above the kink, demand is relatively elastic because all other firms' prices remain unchanged. Below the kink, demand is relatively inelastic because all other firms will introduce a similar price cut, eventually leading to a price war. Therefore, the best option for the oligopolist is to produce at point E which is the equilibrium point and the kink point. This is a theoretical model proposed in 1947, which has failed to receive conclusive evidence for support.

In an oligopoly, firms operate under imperfect competition. With the fierce price competitiveness created by this sticky-upward demand curve, firms use non-price competition in order to accrue greater revenue and market share.

"Kinked" demand curves are similar to traditional demand curves, as they are downward-sloping. They are distinguished by a hypothesized convex bend with a discontinuity at the bend–"kink". Thus the first derivative at that point is undefined and leads to a jump discontinuity in the marginal revenue curve.

Classical economic theory assumes that a profit-maximizing producer with some market power (either due to oligopoly or monopolistic competition) will set marginal costs equal to marginal revenue. This idea can be envisioned graphically by the intersection of an upward-sloping marginal cost curve and a downward-sloping marginal revenue curve (because the more one sells, the lower the price must be, so the less a producer earns per unit). In classical theory, any change in the marginal cost structure (how much it costs to make each additional unit) or the marginal revenue structure (how much people will pay for each additional unit) will be immediately reflected in a new price and/or quantity sold of the item. This result does not occur if a "kink" exists. Because of this jump discontinuity in the marginal revenue curve, marginal costs could change without necessarily changing the price or quantity.

The motivation behind this kink is the idea that in an oligopolistic or monopolistically competitive market, firms will not raise their prices because even a small price increase will lose many customers. This is because competitors will generally ignore price increases, with the hope of gaining a larger market share as a result of now having comparatively lower prices. However, even a large price decrease will gain only a few customers because such an action will begin a price war with other firms. The curve is therefore more price-elastic for price increases and less so for price decreases. Theory predicts that firms will enter the industry in the long run.

Types of Oligopoly Market

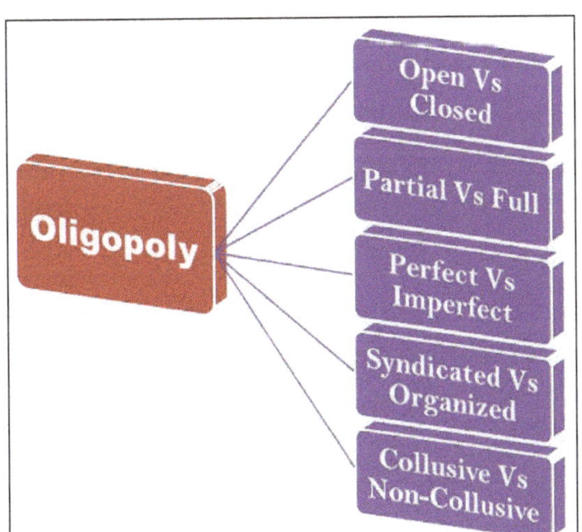

1. Open vs. Closed Oligopoly: This classification is made on the basis of freedom to enter into the new industry. An open Oligopoly is the market situation wherein firm can enter into the industry any time it wants, whereas, in the case of a closed Oligopoly, there are certain restrictions that act as a barrier for a new firm to enter into the industry.

2. Partial vs. Full Oligopoly: This classification is done on the basis of price leadership. The partial Oligopoly refers to the market situation, wherein one large firm dominates the market

and is looked upon as a price leader. Whereas in full Oligopoly, the price leadership is conspicuous by its absence.

3. Perfect (Pure) vs. Imperfect (Differential) Oligopoly: This classification is made on the basis of product differentiation. The Oligopoly is perfect or pure when the firms deal in the homogeneous products. Whereas the Oligopoly is said to be imperfect, when the firms deal in heterogeneous products, i.e. products that are close but are not perfect substitutes.
4. Syndicated vs. Organized Oligopoly: This classification is done on the basis of a degree of coordination found among the firms. When the firms come together and sell their products with the common interest is called as a Syndicate Oligopoly. Whereas, in the case of an Organized Oligopoly, the firms have a central association for fixing the prices, outputs, and quotas.
5. Collusive vs. Non-Collusive Oligopoly: This classification is made on the basis of agreement or understanding between the firms. In Collusive Oligopoly, instead of competing with each other, the firms come together and with the consensus of all fixes the price and the outputs. Whereas in the case of a non-collusive Oligopoly, there is a lack of understanding among the firms and they compete against each other to achieve their respective targets.
6. Thus, oligopoly market is a market structure that lies between the monopolistic competition and a pure monopoly.

Kinked Demand

The Kinked-Demand curve theory is an economic theory regarding oligopoly and monopolistic competition. Kinked demand was an initial attempt to explain sticky prices.

"Kinked" demand curves and traditional demand curves are similar in that they are both downward-sloping. They are distinguished by a hypothesized concave bend with a discontinuity at the bend - the "kink." Therefore, the first derivative at that point is undefined and leads to a jump discontinuity in the marginal revenue curve.

Classical economic theory assumes that a profit-maximizing producer with some market power (either due to oligopoly or monopolistic competition) will set marginal costs equal to marginal revenue. This idea can be envisioned graphically by the intersection of an upward-sloping marginal cost curve and a downward-sloping marginal revenue curve . In classical theory, any change in the marginal cost structure or the marginal revenue structure will be immediately reflected in a new price and/or quantity sold of the item. This result does not occur if a "kink" exists. Because of this jump discontinuity in the marginal revenue curve, marginal costs could change without necessarily changing the price or quantity.

Formulation

The two seminal papers on kinked demand were written nearly simultaneously in 1939 on both sides of the Atlantic. Sweezy argued that an ordinary demand curve does not apply to oligopoly markets and promotes a kinked demand curve.

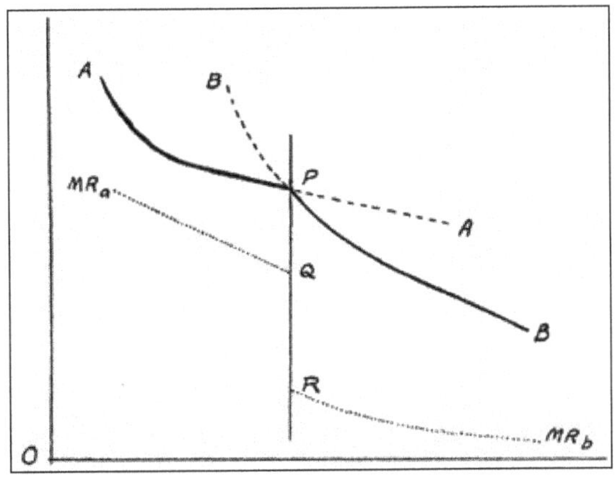

Hall and Hitch's graphical illustration of kinked demand

Hall and Hitch further present a hypothesis for the initial setting of prices; this explains why the "kink" in the curve is located where it is. They base this on a notion of "full cost" - marginal cost of each unit plus a percent of overhead costs or fixed costs with an additional percent added for profit. They emphasize the importance of industry tradition in history in determining this initial price, noting further, "An overwhelming majority of the entrepreneurs thought that a price based on full average cost was the 'right' price, the one which 'ought' to be charged."

Criticism

New classical economists, led by Chicago's George Stigler, worked to discredit the kinked demand models. Stigler first argues that the kinked demand models are not useful, as Hall and Hitch's model only explains observed phenomenon and is not predictive. He further explains that the kinked demand analysis only suggests why prices remain sticky and does not describe the mechanism that establishes the kink and how the kink can reform once prices change. Stigler also asserts that the model is unnecessary because Chicago theory already included allowances for short-run sticky prices due to collusion, menu costs, and regulatory or bureaucratic inefficiencies in markets.

Monopolistic Competition

Monopolistic competition characterizes an industry in which many firms offer products or services that are similar, but not perfect substitutes. Barriers to entry and exit in a monopolistic competitive industry are low, and the decisions of any one firm do not directly affect those of its competitors. Monopolistic competition is closely related to the business strategy of brand differentiation.

Monopolistic competition is a middle ground between monopoly and perfect competition (a purely theoretical state), and combines elements of each. All firms in monopolistic competition have the same, relatively low degree of market power; they are all price makers. In the long run, demand is highly elastic, meaning that it is sensitive to price changes. In the short run, economic profit is positive, but it approaches zero in the long run. Firms in monopolistic competition tend to advertise heavily.

Monopolistic competition is a form of competition that characterizes a number of industries that are familiar to consumers in their day-to-day lives. Examples include restaurants, hair salons, clothing, and consumer electronics. To illustrate the characteristics of monopolistic competition, we'll use the example of household cleaning products.

Number of Firms

Say you've just moved into a new house and want to stock up on cleaning supplies. Go to the appropriate aisle in a grocery store, and you'll see that any given item—dish soap, hand soap, laundry detergent, surface disinfectant, toilet bowl cleaner, etc.—is available in a number of varieties. For each purchase you need to make, perhaps five or six firms will be competing for your business.

Product Differentiation

Because the products all serve the same purpose, there are relatively few options for sellers to differentiate their offerings from other firms'. There might be "discount" varieties that are of lower quality, but it is difficult to tell whether the higher-priced options are in fact any better. This uncertainty results from imperfect information: the average consumer does not know the precise differences between the various products, or what the fair price for any of them is.

Monopolistic competition tends to lead to heavy marketing, because different firms need to distinguish broadly similar products. One company might opt to lower the price of their cleaning product, sacrificing a higher profit margin in exchange—ideally—for higher sales. Another might take the opposite route, raising the price and using packaging that suggests quality and sophistication. A third might sell itself as more eco-friendly, using "green" imagery and displaying a stamp of approval from an environmental watchdog (which the other brands might qualify for as well, but don't display). In reality, every one of the brands might be equally effective.

Decision-Making

Monopolistic competition implies that there are enough firms in the industry that one firm's decision does not set off a chain reaction. In an oligopoly, a price cut by one firm can set off a price war, but this is not the case for monopolistic competition.

Pricing Power

As in a monopoly, firms in monopolistic competition are price setters or makers, rather than price takers. However, the firms nominal ability to set their prices is effectively offset by the fact that demand for their products is highly price elastic. In order to actually raise their prices, the firms must be able to differentiate their product from their competitors by increasing its quality, real or perceived.

Demand Elasticity

Due to the range of similar offerings, demand is highly elastic in monopolistic competition. In other words, demand is very responsive to price changes. If your favorite multipurpose surface cleaner suddenly costs 20% more, you probably won't hesitate to switch to an alternative, and your counter tops probably won't know the difference.

Economic Profit

In the short run, firms can make excess economic profits. However, because barriers to entry are low, other firms have an incentive to enter the market, increasing the competition, until overall economic profit is zero. Note that economic profits are not the same as accounting profits; a firm that posts a positive net income can have zero economic profit, since the latter incorporates opportunity costs.

Advertising in Monopolistic Competition

Economists who study monopolistic competition often highlight the social cost of this type of market structure. Firms in monopolistic competition expend large amounts real resources on advertising and other forms of marketing. When there is a real difference between the products of different firms, which the consume might not be aware of, these expenditures can be useful. However, if it is instead the case that the products are near perfect substitutes, which is likely in monopolistic competition, then real resources spent on advertising and marketing represent a kind of wasteful rent-seeking behavior, which produces a deadweight loss to society.

Features of Monopolistic Competition

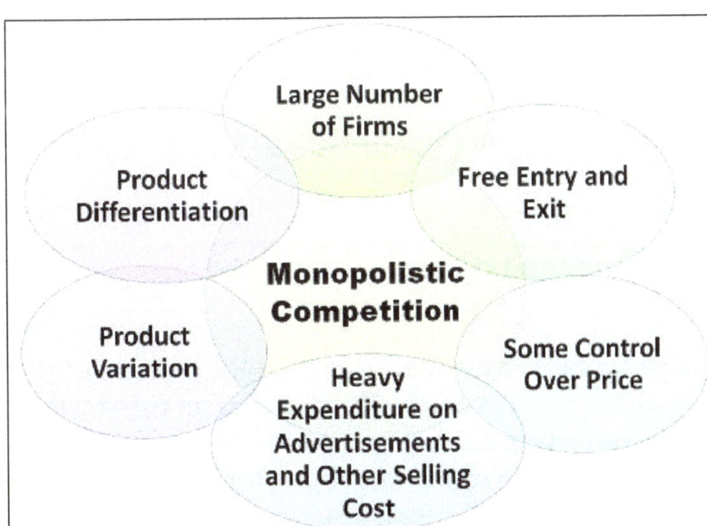

1. Product Differentiation: This is one of the major features of the firms operating under the monopolistic competition, that produces the product which is not identical but is slightly different from each other. The products being slightly different from each other remain close substitutes of each other and hence cannot be priced very differently from each other.

2. Large number of firms: A large number of firms operate under the monopolistic competition, and there is a stiff competition between the existing firms. Unlike the perfect competition, the firms produce the differentiated products which are substitutes for each other, thus make the competition among the firms a real and a tough one.

3. Free Entry and Exit: With an intense competition among the firms, the entity incurring the loss can move out of the industry at any time it wants. Similarly, the new firms can enter into the industry freely, provided it comes up with the unique feature and different variety of products to outstand in the market and meet with the competition already existing in the industry.

4. Some control over price: Since, the products are close substitutes for each other, if a firm lowers the price of its product, then the customers of other products will switch over to it. Conversely, with the increase in the price of the product, it will lose its customers to others. Thus, under the monopolistic competition, an individual firm is not a price taker but has some influence over the price of its product.

5. Heavy expenditure on Advertisement and other Selling Costs: Under the monopolistic competition, the firms incur a huge cost on advertisements and other selling costs to promote the sale of their products. Since the products are different and are close substitutes for each other; the firms need to undertake the promotional activities to capture a larger market share.

6. Product Variation: Under the monopolistic competition, there is a variation in the products offered by several firms. To meet the needs of the customers, each firm tries to adjust its product accordingly. The changes could be in the form of new design, better quality, new packages or container, better materials, etc. Thus, the amount of product a firm is selling in the market depends on the uniqueness of its product and the extent to which it differs from the other products.

The monopolistic competition is also called as imperfect competition because this market structure lies between the pure monopoly and the pure competition.

Characteristics of Monopolistic Competition

Monopolistically competitive markets exhibit the following characteristics:

1. Each firm makes independent decisions about price and output, based on its product, its market, and its costs of production.

2. Knowledge is widely spread between participants, but it is unlikely to be perfect. For example, diners can review all the menus available from restaurants in a town, before they make their choice. Once inside the restaurant, they can view the menu again, before ordering. However, they cannot fully appreciate the restaurant or the meal until after they have dined.

3. The entrepreneur has a more significant role than in firms that are perfectly competitive because of the increased risks associated with decision making.

4. There is freedom to enter or leave the market, as there are no major barriers to entry or exit.

5. A central feature of monopolistic competition is that products are differentiated. There are four main types of differentiation:

    a. Physical product differentiation, where firms use size, design, colour, shape, performance, and features to make their products different. For example, consumer electronics can easily be physically differentiated.

b. Marketing differentiation, where firms try to differentiate their product by distinctive packaging and other promotional techniques. For example, breakfast cereals can easily be differentiated through packaging.

c. Human capital differentiation, where the firm creates differences through the skill of its employees, the level of training received, distinctive uniforms, and so on.

d. Differentiation through distribution, including distribution via mail order or through internet shopping, such as Amazon.com, which differentiates itself from traditional bookstores by selling online.

6. Firms are price makers and are faced with a downward sloping demand curve. Because each firm makes a unique product, it can charge a higher or lower price than its rivals. The firm can set its own price and does not have to 'take' it from the industry as a whole, though the industry price may be a guideline, or becomes a constraint. This also means that the demand curve will slope downwards.

7. Firms operating under monopolistic competition usually have to engage in advertising. Firms are often in fierce competition with other (local) firms offering a similar product or service, and may need to advertise on a local basis, to let customers know their differences. Common methods of advertising for these firms are through local press and radio, local cinema, posters, leaflets and special promotions.

8. Monopolistically competitive firms are assumed to be profit maximisers because firms tend to be small with entrepreneurs actively involved in managing the business.

9. There are usually a large numbers of independent firms competing in the market.

Equilibrium Under Monopolistic Competition

In the short run supernormal profits are possible, but in the long run new firms are attracted into the industry, because of low barriers to entry, good knowledge and an opportunity to differentiate.

Monopolistic Competition in the Short Run

At profit maximisation, MC = MR, and output is Q and price P. Given that price (AR) is above ATC at Q, supernormal profits are possible (area PABC).

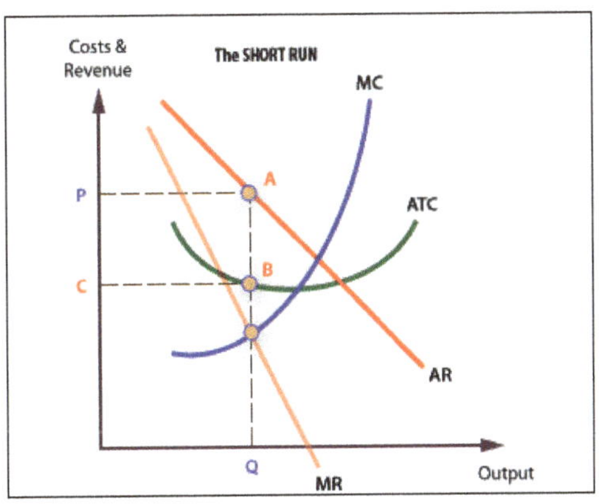

As new firms enter the market, demand for the existing firm's products becomes more elastic and the demand curve shifts to the left, driving down price. Eventually, all super-normal profits are eroded away.

Monopolistic Competition in the Long Run

Super-normal profits attract in new entrants, which shifts the demand curve for existing firm to the left. New entrants continue until only normal profit is available. At this point, firms have reached their long run equilibrium.

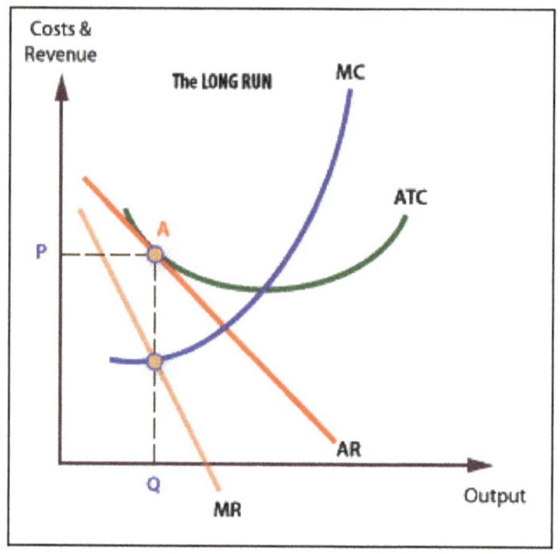

Clearly, the firm benefits most when it is in its short run and will try to stay in the short run by innovating, and further product differentiation.

Examples of Monopolistic Competition

Examples of monopolistic competition can be found in every high street.

Monopolistically competitive firms are most common in industries where differentiation is possible, such as:

1. The restaurant business
2. Hotels and pubs
3. General specialist retailing
4. Consumer services, such as hairdressing

Survival of Small Firms

The existence of monopolistic competition partly explains the survival of small firms in modern economies. The majority of small firms in the real world operate in markets that could be said to be monopolistically competitive.

Monopolistic competition can bring the following advantages:

1. There are no significant barriers to entry; therefore markets are relatively contestable.

2. Differentiation creates diversity, choice and utility. For example, a typical high street in any town will have a number of different restaurants from which to choose.

3. The market is more efficient than monopoly but less efficient than perfect competition - less allocatively and less productively efficient. However, they may be dynamically efficient, innovative in terms of new production processes or new products. For example, retailers often constantly have to develop new ways to attract and retain local custom.

There are several potential disadvantages associated with monopolistic competition, including:

Some differentiation does not create utility but generates unnecessary waste, such as excess packaging. Advertising may also be considered wasteful, though most is informative rather than persuasive.

As the diagram illustrates, assuming profit maximisation, there is allocative inefficiency in both the long and short run. This is because price is above marginal cost in both cases. In the long run the firm is less allocatively inefficient, but it is still inefficient.

Inefficiency

The firm is allocatively and productively inefficient in both the long and short run.

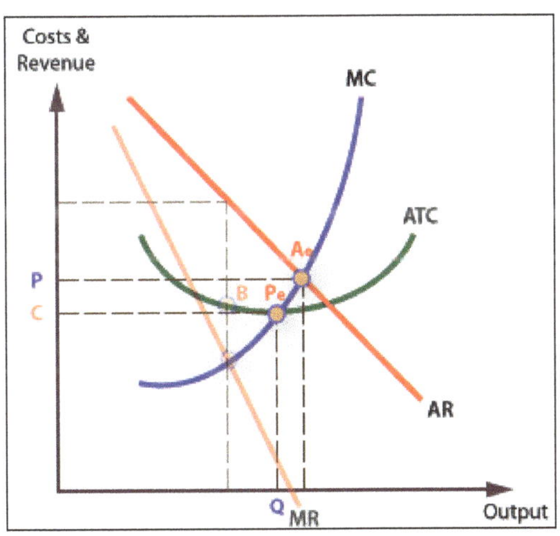

There is a tendency for excess capacity because firms can never fully exploit their fixed factors because mass production is difficult. This means they are productively inefficient in both the long and short run. However, this is may be outweighed by the advantages of diversity and choice.

As an economic model of competition, monopolistic competition is more realistic than perfect competition - many familiar and commonplace markets have many of the characteristics of this model.

References

- Perfectcompetition.asp, terms: investopedia.com, Retrieved 19 April, 2019
- Baten, bianchi, moser (2017). "compulsory licensing and innovation – historical evidence from german patents after wwi". Journal of development economics. 126: 231–242. Doi:10.1016/j.jdeveco.2017.01.002

- Imperfect-competition.asp, terms: investopedia.com, Retrieved 18 May, 2019
- Riggs, Thomas; Bonk, Mary, eds. (2008). Government-Granted Monopoly. Everyday Finance: Economics, Personal Money Management, and Entrepreneurship. Detroit: Gale Cengage Learning. ISBN 978-1-4144-1049-4. LCCN 2007035070. OL 21557400M. Retrieved 6 November 2018
- Imperfect-competition/top-six-characteristics-of-imperfect-competition-7112: economicsdiscussion.net, Retrieved 20 June, 2019
- Leo Cendrowicz (2008-02-27). "Microsoft Gets Mother Of All EU Fines". Forbes. Retrieved 2008-03-1
- Perfect-competition: businessjargons.com, Retrieved 17 March, 2019
- Purnanandam, amiyatosh; weagley, daniel (14 january 2016). "can markets discipline government agencies? Evidence from the weather derivatives market". The journal of finance. 71 (1): 303–334. Doi:10.1111/jofi.12366. Issn 0022-1082
- Types-of-oligopoly-market: businessjargons.com, Retrieved 21 July, 2019
- Mosca, M. 2008. On the origins of the concept of natural monopoly, The European Journal of the History of Economic Thought, 45 (2), 317-353
- Monopolisticmarket.asp, terms: investopedia.com, Retrieved 22 August, 2019
- Saidu, balkisu (8 may 2009). "regulating the abuse of the natural monopoly of pipelines in the gas industry vis-à-vis the provision of third party access". 13 (4): 105–112. Doi:10.3905/jsf.13.4.105
- Monopolistic-competition, businessjargons.com, Retrieved 23 January, 2019
- Monopolistic-competition, business-economics: economicsonline.co.uk, Retrieved 24 February, 2019

Services Marketing 5

- **Relationship Marketing**
- **Customer Relationship Management**
- **Customer Satisfaction**
- **Customer Experience**

The specialized branch of marketing that is involved in identifying, creating, communicating and delivering value to customers is known as services marketing. Some of its major focus areas are relationship marketing, customer satisfaction and customer experience. This chapter discusses in detail these aspects of service marketing.

The world economy nowadays is increasingly characterized as a service economy. This is primarily due to the increasing importance and share of the service sector in the economies of most developed and developing countries. In fact, the growth of the service sector has long been considered as indicative of a country's economic progress.

Economic history tells us that all developing nations have invariably experienced a shift from agriculture to industry and then to the service sector as the main stay of the economy.

This shift has also brought about a change in the definition of goods and services themselves. No longer are goods considered separate from services. Rather, services now increasingly represent an integral part of the product and this interconnectedness of goods and services is represented on a goods-services continuum.

Characteristics of Services

The American Marketing Association defines services as - "Activities, benefits and satisfactions which are offered for sale or are provided in connection with the sale of goods."

The defining characteristics of a service are:

1. Intangibility: Services are intangible and do not have a physical existence. Hence services cannot be touched, held, tasted or smelt. This is most defining feature of a service and that which primarily differentiates it from a product. Also, it poses a unique challenge to those

engaged in marketing a service as they need to attach tangible attributes to an otherwise intangible offering.

2. Heterogeneity/Variability: Given the very nature of services, each service offering is unique and cannot be exactly repeated even by the same service provider. While products can be mass produced and be homogenous the same is not true of services. eg: All burgers of a particular flavor at McDonalds are almost identical. However, the same is not true of the service rendered by the same counter staff consecutively to two customers.

3. Perishability: Services cannot be stored, saved, returned or resold once they have been used. Once rendered to a customer the service is completely consumed and cannot be delivered to another customer. eg: A customer dissatisfied with the services of a barber cannot return the service of the haircut that was rendered to him. At the most he may decide not to visit that particular barber in the future.

4. Inseparability/Simultaneity of production and consumption: This refers to the fact that services are generated and consumed within the same time frame. Eg: a haircut is delivered to and consumed by a customer simultaneously unlike, say, a takeaway burger which the customer may consume even after a few hours of purchase. Moreover, it is very difficult to separate a service from the service provider. Eg: the barber is necessarily a part of the service of a haircut that he is delivering to his customer.

Types of Services

1. Core Services: A service that is the primary purpose of the transaction. Eg: a haircut or the services of lawyer or teacher.

2. Supplementary Services: Services that are rendered as a corollary to the sale of a tangible product. Eg: Home delivery options offered by restaurants above a minimum bill value.

Difference between Goods and Services

Given below are the fundamental differences between physical goods and services:

Goods	Services
A physical commodity	A process or activity
Tangible	Intangible
Homogenous	Heterogeneous
Production and distribution are separation from their consumption	Production, distribution and consumption are simultaneous processes
Can be stored	Cannot be stored
Transfer of ownership is possible	Transfer of ownership is not possible

The 7 P's of Services Marketing

The first four elements in the services marketing mix are the same as those in the traditional marketing mix. However, given the unique nature of services, the implications of these are slightly different in case of services.

1. Product: In case of services, the 'product' is intangible, heterogeneous and perishable. Moreover, its production and consumption are inseparable. Hence, there is scope for customizing the offering as per customer requirements and the actual customer encounter therefore assumes particular significance. However, too much customization would compromise the standard delivery of the service and adversely affect its quality. Hence particular care has to be taken in designing the service offering.

2. Pricing: Pricing of services is tougher than pricing of goods. While the latter can be priced easily by taking into account the raw material costs, in case of services attendant costs - such as labor and overhead costs - also need to be factored in. Thus a restaurant not only has to charge for the cost of the food served but also has to calculate a price for the ambience provided. The final price for the service is then arrived at by including a mark up for an adequate profit margin.

3. Place: Since service delivery is concurrent with its production and cannot be stored or transported, the location of the service product assumes importance. Service providers have to give special thought to where the service would be provided. Thus, a fine dine restaurant is better located in a busy, upscale market as against on the outskirts of a city. Similarly, a holiday resort is better situated in the countryside away from the rush and noise of a city.

4. Promotion: Since a service offering can be easily replicated promotion becomes crucial in differentiating a service offering in the mind of the consumer. Thus, service providers offering identical services such as airlines or banks and insurance companies invest heavily in advertising their services. This is crucial in attracting customers in a segment where the services providers have nearly identical offerings.

We now look at the 3 new elements of the services marketing mix - people, process and physical evidence - which are unique to the marketing of services.

5. People: People are a defining factor in a service delivery process, since a service is inseparable from the person providing it. Thus, a restaurant is known as much for its food as for the service provided by its staff. The same is true of banks and department stores. Consequently, customer service training for staff has become a top priority for many organizations today.

6. Process: The process of service delivery is crucial since it ensures that the same standard of service is repeatedly delivered to the customers. Therefore, most companies have a service blue print which provides the details of the service delivery process, often going down to even defining the service script and the greeting phrases to be used by the service staff.

7. Physical Evidence: Since services are intangible in nature most service providers strive to incorporate certain tangible elements into their offering to enhance customer experience.

Thus, there are hair salons that have well designed waiting areas often with magazines and plush sofas for patrons to read and relax while they await their turn. Similarly, restaurants invest heavily in their interior design and decorations to offer a tangible and unique experience to their guests.

Features of Services Marketing

Intangibility

A physical product is visible and concrete. Services are intangible. The service cannot be touched or viewed, so it is difficult for clients to tell in advance what they will be getting. For example, banks promote the sale of credit cards by emphasizing the conveniences and advantages derived from possessing a credit card.

Inseparability

Personal services cannot be separated from the individual. Services are created and consumed simultaneously. The service is being produced at the same time that the client is receiving it; for example, during an online search or a legal consultation. Dentist, musicians, dancers, etc. create and offer services at the same time.

Heterogeneity (or Variability)

Services involve people, and people are all different. There is a strong possibility that the same enquiry would be answered slightly differently by different people (or even by the same person at different times). It is important to minimize the differences in performance (through training, standard setting and quality assurance). The quality of services offered by firms can never be standardized.

Perishability

Services have a high degree of perishability. Unused capacity cannot be stored for future use. If services are not used today, it is lost forever. For example, spare seats in an aeroplane cannot be transferred to the next flight. Similarly, empty rooms in five-star hotels and credits not utilized are examples of services leading to economic losses. As services are activities performed for simultaneous consumption, they perish unless consumed.

Changing Demand

The demand for services has wide fluctuations and may be seasonal. Demand for tourism is seasonal, other services such as demand for public transport, cricket field and golf courses have fluctuations in demand.

Pricing of Services

Quality of services cannot be standardized. The pricing of services are usually determined on the basis of demand and competition. For example, room rents in tourist spots fluctuate as per demand and season and many of the service providers give off-season discounts.

Direct Channel

Usually, services are directly provided to the customer. The customer goes directly to the service provider to get services such as bank, hotel, doctor, and so on. A wider market is reached through franchising such as McDonald's and Monginis.

Problems in Marketing Services

1. A service cannot be demonstrated.
2. Sale, production and consumption of services takes place simultaneously.
3. A service cannot be stored. It cannot be produced in anticipation of demand.
4. Services cannot be protected through patents.
5. Services cannot be separated from the service provider.
6. Services are not standardized and are inconsistent.
7. Service providers appointing franchisees may face problems of quality of services.
8. The customer perception of service quality is more directly linked to the morale, motivation and skill of the frontline staff of any service organization.

Relationship Marketing

Relationship marketing is a form of marketing developed from direct response marketing campaigns that emphasises customer retention and satisfaction rather than sales transactions. It differs from other forms of marketing in that it recognises the long-term value of customer relationships and extends communication beyond intrusive advertising and sales promotional messages. With the growth of the Internet and mobile platforms, relationship marketing has continued to evolve as technology opens more collaborative and social communication channels such as tools for managing relationships with customers that go beyond demographics and customer service data collection. Relationship marketing extends to include inbound marketing, a combination of search optimization and strategic content, public relations, social media and application development.

Development

Relationship marketing refers to an arrangement where both the buyer and seller have an interest in a more satisfying exchange. This approach aims to transcend the post-purchase-exchange process with a customer in order to make richer contact by providing a more personalised purchase, using the experience to create stronger ties. A main focus on a long-term relationship with customers differentiates relationship marketing from other marketing techniques.

The technique was first proposed by American marketing scholars Berry and Jackson. Berry argued in a conference about the field of service marketing that relationship marketing is a marketing activity for enterprises to obtain, maintain and promote effective relationships with customers. After a long-term study on the marketing process of the service industry, it was concluded that the ultimate goal of enterprise marketing is not only to develop new customers but also to focus on maintaining existing customers. Ultimately, the goal is to improve the long-term interests of both parties through cooperative relationships. The study also argues that the cost of maintaining an old customer is far lower than the cost of developing a new customer and that maintaining a relationship with old consumers is more economical than developing new customers. Jackson further modified the concept in the aspect of industry marketing. He argued that the essence of relationship marketing is to attract, establish and maintain a close relationship with enterprise customers. Furthermore, other studies have concluded that the essence of relationship marketing is the actual maintenance of existing customers, which creates long-term interest in a product. This research conclusion has been generally recognised after the original proposal of relationship marketing. The research scope, however, is limited to the relationship with old customers, easily ignoring the dynamic development of customers because long-term customers are developed from new customers. If an enterprise is restricted to the maintenance of existing customers, it is impossible for it to achieve any progress or compete in the market since it cannot attract long-term customers in the first place.

From a social anthropological perspective, relationship marketing theory and practice can be interpreted as commodity exchange that instrumentalises features of gift exchange. Marketers, consciously or intuitively, are recognizing reciprocity, a 'pre-modern' form of exchange, and have begun to use it.

Thus relationship marketing revolves around gaining loyal customers. According to Liam Alvey, relationship marketing can be applied where there are competitive product alternatives for customers to choose from and an ongoing desire for that product. Research studying relationship marketing suggests that companies can do this through one of the three value strategies: best price, best product or best service. Hence companies can relay their relationship marketing message through value statements.

The practice of relationship marketing has been facilitated by several generations of customer relationship management software, which track and analyze each customer's preferences and activities. For example, an automobile manufacturer maintaining a database of when and how repeat customers buy their products, including data concerning their choices and purchase financing, can more efficiently develop one-to-one marketing offers and product benefits. Moreover, extensive use of such software is found in web applications. A consumer shopping profile can be built as a person shops online and is then used to compute his likely preferences. These predicted offerings can then be presented to the customer through cross-sell, email recommendation and other channels.

Relationship marketing has also migrated back into direct mail. Marketers can use the technological capabilities of digital, toner-based printing presses to produce unique, personalised pieces for each recipient through variable data printing. They can personalise documents by information contained in their databases, including name, address, demographics, purchase history and dozens to hundreds of other variables. The result is a printed piece that reflects the individual needs and preferences of each recipient, increasing the relevance of the piece and increasing the response rate.

Scope

Additionally, relationship marketing has been strongly influenced by reengineering. According to process reengineering theory, organizations should be structured according to complete tasks and processes rather than functions. Thus cross-function teams should be responsible for a whole process from beginning to end rather than having the work go from one functional department to another, whereas traditional marketing uses the functional (or 'silo') department approach where stages of production are handled by different departments. The legacy of traditional marketing can still be seen in the traditional four Ps of the marketing mix: pricing, product management, promotion, and placement. According to Gordon, the marketing mix approach is too limited to provide a usable framework for assessing and developing customer relationships in many industries and should be replaced by the relationship marketing alternative model where the focus is on customers, relationships and interaction over time rather than markets and products.

In contrast, relationship marketing is cross-functional, organised around processes that involve all aspects of an organization. In fact, some commentators prefer to call relationship marketing 'relationship management' because it involves much more than that which is included in normal marketing.

Because of its broad scope, relationship marketing can be effective in many contexts. As well as being relevant to 'for profit' businesses, research indicates that relationship marketing can be useful for organizations in the voluntary sector and in the public sector.

Martin Christopher, Adrian Payne and David Ballantyne at the Cranfield School of Management claim that relationship marketing has the potential to forge a synthesis between quality management, customer service management and marketing.

Approaches

Satisfaction

Relationship marketing relies on the communication and acquisition of consumer requirements solely from existing customers in a mutually beneficial exchange usually involving permission for contact by the customer through an opt-in system. With particular relevance to customer satisfaction, the relative price and quality of goods and services produced or sold through a company alongside customer service generally determine the amount of sales relative to that of competing companies. Although groups targeted through relationship marketing may be large, accuracy of communication and overall relevance to the customer remains higher than that of direct marketing. However, relationship marketing has less potential for generating new leads than direct marketing and is limited to viral marketing for acquiring customers.

Retention

A principle of relationship marketing is the retention of customers in order to ensure repeated trade from preexisting customers by satisfying requirements above those of competing companies through a mutually beneficial relationship. This technique balances new customers and opportunities with current and existing customers to maximise profit and counteracts the leaky bucket theory of business, where new customers in older direct marketing-oriented businesses are gained at the expense of the loss of older customers. This process of 'churning' is less economically viable than retaining all or the majority of customers using both direct and relationship management because securing new customers requires more investment.

Many companies in competing markets redirect or allocate large amounts of resources towards customer retention. In markets with increasing competition, attracting new customers may cost up to five times more than retaining current customers because direct or 'offensive' marketing requires much more to cause defection from competitors. However, it is suggested that because extensive classic marketing theories center on means of attracting customers and creating transactions rather than maintaining them, the predominant usage of direct marketing used in the past is now gradually being used more with relationship marketing as the latter's importance becomes more recognizable.

Reichheld and Sasser claim that a 5% improvement in customer retention can cause an increase in profitability of between 25 and 85 percent in terms of net present value depending on the industry. However, Carrol and Reichheld dispute these calculations, claiming that they result from faulty cross-sectional analysis. Research by John Fleming and Jim Asplund indicates that engaged customers generate 1.7 times more revenue than normal customers while having engaged employees and engaged customers returns a revenue gain of 3.4 times the normal return.

According to Buchanan and Gilles, the increased profitability associated with customer retention efforts occurs because of several factors once a relationship has been established with a customer:

1. The cost of acquisition occurs only at the beginning of a relationship. The longer a relationship, the lower the amortised cost.
2. Account maintenance costs decline as a percentage of total costs or as a percentage of revenue.
3. Long-term customers tend to be less inclined to switch products and also tend to be less price-sensitive. This can result in stable unit sales volume and increases in dollar-sales volume.
4. They also may provide free word-of-mouth promotions and referrals.
5. Furthermore, they are more likely to purchase ancillary products and high-profit margin supplemental products.
6. Customers who stay with a company tend to be satisfied with the relationship and are less likely to switch to competitors, increasing the difficulty for competitors to enter the market or gain market share.
7. Regular customers tend to be less expensive to service because they are familiar with the process, require less 'education' and are consistent in their order placement.
8. Increased customer retention and loyalty makes employees' jobs easier and more satisfying. In turn, happy employees increase customer satisfaction in a virtuous circle.

The relationship ladder of customer loyalty groups types of customers according to their level of loyalty. The ladder's first rung consists of prospects, non-customers who are likely to become customers in the future. This is followed by the successive rungs of customer, client, supporter, advocate, and partner. The relationship marketer's objective is to 'help' customers climb the ladder as high up as possible. This usually involves providing more personalised service and providing service quality that exceeds expectations at each step.

Customer retention efforts involve multiple considerations:

1. Customer valuation – Gordon describes how to value customers and categorise them according to their financial and strategic value so that companies can decide where to invest for deeper relationships and which relationships need to be served differently or even terminated.

2. Customer retention measurement – Dawkins and Reichheld calculated a company's customer retention rate. This is the percentage of customers at the beginning of the year that are still customers by the end of the year. In accordance with this statistic, an increase in retention rate from 80% to 90% is associated with a doubling of the average life of a customer relationship from 5 to 10 years. This ratio can be used to make comparisons between products, between market segments, and over time.

3. Determining reasons for defection – It comprises investigating root causes, not mere symptoms. This involves probing for details when contacting former customers. Other techniques include the analysis of customers' complaints and competitive benchmarking .

4. Developing and implementing a corrective plan – This could involve actions to improve employee practices, using benchmarking to determine best corrective practices, visible endorsement of top management, adjustments to the company's reward and recognition systems, and the use of recovery teams to eliminate the causes of defections.

A technique to calculate the value to a firm of a sustained customer relationship has been developed. This calculation is typically called customer lifetime value, a prediction of the net profit of a customer's relationship with a company.

Retention strategies may also include building barriers to customer switching by product bundling (combining several products or services into one package and offering them at a single price), cross-selling (selling related products to current customers), cross-promotions (giving discounts or other promotional incentives to purchasers of related products), loyalty programs (giving incentives for frequent purchases), increasing switching costs (adding termination costs such as mortgage termination fees), and integrating computer systems of multiple organizations (primarily in industrial marketing).

Many relationship marketers use a team-based approach due to the concept that the more points of contact between the organization and customer, the stronger the bond and the more secure the relationship.

Application

Relationship marketing and traditional or transactional marketing are not mutually exclusive, and there is no need for a conflict between them. In practice, a relationship-oriented marketer still has choices depending on the situation. Most firms blend the two approaches in order to reach a short-term marketing goal or long-term marketing strategy. Many products have a service component to them, which has been growing in recent decades. Relationship marketing aims to strengthen the relationship with clients and secure them. Morgan and Hunt made a distinction between economic and social exchange on the basis of exchange theory and concluded that the basic guarantee of social exchange was the spirit of the contract of trust and commitment. The transition from economic exchange theory to social exchange theory is where the one-time transaction's prevalence is reduced. Besides, the theoretical core of enterprise relationship marketing in this period is the cooperative relationship based on commitment, which defines relationship marketing from the perspective of exchange theory and emphasizes that relationship marketing is an activity related to the progress, maintenance and development of all marketing activities. The theory states that trading enterprises are composed of trust and commitment and that the basis of marketing activities to establish long-term relations.

Factors affecting cooperation from both sides include communication, power, cost and benefit and opportunism behavior; but the relationship effect is mainly formed by trust and commitment. Moreover, Copulsky and Wolf introduced terminology like 'one to one' marketing that leverages IT to target customers with specific offers. Enterprise has an incentive to improve the effect of relationships with customer. When access to data and information that improves the relationship with the customer has a low cost, enterprises pay the cost in order to improve relations with customers. Due to the development of communication and Internet technology, information costs have decreased substantially. Liker and Klamath introduced the relationship between enterprises and suppliers into the scope of relational marketing, claiming that in the marketing process manufacturers make suppliers assume corresponding responsibilities and enable them to exploit technological and resource advantages in the production process, improving their marketing innovation. Meanwhile, Lukas and Ferrell believe that the implementation of customer-oriented marketing can greatly promote marketing innovation and encourage enterprises to break through the traditional relationship model between enterprises and customers and propose new products. Lethe confirms the relationship between enterprises and customers through the observation of the benchmarking customer research, finding a positive correlation to innovation. He posits that good relations between enterprises and customers results in more efficient benchmarking, identifying new potential products, reduce the cost of new product development and increase market acceptance of products. Also he proposes that all relationships established with relevant parties for enterprise marketing are centered on the establishment of good customer relations: the core concept of relationship marketing is maintaining a relationship with customers. Guinness propounds that relationship marketing is a consciousness that regards the marketing process as the interaction between enterprises and various aspects of relationships and networks. According to his research, enterprise faces four relations: its relationship with the macro-environment, that with the micro-environment, market relations and relations with a special market. In addition, enterprises in the implementation of relationship marketing are often able to use networks to promote all aspects of relationship coordination and progress.

Internal Marketing

Relationship marketing stresses internal marketing, which is using a marketing orientation within an organization itself. Many relationship marketing attributes like collaboration, loyalty and trust determine internal customers' words and actions. According to this theory, every employee, team and department in the company is simultaneously a supplier and a customer of services and products. An employee obtains a service at a point in the value chain and then provides a service to another employee further along the value chain. If internal marketing is effective, every employee both provides and receives exceptional service to and from other employees. It also helps employees understand the significance of their roles and how their roles relate to others'. If implemented well, it can encourage every employee to see the process in terms of the customer's perception of value and the organization's strategic mission. Further, an effective internal marketing program is a prerequisite for effective external marketing efforts.

Six Markets Model

Christopher, Payne and Ballantyne identify six markets that they claim to be central to relationship marketing: internal markets, supplier markets, recruitment markets, referral markets, influence markets and customer markets. Referral marketing is the development and implementation of a marketing plan in order to stimulate referrals. Although it may take months before the effect of referral marketing is noticeable, it is often the most effective part of an overall marketing plan and the most efficient use of resources. Marketing to suppliers is aimed at ensuring a long-term conflict-free relationship in which all parties understand the others' needs and exceed their expectations. Such a strategy can reduce costs and improve quality. Meanwhile, Influence markets involve a wide range of sub-markets, including government regulators, standards bodies, lobbyists, stockholders, bankers, venture capitalists, financial analysts, stockbrokers, consumer associations, environmental associations and labor associations. These activities are typically carried out by the public relations department, but relationship marketers believe that marketing to all six markets is the responsibility of everyone in an organization. Each market may require its own explicit strategies and marketing mix.

Live-in Marketing

Live-in marketing (LIM) is a variant of marketing and advertising in which the target consumer is allowed to sample or use a product in a relaxed atmosphere over a long period of time. Much like product placement in film and television, LIM was developed as a means to reach select target demographics in a non-invasive and much less garish manner than traditional advertising.

While LIM represents an entirely untapped avenue of marketing, it is not an entirely novel idea. With the rising popularity of experiential and event marketing in North America and Europe and the relatively high ROI in terms of advertising dollars spent on experiential marketing compared to traditional big media advertising, industry analysts see LIM as a natural progression.

Premise

LIM functions around the premise that marketing or advertising agencies aim to appeal to companies' target demographic. Avenues such as sponsorship or direct product placement and sampling are explored in turn. Unlike traditional event marketing, LIM suggests that end-users can sample the product or service in a comfortable and relaxed atmosphere. The theory posits that the end-user will have as positive as possible an interaction with the given brand, thereby leading to word-of-mouth communication and potential future purchases. If the success of a traditional event and experiential marketing is shared with LIM, a lucrative and low-cost means of product promotion could be demonstrated. However, this means of advertising is still being developed, and more research is required to determine the true success of such campaigns. The first company to explicitly offer LIM services was Hostival Connect in late 2010.

Customer Relationship Management

Customer relationship management (CRM) is an approach to manage a company's interaction with current and potential customers. It uses data analysis about customers' history with a company to improve business relationships with customers, specifically focusing on customer retention and ultimately driving sales growth.

One important aspect of the CRM approach is the systems of CRM that compile data from a range of different communication channels, including a company's website, telephone, email, live chat, marketing materials and more recently, social media. Through the CRM approach and the systems used to facilitate it, businesses learn more about their target audiences and how to best cater to their needs.

The concept of customer relationship management started in the early 1970s, when customer satisfaction was evaluated using annual surveys or by front-line asking. At that time, businesses had to rely on standalone mainframe systems to automate sales, but the extent of technology allowed them to categorize customers in spreadsheets and lists. In 1982, Kate and Robert D. Kestnbaum introduced the concept of Database marketing, namely applying statistical methods to analyze and gather customer data. By 1986, Pat Sullivan and Mike Muhney released a customer evaluation system called ACT! based on the principle of digital rolodex, which offered a contact management service for the first time.

The trend was followed by numerous companies and independent developers trying to maximize leads' potential, including Tom Siebel, who designed the first CRM product Siebel Systems in 1993. In order to compete with these new and quickly growing stand-alone CRM solutions the established enterprise resource planning (ERP) software companies like Oracle, SAP, Peoplesoft and Navision started extending their sales, distribution and customer service capabilities with embedded CRM modules. This included embedding sales force automation or extended customer service (e.g. inquiry, activity management) as CRM features in their ERP.

Customer relationship management was popularized in 1997, due to the work of Siebel, Gartner, and IBM. Between 1997 and 2000, leading CRM products were enriched with shipping and marketing capabilities. Siebel introduced the first mobile CRM app called Siebel Sales Handheld in 1999. The idea of a stand-alone, cloud-hosted and moveable customer bases was soon adopted by other leading providers at the time, including PeopleSoft, Oracle, SAP and Salesforce.com.

The first open-source CRM system was developed by SugarCRM in 2004. During this period, CRM was rapidly migrating to cloud, as a result of which it became accessible to sole entrepreneurs and small teams. This increase in accessibility generated a huge wave of price reduction. Around 2009, developers began considering the options to profit from social media's momentum, and designed tools to help companies become accessible on all users' favorite networks. Many startups at the time benefited from this trend to provide exclusively social CRM solutions, including Base and Nutshell. The same year, Gartner organized and held the first Customer Relationship Management Summit, and summarized the features systems should offer to be classified as CRM solutions. In 2013 and 2014, most of the popular CRM products were linked to business intelligence systems and communication software to improve corporate communication and end-users' experience. The leading trend is to replace standardized CRM solutions with industry-specific ones, or to make them customizable enough to meet the needs of every business.

Types

Strategic

Strategic CRM is concentrated upon the development of a customer-centric business culture.

Operational

The primary goal of customer relationship management systems is to integrate and automate sales, marketing, and customer support. Therefore, these systems typically have a dashboard that gives an overall view of the three functions on a single customer view, a single page for each customer that a company may have. The dashboard may provide client information, past sales, previous marketing efforts, and more, summarizing all of the relationships between the customer and the firm. Operational CRM is made up of 3 main components: sales force automation, marketing automation, and service automation.

1. Sales force automation works with all stages in the sales cycle, from initially entering contact information to converting a prospective client into an actual client. It implements sales promotion analysis, automates the tracking of a client's account history for repeated sales or future sales and coordinates sales, marketing, call centers, and retail outlets. It prevents duplicate efforts between a salesperson and a customer and also automatically tracks all contacts and follow-ups between both parties.

2. Marketing automation focuses on easing the overall marketing process to make it more effective and efficient. CRM tools with marketing automation capabilities can automate repeated tasks, for example, sending out automated marketing emails at certain times to customers, or posting marketing information on social media. The goal with marketing automation is to turn a sales lead into a full customer. CRM systems today also work on customer engagement through social media.

3. Service automation is the part of the CRM system that focuses on direct customer service technology. Through service automation, customers are supported through multiple channels such as phone, email, knowledge bases, ticketing portals, FAQs, and more.

Analytical

The role of analytical CRM systems is to analyze customer data collected through multiple sources and present it so that business managers can make more informed decisions. Analytical CRM systems use techniques such as data mining, correlation, and pattern recognition to analyze the customer data. These analytics help improve customer service by finding small problems which can be solved, perhaps by marketing to different parts of a consumer audience differently. For example, through the analysis of a customer base's buying behavior, a company might see that this customer base has not been buying a lot of products recently. After scanning through this data, the company might think to market to this subset of consumers differently, in order to best communicate how this company's products might benefit this group specifically.

Collaborative

The third primary aim of CRM systems is to incorporate external stakeholders such as suppliers, vendors, and distributors, and share customer information across groups/departments and organisations. For example, feedback can be collected from technical support calls, which could help provide direction for marketing products and services to that particular customer in the future.

Customer Data Platform

A customer data platform (CDP) is a computer system used by marketing departments that assembles data about individual people from various sources into one database, with which other software systems can interact. As of February 2017 there were about twenty companies selling such systems and revenue for them was around US$300 million.

Components

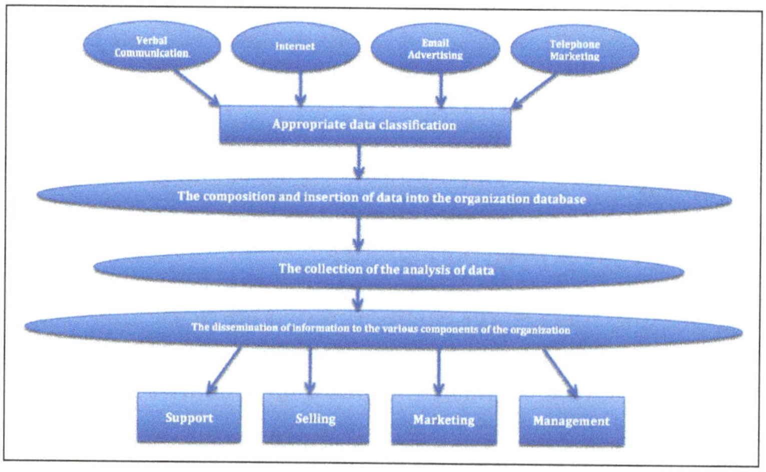

Components in the different types of CRM.

The main components of CRM are building and managing customer relationships through marketing, observing relationships as they mature through distinct phases, managing these relationships at each stage and recognizing that the distribution of value of a relationship to the firm is not homogeneous. When building and managing customer relationships through marketing, firms might benefit from using a variety of tools to help organizational design, incentive schemes, customer structures, and more to optimize the reach of its marketing campaigns. Through the acknowledgement of the distinct phases of CRM, businesses will be able to benefit from seeing the interaction of multiple relationships as connected transactions. The final factor of CRM highlights the importance of CRM through accounting for the profitability of customer relationships. Through studying the particular spending habits of customers, a firm may be able to dedicate different resources and amounts of attention to different types of consumers.

Relational Intelligence, or awareness of the variety of relationships a customer can have with a firm, is an important component to the main phases of CRM. Companies may be good at capturing demographic data, such as gender, age, income, and education, and connecting them with purchasing information to categorize customers into profitability tiers, but this is only a firm's mechanical view of customer relationships. This therefore is a sign that firms believe that customers are still resources that can be used for up-sell or cross-sell opportunities, rather than humans looking for interesting and personalized interactions.

CRM systems include:

1. Data warehouse technology, used to aggregate transaction information, to merge the information with CRM products, and to provide key performance indicators.
2. Opportunity management which helps the company to manage unpredictable growth and demand, and implement a good forecasting model to integrate sales history with sales projections.
3. CRM systems that track and measure marketing campaigns over multiple networks, tracking customer analysis by customer clicks and sales.
4. Some CRM software is available as a software as a service (SaaS), delivered via the internet and accessed via a web browser instead of being installed on a local computer. Businesses using the software do not purchase it, but typically pay a recurring subscription fee to the software vendor.
5. For small businesses a CRM system may consist of a contact manager system that integrates emails, documents, jobs, faxes, and scheduling for individual accounts. CRM systems available for specific markets (legal, finance) frequently focus on event management and relationship tracking as opposed to financial return on investment (ROI).
6. CRM systems for eCommerce, focused on marketing automation tasks, like: cart rescue, re-engage users with email, personalization.
7. Customer-centric relationship management (CCRM) is a nascent sub-discipline that focuses on customer preferences instead of customer leverage. CCRM aims to add value by engaging customers in individual, interactive relationships.
8. Systems for non-profit and membership-based organizations help track constituents, fundraising, sponsors' demographics, membership levels, membership directories, volunteering and communication with individuals.

Effect on Customer Satisfaction

Customer satisfaction has important implications for the economic performance of firms because it has the ability to increase customer loyalty and usage behavior and reduce customer complaints and the likelihood of customer defection. The implementation of a CRM approach is likely to have an effect on customer satisfaction and customer knowledge for a variety of different reasons.

Firstly, firms are able to customize their offerings for each customer. By accumulating information across customer interactions and processing this information to discover hidden patterns, CRM applications help firms customize their offerings to suit the individual tastes of their customers. This customization enhances the perceived quality of products and services from a customer's viewpoint, and because perceived quality is a determinant of customer satisfaction, it follows that CRM applications indirectly affect customer satisfaction. CRM applications also enable firms to provide timely, accurate processing of customer orders and requests and the ongoing management of customer accounts. For example, Piccoli and Applegate discuss how Wyndham uses IT tools to deliver a consistent service experience across its various properties to a customer. Both an improved ability to customize and a reduced variability of the consumption experience enhance perceived quality, which in turn positively affects customer satisfaction. Furthermore, CRM applications also help firms manage customer relationships more effectively across the stages of relationship initiation, maintenance, and termination.

Customer Benefits

With Customer relationship management systems customers are served better on day to day process and with more reliable information their demand of self service from companies will decrease. If there is less need to interact with the company for different problems, customer satisfaction level increases. These central benefits of CRM will be connected hypothetically to the three kinds of equity that are relationship, value and brand, and in the end to customer equity. Eight benefits were recognized to provide value drivers.

1. Enhanced ability to target profitable customers.
2. Integrated assistance across channels
3. Enhanced sales force efficiency and effectiveness
4. Improved pricing
5. Customized products and services
6. Improved customer service efficiency and effectiveness
7. Individualized marketing messages also called campaigns
8. Connect customers and all channels on a single platform.

In 2012, after reviewing the previous studies, someone selected some of those benefits which are more significant in customer's satisfaction and summarized them into the following cases:

1. Improve customer services: In general, customers would have some questions, concerns

or requests. CRM services provide the ability to a company for producing, allocating and managing requests or something made by customers. For example, call center software, which helps to connect a customer to the manager or person who can best assist them with their existing problem, is one of the CRM abilities that can be implemented to increase efficiency.

2. Increased personalized service or one-to-one service: Personalizing customer service or one-to-one service provides companies to improve understanding and gaining knowledge of the customers and also to have better knowledge about their customers' preferences, requirements and demands.
3. Responsive to customer's needs: Customers' situations and needs can be understood by the firms focusing on customer needs and requirements.
4. Customer segmentation: In CRM, segmentation is used to categorize customers, according to some similarity, such as industry, job or some other characteristics, into similar groups. Although these characteristics, can be one or more attributes. It can be defined as a subdividing the customers based on already known good discriminator.
5. Improve customization of marketing: Meaning of customization of marketing is that, the firm or organization adapt and change its services or products based on presenting a different and unique product or services for each customer. With the purpose of ensuring that customer needs and requirements are met Customization is used by the organization. Companies can put investment in information from customers and then customize their products or services to maintain customer interests.
6. Multichannel integration: Multichannel integration shows the point of co creation of customer value in CRM. On the other hand, a company's skill to perform multichannel integration successfully, is heavily dependent on the organization's ability getting together customer information from all channels and incorporate it with other related information.
7. Time saving: CRM will let companies to interact with customers more frequently, by personalized message and communication way which can be produced rapidly and matched on a timely basis, and finally they can better understand their customers and therefore look forward to their needs.
8. Improve customer knowledge: Firms can make and improve products and services through the information from tracking (e.g. via website tracking) customer behaviour to customer tastes and needs. CRM could contribute to a competitive advantage in improving firm's ability of customer information collecting to customize products and services according to customer needs.

Examples:

Research has found a 5% increase in customer retention boosts lifetime customer profits by 50% on average across multiple industries, as well as a boost of up to 90% within specific industries such as insurance. Companies that have mastered customer relationship strategies have the most successful CRM programs. For example, MBNA Europe has had a 75% annual profit growth since

1995. The firm heavily invests in screening potential cardholders. Once proper clients are identified, the firm retains 97% of its profitable customers. They implement CRM by marketing the right products to the right customers. The firm's customers' card usage is 52% above industry norm, and the average expenditure is 30% more per transaction. Also 10% of their account holders ask for more information on cross-sale products.

Amazon has also seen great success through its customer proposition. The firm implemented personal greetings, collaborative filtering, and more for the customer. They also used CRM training for the employees to see up to 80% of customers repeat.

Customer Profile

Customer or consumer profiles are the essence of the data that is collected alongside core data (name, address, company) and processed through customer analytics methods, essentially a type of profiling. A customer is abstracted to information that sums up consumption habits so far and projects them into the future so that they can be grouped for marketing and advertising purposes.

Improving CRM within a Firm

Consultants argue that it is important for companies establishing strong CRM systems to improve their relational intelligence. According to this argument, a company must recognize that people have many different types of relationships with different brands. One research study analyzed relationships between consumers in China, Germany, Spain, and the United States, with over 200 brands in 11 industries including airlines, cars and media. This information is valuable as it provides demographic, behavioral, and value-based customer segmentation. These types of relationships can be both positive and negative. Some customers view themselves as friends of the brands, while others as enemies, and some are mixed with a love-hate relationship with the brand. Some relationships are distant, intimate or anything in between.

Analyzing the Information

Managers must understand the different reasons for the types of relationships, and provide the customer with what they are looking for. Companies can collect this information by using surveys, interviews, and more, with current customers. For example, Frito-Lay conducted many ethnographic interviews with customers to try and understand the relationships they wanted with the companies and the brands. They found that most customers were adults who used the product to feel more playful. They may have enjoyed the company's bright orange color, messiness and shape.

Companies must also improve their relational intelligence of their CRM systems. These days, companies store and receive huge amounts of data through emails, online chat sessions, phone calls, and more. Many companies do not properly make use of this great amount of data, however. All of these are signs of what types of relationships the customer wants with the firm, and therefore companies may consider investing more time and effort in building out their relational intelligence. Companies can use data mining technologies and web searches to understand relational signals. Social media such as social networking sites, blogs and forums can also be used to collect and analyze information. Understanding the customer and capturing this data allows companies to convert customer's signals into information and knowledge that the firm can use to understand a potential customer's desired relations with a brand.

It is also very important to analyze all of this information to determine which relationships prove the most valuable. This helps convert data into profits for the firm. Stronger bonds contribute to building market share. By managing different portfolios for different segments of the customer base, the firm can achieve strategic goals.

Employee Training

Many firms have also implemented training programs to teach employees how to recognize and effectively create strong customer–brand relationships. For example, Harley Davidson sent its employees on the road with customers, who were motorcycle enthusiasts, to help solidify relationships. Other employees have also been trained in social psychology and the social sciences to help bolster strong customer relationships. Customer service representatives must be educated to value customer relationships, and trained to understand existing customer profiles. Even the finance and legal departments should understand how to manage and build relationships with customers.

Application

Applying new technologies while using CRM systems requires changes in infrastructure of the organization as well as deployment of new technologies such as business rules, databases and information technology.

Call Centers

Contact center CRM providers are popular for small and mid-market businesses. These systems codify the interactions between company and customers by using analytics and key performance indicators to give the users information on where to focus their marketing and customer service. This allows agents to have access to a caller's history to provide personalized customer communication. The intention is to maximize average revenue per user, decrease churn rate and decrease idle and unproductive contact with the customers.

Growing in popularity is the idea of gamifying, or using game design elements and game principles in a non-game environment such as customer service environments. The gamification of customer service environments includes providing elements found in games like rewards and bonus points to customer service representatives as a method of feedback for a job well done. Gamification tools can motivate agents by tapping into their desire for rewards, recognition, achievements, and competition.

Contact-center Automation

Contact-center automation, the practice of having an integrated system that coordinates contacts between an organization and the public, is designed to reduce the repetitive and tedious parts of a contact center agent's job. Automation prevents this by having pre-recorded audio messages that help customers solve their problems. For example, an automated contact center may be able to re-route a customer through a series of commands asking him or her to select a certain number in order to speak with a particular contact center agent who specializes in the field in which the customer has a question. Software tools can also integrate with the agent's desktop tools to handle customer questions and requests. This also saves time on behalf of the employees.

Social Media

Social CRM involves the use of social media and technology to engage and learn from consumers. Because the public, especially young people, are increasingly using social networking sites, companies use these sites to draw attention to their products, services and brands, with the aim of building up customer relationships to increase demand.

Some CRM systems integrate social media sites like Twitter, LinkedIn and Facebook to track and communicate with customers. These customers also share their own opinions and experiences with a company's products and services, giving these firms more insight. Therefore, these firms can both share their own opinions and also track the opinions of their customers.

Enterprise feedback management software platforms combine internal survey data with trends identified through social media to allow businesses to make more accurate decisions on which products to supply.

Location-based Services

CRM systems can also include technologies that create geographic marketing campaigns. The systems take in information based on a customer's physical location and sometimes integrates it with popular location-based GPS applications. It can be used for networking or contact management as well to help increase sales based on location.

Business-to-business Transactions

Despite the general notion that CRM systems were created for the customer-centric businesses, they can also be applied to B2B environments to streamline and improve customer management conditions. For the best level of CRM operation in a B2B environment, the software must be personalized and delivered at individual levels.

The main differences between business-to-consumer (B2C) and business-to-business CRM systems concern aspects like sizing of contact databases and length of relationships. Business-to-business companies tend to have smaller contact databases than business-to-consumer, the volume of sales in business-to-business is relatively small. There are fewer figure propositions in business-to-business, but in some cases, they cost a lot more than business-to-consumer items and relationships in business-to-business environment are built over a longer period of time. Furthermore, business-to-business CRM must be easily integrated with products from other companies. Such integration enables the creation of forecasts about customer behavior based on their buying history, bills, business success, etc. An application for a business-to-business company must have a function to connect all the contacts, processes and deals among the customers segment and then prepare a paper. Automation of sales process is an important requirement for business-to-business products. It should effectively manage the deal and progress it through all the phases towards signing. Finally, a crucial point is personalization. It helps the business-to-business company to create and maintain strong and long-lasting relationship with the customer.

Market Trends

In the Gartner CRM Summit 2010 challenges like "system tries to capture data from social networking traffic like Twitter, handles Facebook page addresses or other online social networking sites" were discussed and solutions were provided that would help in bringing more clientele. Many CRM vendors offer subscription-based web tools (cloud computing) and SaaS. Some CRM systems are equipped with mobile capabilities, making information accessible to remote sales staff. Salesforce.com was the first company to provide enterprise applications through a web browser, and has maintained its leadership position.

Traditional providers have recently moved into the cloud-based market via acquisitions of smaller providers: Oracle purchased RightNow in October 2011 and SAP acquired SuccessFactors in December 2011.

The era of the "social customer" refers to the use of social media by customers. CRM philosophy and strategy has shifted to encompass social networks and user communities.

Sales forces also play an important role in CRM, as maximizing sales effectiveness and increasing sales productivity is a driving force behind the adoption of CRM. Empowering sales managers was listed as one of the top 5 CRM trends in 2013.

Another related development is vendor relationship management (VRM), which provide tools and services that allow customers to manage their individual relationship with vendors. VRM development has grown out of efforts by ProjectVRM at Harvard's Berkman Center for Internet & Society and Identity Commons' Internet Identity Workshops, as well as by a growing number of startups and established companies.

Pharmaceutical companies were some of the first investors in sales force automation (SFA) and some are on their third- or fourth-generation implementations. However, until recently, the deployments did not extend beyond SFA—limiting their scope and interest to Gartner analysts.

Another trend worth noting is the rise of Customer Success as a discipline within companies. More and more companies establish Customer Success teams as separate from the traditional Sales team and task them with managing existing customer relations. This trend fuels demand for additional capabilities for more holistic understanding of the customer health, which is a limitation for many existing vendors in the space. As a result, a growing number of new entrants enter the market, while existing vendors add capabilities in this area to their suites. In 2017, artificial intelligence and predictive analytics were identified as the newest trends in CRM.

Customer Satisfaction

Customer satisfaction (often abbreviated as CSAT, more correctly CSat) is a term frequently used in marketing. It is a measure of how products and services supplied by a company meet or surpass customer expectation. Customer satisfaction is defined as "the number of customers, or percentage of total customers, whose reported experience with a firm, its products, or its services (ratings) exceeds specified satisfaction goals."

The Marketing Accountability Standards Board (MASB) endorses the definitions, purposes, and constructs of classes of measures that appear in Marketing Metrics as part of its ongoing Common Language in Marketing Project. In a survey of nearly 200 senior marketing managers, 71 percent responded that they found a customer satisfaction metric very useful in managing and monitoring their businesses.

It is seen as a key performance indicator within business and is often part of a Balanced Scorecard. In a competitive marketplace where businesses compete for customers, customer satisfaction is seen as a key differentiator and increasingly has become a key element of business strategy.

Purpose

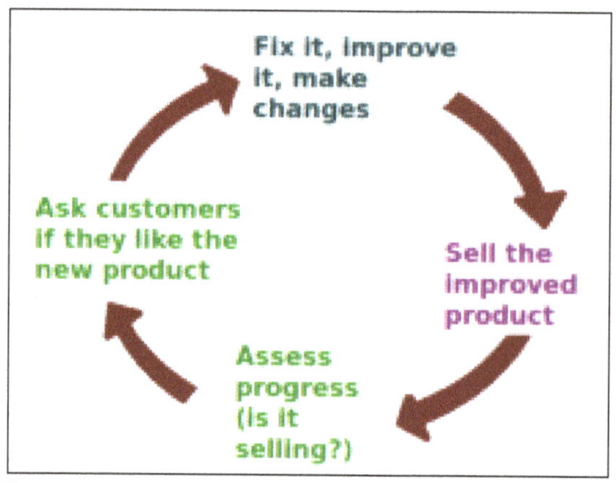

A business ideally is continually seeking feedback to improve customer satisfaction.

Customer satisfaction provides a leading indicator of consumer purchase intentions and loyalty. Customer satisfaction data are among the most frequently collected indicators of market perceptions. Their principal use is twofold:

1. Within organizations, the collection, analysis and dissemination of these data send a message about the importance of tending to customers and ensuring that they have a positive experience with the company's goods and services.

2. Although sales or market share can indicate how well a firm is performing currently, satisfaction is perhaps the best indicator of how likely it is that the firm's customers will make further purchases in the future. Much research has focused on the relationship between customer satisfaction and retention. Studies indicate that the ramifications of satisfaction are most strongly realized at the extremes.

On a five-point scale, individuals who rate their satisfaction level as '5' are likely to become return customers and might even evangelize for the firm. (A second important metric related to satisfaction is willingness to recommend. This metric is defined as "The percentage of surveyed customers who indicate that they would recommend a brand to friends. When a customer is satisfied with a product, he or she might recommend it to friends, relatives and colleagues. This can be a powerful marketing advantage.) Individuals who rate their satisfaction level as '1,' by contrast, are unlikely to return. Further, they can hurt the firm by making negative comments about it to prospective customers. Willingness to recommend is a key metric relating to customer satisfaction.

Theoretical Ground

In literature antecedents of satisfaction are studied from different aspects. The considerations extend from psychological to physical and from normative to positive aspects. However, in most of the cases the consideration is focused on two basic constructs as customers expectations prior to purchase or use of a product and his relative perception of the performance of that product after using it.

A customer's expectations about a product tell us how he or she anticipates how that product will perform. As it is suggested in the literature, consumers may have various "types" of expectations when forming opinions about a product's anticipated performance. For example, four types of expectations are identified by Miller: ideal, expected, minimum tolerable, and desirable. While, Day indicated among expectations, the ones that are about the costs, the product nature, the efforts in obtaining benefits and lastly expectations of social values. Perceived product performance is considered as an important construct due to its ability to allow making comparisons with the expectations.

It is considered that customers judge products on a limited set of norms and attributes. Olshavsky and Miller and Olson and Dover designed their researches as to manipulate actual product performance, and their aim was to find out how perceived performance ratings were influenced by expectations. These studies took out the discussions about explaining the differences between expectations and perceived performance.

In some research studies, scholars have been able to establish that customer satisfaction has a strong emotional, i.e., affective, component. Still others show that the cognitive and affective components of customer satisfaction reciprocally influence each other over time to determine overall satisfaction.

Especially for durable goods that are consumed over time, there is value to taking a dynamic perspective on customer satisfaction. Within a dynamic perspective, customer satisfaction can evolve over time as customers repeatedly use a product or interact with a service. The satisfaction experienced with each interaction (transactional satisfaction) can influence the overall, cumulative satisfaction. Scholars showed that it is not just overall customer satisfaction, but also customer loyalty that evolves over time.

Disconfirmation Model

"The Disconfirmation Model is based on the comparison of customers' expectations and their perceived performance ratings. Specifically, an individual's expectations are confirmed when a product performs as expected. It is negatively confirmed when a product performs more poorly than expected. The disconfirmation is positive when a product performs over the expectations. There are four constructs to describe the traditional disconfirmation paradigm mentioned as expectations, performance, disconfirmation and satisfaction." "Satisfaction is considered as an outcome of purchase and use, resulting from the buyers' comparison of expected rewards and incurred costs of the purchase in relation to the anticipated consequences. In operation, satisfaction is somehow similar to attitude as it can be evaluated as the sum of satisfactions with some features of a product." In the literature, cognitive and affective models of satisfaction are also developed and considered as alternatives.

Construction

Organizations need to retain existing customers while targeting non-customers. Measuring customer satisfaction provides an indication of how successful the organization is at providing products and/or services to the marketplace.

Customer satisfaction is measured at the individual level, but it is almost always reported at an aggregate level. It can be, and often is, measured along various dimensions. A hotel, for example, might ask customers to rate their experience with its front desk and check-in service, with the room, with the amenities in the room, with the restaurants, and so on. Additionally, in a holistic sense, the hotel might ask about overall satisfaction 'with your stay.'

As research on consumption experiences grows, evidence suggests that consumers purchase goods and services for a combination of two types of benefits: hedonic and utilitarian. Hedonic benefits are associated with the sensory and experiential attributes of the product. Utilitarian benefits of a product are associated with the more instrumental and functional attributes of the product.

Customer satisfaction is an ambiguous and abstract concept and the actual manifestation of the state of satisfaction will vary from person to person and product/service to product/service. The state of satisfaction depends on a number of both psychological and physical variables which correlate with satisfaction behaviors such as return and recommend rate. The level of satisfaction can also vary depending on other options the customer may have and other products against which the customer can compare the organization's products.

Work done by Parasuraman, Zeithaml and Berry (Leonard L) between 1985 and 1988 provides the basis for the measurement of customer satisfaction with a service by using the gap between the customer's expectation of performance and their perceived experience of performance. This provides the measurer with a satisfaction "gap" which is objective and quantitative in nature. Work done by Cronin and Taylor propose the "confirmation/disconfirmation" theory of combining the "gap" described by Parasuraman, Zeithaml and Berry as two different measures (perception and expectation of performance) into a single measurement of performance according to expectation.

The usual measures of customer satisfaction involve a survey using a Likert scale. The customer is asked to evaluate each statement in terms of their perceptions and expectations of performance of the organization being measured.

Good quality measures need to have high satisfaction loadings, good reliability, and low error variances. In an empirical study comparing commonly used satisfaction measures it was found that two multi-item semantic differential scales performed best across both hedonic and utilitarian service consumption contexts. A study by Wirtz & Lee, found that a six-item 7-point semantic differential scale, which is a six-item 7-point bipolar scale, consistently performed best across both hedonic and utilitarian services. It loaded most highly on satisfaction, had the highest item reliability, and had by far the lowest error variance across both studies. In the study, the six items asked respondents' evaluation of their most recent experience with ATM services and ice cream restaurant, along seven points within these six items: "pleased me to displeased me", "contented with to disgusted with", "very satisfied with to very dissatisfied with", "did a good job for me to did a poor job for me", "wise choice to poor choice" and "happy with to unhappy with". A semantic differential (4 items) scale , which is a four-item 7-point bipolar scale, was the second best performing measure, which was again consistent across both contexts. In the study, respondents were asked to evaluate their experience with both products, along seven points within these four items: "satisfied to dissatisfied", "favorable to unfavorable", "pleasant to unpleasant" and "I like it very much to I didn't like it at all". The third best scale was single-item percentage measure, a one-item 7-point bipolar scale. Again, the respondents were asked to evaluate their experience on both ATM services and ice cream restaurants, along seven points within "delighted to terrible".

Finally, all measures captured both affective and cognitive aspects of satisfaction, independent of their scale anchors. Affective measures capture a consumer's attitude (liking/disliking) towards a product, which can result from any product information or experience. On the other hand, cognitive element is defined as an appraisal or conclusion on how the product's performance compared against expectations (or exceeded or fell short of expectations), was useful (or not useful), fit the situation (or did not fit), exceeded the requirements of the situation (or did not exceed).

Recent research shows that in most commercial applications, such as firms conducting customer surveys, a single-item overall satisfaction scale performs just as well as a multi-item scale. Especially in larger scale studies where a researcher needs to gather data from a large number of customers, a single-item scale may be preferred because it can reduce total survey error.

Methodologies

American Customer Satisfaction Index (ACSI) is a scientific standard of customer satisfaction. Academic research has shown that the national ACSI score is a strong predictor of Gross Domestic Product (GDP) growth, and an even stronger predictor of Personal Consumption Expenditure (PCE) growth. On the microeconomic level, academic studies have shown that ACSI data is related to a firm's financial performance in terms of return on investment (ROI), sales, long-term firm value (Tobin's *q*), cash flow, cash flow volatility, human capital performance, portfolio returns, debt financing, risk, and consumer spending. Increasing ACSI scores have been shown to predict loyalty, word-of-mouth recommendations, and purchase behavior. The ACSI measures customer satisfaction annually for more than 200 companies in 43 industries and 10 economic sectors. In addition to quarterly reports, the ACSI methodology can be applied to private sector companies and government agencies in order to improve loyalty and purchase intent.

The Kano model is a theory of product development and customer satisfaction developed in the 1980s by Professor Noriaki Kano that classifies customer preferences into five categories: Attractive, One-Dimensional, Must-Be, Indifferent, Reverse. The Kano model offers some insight into the product attributes which are perceived to be important to customers.

SERVQUAL or RATER is a service-quality framework that has been incorporated into customer-satisfaction surveys (e.g., the revised Norwegian Customer Satisfaction Barometer) to indicate the gap between customer expectations and experience.

J.D. Power and Associates provides another measure of customer satisfaction, known for its top-box approach and automotive industry rankings. J.D. Power and Associates' marketing research consists primarily of consumer surveys and is publicly known for the value of its product awards.

Other research and consulting firms have customer satisfaction solutions as well. These include A.T. Kearney's Customer Satisfaction Audit process, which incorporates the Stages of Excellence framework and which helps define a company's status against eight critically identified dimensions.

For B2B customer satisfaction surveys, where there is a small customer base, a high response rate to the survey is desirable. The American Customer Satisfaction Index found that response rates for paper-based surveys were around 10% and the response rates for e-surveys (web, wap and e-mail) were averaging between 5% and 15% - which can only provide a straw poll of the customers' opinions.

In the European Union member states, many methods for measuring impact and satisfaction of e-government services are in use, which the eGovMoNet project sought to compare and harmonize.

These customer satisfaction methodologies have not been independently audited by the Marketing Accountability Standards Board (MASB) according to MMAP (Marketing Metric Audit Protocol).

Recently there has been a growing interest in predicting customer satisfaction using big data and machine learning methods (with behavioral and demographic features as predictors) to take targeted preventive actions aimed at avoiding churn, complaints and dissatisfaction.

Customer Experience

In commerce, customer experience (CX) is the product of an interaction between an organization and a customer over the duration of their relationship. This interaction is made up of three parts: the customer journey, the brand touchpoints the customer interacts with, and the environments the customer experiences (including digital environment) during their experience. A good customer experience means that the individual's experience during all points of contact matches the individual's expectations. Gartner asserts the importance of managing the customer's experience.

Customer experience implies customer involvement at different levels – such as rational, emotional, sensorial, physical, and spiritual. Customers respond diversely to direct and indirect contact with a company. Direct contact usually occurs when the purchase or use is initiated by the customer. Indirect contact often involves advertising, news reports, unplanned encounters with sales representatives, word-of-mouth recommendations or criticisms.

Customer experience encompasses every aspect of a company's offering—the quality of customer care, but also advertising, packaging, product and service features, ease of use, and reliability. Creating direct relationships in the place where customers buy, use and receive services by a business intended for customers such as instore or face to face contact with the customer which could be seen through interacting with the customer through the retail staff. We then have indirect relationships which can take the form of unexpected interactions through a company's product representative, certain services or brands and positive recommendations – or it could even take the form of "criticism, advertising, news, reports" and many more along that line.

Customer experience is created by the contribution of not only the customers' values but also by the contribution of the company providing the experience.

All of the events experienced by customers before and after a purchase are part of the customer experience. What a customer experiences is personal and may involve sensory, emotional, rational and physical aspects to create a memorable experiencer. In the retail industry, both company and customers play a big role in creating a customer experience.

Forbes describes the customer experience as the "cumulative impact of multiple touchpoints" over the course of a customer's interaction with an organization. Some companies are known to segment the customer experience into interactions through the web and social media, while others define human interaction such as over-the-phone customer service or face-to-face retail service as the customer experience.

According to Forrester Research, the six disciplines for great customer experience are strategy, customer understanding, design, measurement, governance and culture. A company's ability to deliver an experience that sets it apart in the eyes of its customers will increase the amount of consumer spending with the company and inspire loyalty to its brand. According to Jessica Sebor, "loyalty is now driven primarily by a company's interaction with its customers and how well it delivers on their wants and needs."

Wharton's Professor of Marketing Barbara E. Kahn has established an evolutional approach to customer experience as the third of four stages of any company in terms of its customer centricity maturity. These progressive phases are:

1. Product orientation: Companies just manufacture goods and offer them the best way possible.
2. Market orientation: Some consideration on customer needs and segmentation arises, developing different marketing mix bundles for each one.
3. Customer experience: Adding to the other two factors some recognition of the importance of providing an emotionally positive experience to customers.
4. Authenticity: This is the top maturity stage of companies. Products and service emerge from real soul of brand and connect naturally and on long term sustainable basis with clients and other stakeholders.

In today's competitive climate, more than just low prices and innovative products are required to survive in retail business. Customer experience involves every point of contact you have with a customer and the interactions with the products or service of the business. Customer experience has emerged as a vital strategy for all retail businesses that are facing competition. According to Holbrook & Hirschman studies customer experience can be defined as a whole event that a customer comes into contact with when interacting with a certain business. This experience often affects the emotions of the customer. The whole experience occurs when the interaction takes place through the stimulation of goods and services consumed.

The type experience seen through a marketing perspective is put forward by Pine & Gilmore which they state that an experience can be unique which may mean different individuals will not have the same level experience that may not be memorable to the person therefore it won't be remembered over a period of time. Certain types of experiences may involve different aspects of the individual person such as emotional, physical, intellectual or even spiritual.

Customer experience is the stimulation a company creates for the senses of the consumers, this means that the companies and that particular brand can control the stimuli that they have given to the consumers senses which the companies can then control the consumers reaction resulting from the stimulation process, giving more acquisition of the customer experience as expected by company.

Customer experience is about, adding value for customers buying products and services through customer participation and connection, by managing all aspects of the encounter. The encounter includes touchpoints. Businesses can create and modify touchpoints so that they are suited to their consumers which changes/enhances the customers' experience. Creating an experience for the customer can lead to greater brand loyalty and brand recognition in the form of logos, colour, smell, touch, taste, etc.

Development

There are many elements in the shopping experience associated with a customer's experience. Customer service, a brand's ethical ideals and the shopping environment are examples of factors that effect a customer's experience. Understanding and effectively developing a positive customer experience has become a staple within businesses and brands to combat growing competition Many consumers are well informed, they are able to easily compare two similar products or services together. Therefore, consumers are looking for experiences that can fulfil their intentions A brand that can provide this gains a competitive advantage over their competition. A study by Ali found that developing a positive behavioural culture created a greater competitive advantage in the long term. He looked at the customer experience at resort hotels and discovered that providing the best hotel service was not sufficient. To optimise a customer's experience, management must also consider peace of mind and relaxation, recognition and escapism, involvement, and hedonics. The overall customer experience must be considered. The development of a positive customer experience is important as it increases the chances of a customer to make continued purchases and develops brand loyalty. Brand loyalty can turn customers into advocates, resulting in a long term relationship between both parties. This promotes word-of-mouth and turns the customer into a touchpoint for the brand. Potential customers can develop opinions through another's experiences. Males and females both respond differently to brands and therefore, will experience the same brand differently. Males respond effectively to relational, behavioural and cognitive experiences whereas females respond greater to behavioural, cognitive and effective experiences in relation to branded apps. If female consumers are the target market, an app advert focused on the emotion of the product will provide an effective customer experience.

Today, retail stores tend to exist in shopping area's such as malls or shopping districts. Very few operate in areas alone Customer experience is not limited to the purchase alone. It includes all activities that may influence a customer's experience with a brand. Therefore, a shopping centre's reputation that a store is located in will effect a brands customer experience. This is an example of the shopping environment effecting a customer's experience. A study by Hart, Stachow and Cadogan found that a consumer's opinion of a town centre can affect the opinion of the retail stores operating within both negatively and positively. They shared an example of a town centre's management team developing synergy between the surrounding location and the retail stores. A location bound with historical richness could provide an opportunity for the town centre and local businesses to connect at deeper level with their customers. They suggested that town centre management and retail outlets should work cooperatively to develop an effective customer experience. This will result in all stores benefiting from customer retention and loyalty.

Another effective way to develop a positive customer experience is by actively engaging a customer with an activity. Human and physical components of an experience are very important. Customers are able to recall active, hands-on experiences much more effectively and accurately than passive activities. Participants within a study were able to recount previous luxury driving experiences due to its high involvement. However, this can also have a negative effect on the customer's experience. Just as active, hands-on experiences can greatly develop value creation, it can also greatly facilitate value destruction. This is related to a customer's satisfaction of their experience. By understanding what causes satisfaction or dissatisfaction of a customer's experience, management can appropriately implement changes within their approach. A study on the customer experience in budget hotels revealed interesting results. Customer satisfaction was largely influenced by tangible and sensory dimensions. This included cleanliness, shower comfortability and room temperature, just to name a few. As budget hotels are cheap, customers expected the basic elements to be satisfactory and the luxury elements to be non-existent. If these dimensions did not reach an appropriate standard, satisfaction would decline, resulting in a negative experience. These dimensions also relate to the statement above about how participants were able to recall their luxury driving experiences. Luxury driving exhibits both tangible and sensory dimensions, therefore, it is not surprising that these experiences were easily recalled. A change in a company's culture is an effective way to improve the customer's experience on a large scale. DHL freight, a road transportation solutions company, decided to prioritize the customer's experience. Throughout the whole organisation which is based in multiple locations, they implemented this change. The change included a vision and purpose evaluation and improved customer interactions. This improved customer perception, changed employee's mind-set, and improved customer dialogues. Customer experience can only be changed when it becomes a business's top priority.

Management

Customer experience management (CEM or CXM) is the process that companies use to oversee and track all interactions with a customer during their relationship. This involves the strategy of building around the needs of individual customers. According to Jeananne Rae, companies are realizing that "building great consumer experiences is a complex enterprise, involving strategy, integration of technology, orchestrating business models, brand management and CEO commitment."

According to Bernd Schmitt, "the term 'Customer Experience Management' represents the discipline, methodology and/or process used to comprehensively manage a customer's cross-channel exposure, interaction and transaction with a company, product, brand or service." A company must define and understand all dimensions of the customer experience in order to have long-term success.

Although 80% of businesses state that they offer a "great customer experience," according to author James Allen, this contrasts with the 8% of customers expressing satisfaction with their experience. Allen asserts that for companies to meet the demands of providing an exceptional customer experience, they must be able to execute the "Three Ds":

1. Designing the correct incentive for the correctly identified consumer, offered in an enticing environment.
2. Delivery: A company's ability to focus the entire team across various functions to deliver the proposed experience.
3. Development ultimately determines a company's success, with an emphasis on developing consistency in execution.

CEM has been recognized as the future of the customer service and sales industry. Companies are using this approach to anticipate customer needs and adopt the mindset of the customer.

CEM depicts a business strategy designed to manage the customer experience and gives benefits to both retailers and customers. CEM can be monitored through surveys, targeted studies, observational studies, or "voice of customer" research. It captures the instant response of the customer to its encounters with the brand or company. Customer surveys, customer contact data, internal operations process and quality data, and employee input are all sources of "voice of customer" data that can be used to quantify the cost of inaction on customer experience issues.

The aim of CEM is to optimize the customer experience through gaining the loyalty of the current customers in a multi-channel environment and ensure they are completely satisfied. Its also to create advocates of their current customers with potential customers as a word of mouth form of marketing. However, common efforts at improving CEM can have the opposite effect.

Utilizing surroundings includes using visuals, displays and interactivity to connect with customers and create an experience. CEM can be related to customer journey mapping, a concept pioneered by Ron Zemke and Chip Bell. Customer journey mapping is a design tool used to track customers' movements through different touchpoints with the business in question. It maps out the first encounters people may have with the brand and shows the different route people can take through the different channels or marketing (e.g. online, television, magazine, newspaper). Integrated marketing communications (IMC) is also being used to manage the customer experience; IMC is about sending a consistent message amongst all platforms; these platforms include: Advertising, personal selling, public relations, direct marketing, and sales promotion.

CEM holds great importance in terms of research and showing that academia is not as applicable and usable as the practice behind it. Typically, to make the best use of CEM and ensure its accuracy, the customer journey must be viewed from the actual perspective of customers, not the business or organization. It needs to be noted that there isn't a specific set of rules or steps to follow as companies (in their various industries) will have different strategies. Therefore, development into the conceptual and theoretical aspects are needed, based from customers' perspective on the brand experience. This can be seen through different scholarly research. The reasoning behind the interest in CEM increasing so significantly is because businesses are looking for competitive differentiation. Businesses want to be more profitable and see this as a means to do so. Hence why businesses want to offer a better experience to their customers and want to manage this process efficiently. In order to gain success as a business customers need to be understood. In order to fully utilise the models used in practice, academic research that is conducted can assist the practical aspect. This along with recognising past customer experiences can help manage future experiences.

A good indicator of customer satisfaction is the Net Promoter Score (NPS). This indicates out of a score of ten if a customer would recommend a business to other people. With scores of nine and ten these people are called protractors and will recommend other to the given product but on the other end of the spectrum are detractors, those who give the score zero to six. Subtracting the detractors from the protractors gives the calculation of advocacy. Those businesses with higher scores are likely to be more successful and give a better customer experience.

Not all aspects of CEM can be controlled by the business (e.g. other people and the influence they have). Besides, there is not much substantial information to support CEM claims in terms of academic research.

Managing the Communication

The classical linear communication model includes having one sender or source sending out a message that goes through the media (television, magazines) then to the receiver. The classical linear model is a form of mass marketing which targets a large number of people where only a few may be customers; this is a form non-personal communication. The adjusted model shows the source sending a message either to the media or directly to an opinion leader/s and/or opinion former (Model, actress, credible source, trusted figure in society, YouTuber/reviewer), which send a decoded message to the receiver. The adjusted model is a form of interpersonal communication where feedback is almost instantaneous with receiving the message. The adjusted model means that there are many more platforms of marketing with the use of social media, which connects people with more touchpoints. Marketers use digital experience to enhance the customer experience. Enhancing digital experiences influences changes to the CEM, the customer journey map and IMC. The adjusted model allows marketers to communicate a message designed specifically for the 'followers' of the particular opinion leader or opinion former, sending a personalised message and creating a digital experience.

Persuasion Techniques

Persuasion techniques are used when trying to send a message in order for an experience to take place. Marcom Projects came up with five mind shapers to show how humans view things. The five mind shapers of persuasion include:

1. Frames – Only showing what they want you to see (a paid ad post).

2. Setting and context – The surrounding objects of items for sale.
3. Filters – Previous beliefs that shape thoughts after an interaction.
4. Social influence – How behaviours of others impact us.
5. Belief (placebo effect) – The expectation.

Mind shapers can be seen through the use of the adjusted communication model, it allows the source/sender to create a perception for the receiver. Mind shapers can take two routes for persuasion:

1. Central route, this route requires a thought process to occur, the content of the message is important. People think thoroughly about their reaction/reply. This can be seen in the purchase of homes, Internet providers, insurance companies.
2. Peripheral route, does not require very much thought, the brain makes the connection. Marketers use recognisable cues like logos, colours and sounds. This type of marketing is used when the decision is about something simple like choosing a drink, food.

Marketers can use human thought processes and target these to create greater experiences, they can do so by either maker the process more simple and creating interactive steps to help the process.

Customer Relationship Management

According to Das , customer relationship management (CRM) is the "establishment, development, maintenance and optimization of long-term mutually valuable relationships between consumers and organizations". The official definition of CRM by the Customer Relationship Management Research Center is "a strategy used to learn more about the customers need and behaviours in order to develop stronger relationships with them". The purpose of this strategy is to change the approach to customers and improving the experience for the consumer by making the supplier more aware of their buying habits and frequencies.

The D4 Company Analysis is an audit tool that considers the four aspects of strategy, people, technology and processes in the design of a CRM strategy. The analysis includes four main steps.

1. Define the existing customer relationship management processes within the company.
2. Determine the perceptions of how the company manages their customer relationships, both internally and externally.
3. Design the ideal customer relationship management solutions relative to the company or industry.
4. Deliver a strategy for the implementation of the recommendations based on the findings.

Digital Customer Journey

In the classical marketing model, marketing is deemed to a funnel: at the beginning of the process (in the "awareness" stage) there are many branches competing for the attention of the customer, and this number is reduced through the different purchasing stages. Marketing is an action of "pushing" the brand through few touch points (for example through TV ads).

Since the rise of the World Wide Web and smartphone applications, there are many more touch points from new content serving platforms (Facebook, Twitter, YouTube etc.), individual online presences (such as websites, forums, blogs, etc.) and dedicated smartphone applications.

As a result, this process has become a type of "journey":

1. The number of brands does not decrease during the process of evaluating and purchasing a product.
2. Brands not taken into account in the "awareness" stage may be added during the evaluation or even purchase stage.
3. Following the post-purchase stage, there is a return to the first step in the process, thus feeding the brand awareness.

In relation to customers and the channels which are associated with sales, these are multichannel in nature. Due to the growth and importance of social media and digital advancement, these aspects need to be understood by businesses to be successful in this era of customer journeys. With tools such as Facebook and Twitter having such prominence, there is a constant stream of data that needs to be analysed to understand this journey. Business flexibility and responsiveness is vital in the ever-changing digital customer environment, as customers are constantly connected to businesses and their products. Customers are now instant product experts due to various digital outlets and form their own opinions on how and where to consume products and services. Businesses use customer values and create a plan to gain a competitive advantage. Businesses use the knowledge of customers to guide the customer journey to their products and services.

Due to the shift in customer experience, in 2014 Wolny & Charoensuksai highlight three behaviours that show how decisions can be made in this digital journey. The Zero Moment of truth is the first interaction a customer has in connection with a service or product. This moment affects the consumer's choice to explore a product further or not at all. These moments can occur on any digital device. Showrooming highlights how a consumer will view a product in a physical store but then decide to exit the store empty handed and buy online instead. This consumer decision may be due to the ability to compare multiple prices online. On the opposing end of the spectrum is webrooming. Consumers will research about a product online in regards to quality and price but then decide to purchase in store. These three channels need to be understood by businesses because customers expect businesses to be readily available to cater to their specific customer needs and purchasing behaviours.

Customer Journey Mapping

The customer journey mapping approach for service design was first introduced by OxfordSM (at the time called Oxford Corporate Consultants) in 1998, in support of Eurostar to establish and implement their corporate mission and brand proposition. OxfordSM went on to use the approach widely, including with the UK Government, through which the guidance on the technique was publicly published. It has subsequently become one of the most widely used tools for service design and have been utilized as a tool for visualizing intangible services. A customer journey map shows the story of the customer's experience. It not only identifies key interactions that the customer has with the organization, but it also brings user's feelings, motivations and questions for each of the touchpoints. Finally, a customer journey map has the objective of teaching organizations more about their customers. To map a customer journey is important to consider the company's customers (buyer persona), the customer journey's time frame, channels (telephone, email, in-app messages, social media, forums, recommendations), first actions (problem acknowledgement) and last actions (recommendations or subscription renewal, f.i.). Customer Journey Maps are good storytelling conduits – they communicate to the brand the journey, along with the emotional quotient, that customer experiences at every stage of the buyer journey.

Customer journey maps take into account people's mental models (how things should behave), the flow of interactions and possible touch points. They may combine user profiles, scenarios, and user flows; and reflect the thought patterns, processes, considerations, paths, and experiences that people go through in their daily lives.

Benefits

Mapping the customer journey helps organisations understand how prospects and customers use the various channels and touchpoints, how the organisation's is perceived and how the organisation would like its customers and prospects' experiences to be. By understanding the latter, it is possible to design an optimal experience that meets the expectations of major customer groups, achieves competitive advantage and supports attainment of desired customer experience objectives.

Retail Environment

Retail environment factors include social features, design, and ambience. This can result in enhanced pleasure while shopping, thus positive customer experience and more likely chances of the customer revisiting the store in the future. The same retail environment may produce varied outcomes and emotions, depending on what the consumer is looking for. For example, a crowded retail environment may be exciting for a consumer seeking entertainment, but create an impression of inattentive customer service and frustration to a consumer who may need help looking for a specific product to meet an immediate need.

Environmental stimuli such as lighting and music, can influence a consumer's decision to stay longer in the store, therefore increasing the chances of purchasing. For example, a retail store may have dim lights and soothing music which may lead a consumer to experience the store as relaxing and calming.

Today's consumers are consistently connected through the development of technological innovation in the retail environment. This has led to the increased use of digital-led experiences in their purchase journey both in-store and online that inspire and influence the sales process. For example, Rebecca Minkoff has installed smart mirrors in their fitting rooms that allows the customers to browse for products that may compliment what they are trying on. These mirrors also hold an extra feature, a self-checkout system where the customer places the item on an RFID-powered table, this the sends the products to an iPad that is then used to checkout.

External and internal variables in a retail environment can also affect a consumer's decision to visit the store. External variables include window displays such as posters and signage, or product exposure that can be seen by the consumer from outside of the store. Internal variables include flooring, decoration and design. These attributes of a retail environment can either encourage or discourage a consumer from approaching the store.

Sales Experience

Sales experience is a subset of the customer experience. Whereas customer experience encompasses the sum of all interactions between an organization and a customer over the entire relationship, sales experience is focused exclusively on the interactions that take place during the sales process and up to the point that a customer decides to buy.

Customer experience tends to be owned by the Marketing function within an organization and therefore has little control or focus on what happens before a customer decides to buy.

Sales experience is concerned with the buyer journey up to and including the point that the buyer makes a purchase decision. Sales is a very important touch-point for overall customer experience as this is where the most human interaction takes place.

References

- Lakshman Jha (2008). Customer Relationship Management: A Strategic Approach. ISBN 9788190721127. Retrieved 8 June 2017
- Definition-and-characteristics-of-services: managementstudyguide.com, Retrieved 25 March, 2019
- Berry, leonard l. (2002). "relationship marketing of services perspectives from 1983 and 2000". Journal of relationship marketing. 1 (1): 59–77. Doi:10.1300/j366v01n01_05. Issn 1533-2667
- Service-marketing-definition-features-and-problem-faced-in-marketing-services-32336, marketing: yourarticlelibrary.com, Retrieved 26 April, 2019
- Watkins, diane. "transactional vs. Relational marketing". Small business chron. Retrieved 20 August 2019
- Fornell, C., S. Mithas, F.V. Morgeson III, and M.S. Krishnan (2006). "Customer Satisfaction and Stock Prices: High Returns, Low Risk," Journal of Marketing, 70(1), 3–14
- Reinartz, werner; krafft, manfred; hoyer, wayne d. (August 2004). "the customer relationship management process: its measurement and impact on performance". Journal of marketing research. 41 (3): 293–305. Doi:10.1509/jmkr.41.3.293.35991

PERMISSIONS

All chapters in this book are published with permission under the Creative Commons Attribution Share Alike License or equivalent. Every chapter published in this book has been scrutinized by our experts. Their significance has been extensively debated. The topics covered herein carry significant information for a comprehensive understanding. They may even be implemented as practical applications or may be referred to as a beginning point for further studies.

We would like to thank the editorial team for lending their expertise to make the book truly unique. They have played a crucial role in the development of this book. Without their invaluable contributions this book wouldn't have been possible. They have made vital efforts to compile up to date information on the varied aspects of this subject to make this book a valuable addition to the collection of many professionals and students.

This book was conceptualized with the vision of imparting up-to-date and integrated information in this field. To ensure the same, a matchless editorial board was set up. Every individual on the board went through rigorous rounds of assessment to prove their worth. After which they invested a large part of their time researching and compiling the most relevant data for our readers.

The editorial board has been involved in producing this book since its inception. They have spent rigorous hours researching and exploring the diverse topics which have resulted in the successful publishing of this book. They have passed on their knowledge of decades through this book. To expedite this challenging task, the publisher supported the team at every step. A small team of assistant editors was also appointed to further simplify the editing procedure and attain best results for the readers.

Apart from the editorial board, the designing team has also invested a significant amount of their time in understanding the subject and creating the most relevant covers. They scrutinized every image to scout for the most suitable representation of the subject and create an appropriate cover for the book.

The publishing team has been an ardent support to the editorial, designing and production team. Their endless efforts to recruit the best for this project, has resulted in the accomplishment of this book. They are a veteran in the field of academics and their pool of knowledge is as vast as their experience in printing. Their expertise and guidance has proved useful at every step. Their uncompromising quality standards have made this book an exceptional effort. Their encouragement from time to time has been an inspiration for everyone.

The publisher and the editorial board hope that this book will prove to be a valuable piece of knowledge for students, practitioners and scholars across the globe.

INDEX

CPSIA information can be obtained
at www.ICGtesting.com
Printed in the USA
LVHW060900030122
707669LV00002B/271